MARISSA MAYER

AND THE FIGHT TO SAVE

YAHOO!

NICHOLAS CARLSON

TWELVE

NEW YORK   BOSTON

Some sections of the book were previously published in a different form in *Business Insider*.

Twelve
Hachette Book Group
1290 Avenue of the Americas
New York, NY 10104

HachetteBookGroup.com

Printed in the United States of America

RRD-C

Originally published in hardcover by Twelve.

First Trade Edition: January 2016
10 9 8 7 6 5 4 3 2 1

Twelve is an imprint of Grand Central Publishing.
The Twelve name and logo are trademarks of Hachette Book Group, Inc.

The Hachette Speakers Bureau provides a wide range of authors for speaking events. To find out more, go to www.hachettespeakersbureau.com or call (866) 376-6591.

The publisher is not responsible for websites (or their content) that are not owned by the publisher.

Library of Congress Cataloging-in-Publication Data

Carlson, Nicholas.
Marissa Mayer and the fight to save Yahoo! / Nicholas Carlson.
    pages cm
Includes index.
    Summary: "A page-turning, warts-and-all narrative about Marissa Mayer's efforts to remake Yahoo as well as her own rise from Stanford University undergrad to CEO of a $30 billion corporation by the age of 38"—Provided by publisher.
    ISBN 978-1-4555-5661-8 (hardback) — ISBN 978-1-4555-8892-3 (international trade paperback) — ISBN 978-1-4789-0067-2 (audio download) — ISBN 978-1-4789-8689-8 (audio book)
    1. Yahoo! Inc.   2. Mayer, Marissa, 1975–   3. Internet industry—United States—Management.   4. Women chief executive officers—United States—Biography.   I. Title.
    HD9696.8.U64Y3437 2015
    338.7'6102504092—dc23
    [B]
                                      2014040842

ISBN 978-1-4555-5660-1 (pbk.)

For Mom, another book to read so we can talk about it

Contents

Bobbie Had a Nickel

Nearly four thousand Yahoo employees sat and waited for Marissa Mayer to explain herself.

It was around ten thirty on Thursday morning, November 7, 2013.

Some of the employees, those in Yahoo's Santa Monica and New York offices, sat at their desks watching a video feed on their computer monitors.

At Yahoo's headquarters in Sunnyvale, California, just off US 101 in the heart of Silicon Valley, almost two thousand employees sat in a huge cafeteria.

The sunlit, windowed cafeteria was called URLs. It was named that because, when Yahoo was founded almost twenty years before, all it did was serve up URLs, website addresses. The earliest version of Yahoo was a directory of links on a gray web page with a friendly logo up top.

The name also worked because URLs sounded like Earl's, and that suited the cafeteria's 1950s diner motif. Walking into the cafeteria, you see a sign that reads: "Eat at URLs." The sign is one whimsical touch among many in Yahoo's headquarters. The campus is called the Hoo. The employees call themselves Yahoos. A statue of a purple cow greets visitors in the lobby. There's an exclamation point at the end of every Yahoo logo.

The mood of Yahoo employees that day in November 2013 was not whimsical.

Some of the people in the room were angry—angry about refused promotions and pay raises, angry that their jobs now seemed to entail an endless series of tasks done only because "Marissa said so," or angry that new employees were coming into the company and making a lot more money. They were angry because, to them, it seemed like Marissa Mayer had said one thing and done another.

Most of the gathered Yahoo employees and executives weren't so mad. They were just confused. They believed Mayer was brilliant, hardworking, and sincerely interested in the welfare of Yahoo, its employees, and its users. They'd decided this after Mayer came to Yahoo from Google in July 2012 and brought with her sweeping changes that reenergized the entire company.

Before Mayer joined, Yahoo's parking lots were empty for the weekend by 4:30 p.m. Thursday. It took years for Yahoo to refresh its products, while competitors took months or just weeks. Yahoo's apps for Android and iPhone were embarrassing.

Within weeks of Mayer's arrival, the lots were packed and the headquarters was humming till Friday evenings. Within months, Yahoo was launching products at a pace it hadn't hit in more than a decade. Within a year, Yahoo was winning awards and praise from the press for its product design. By the summer of 2013, tens of thousands of people were applying for Yahoo jobs every quarter. Yahoo finally had a team of hundreds working on apps for smartphones.

Now, in November 2013, the many Yahoos who had admired all Mayer's progress wondered: Why was Mayer throwing away all the goodwill she had earned with a series of policies that were, at best, poorly rolled out and badly explained to employees or, at worst, plain mistakes. They wondered, more seriously than at any time since she joined, if Mayer was actually up for the job of saving Yahoo.

Mayer sat in front of them all, in a chair on a stage at the far end of the cafeteria. Next to her chair was a small table. Mayer had something with her. It looked like a book or a folder with an illustration on it.

A couple months before, fashion magazine *Vogue* published a photo of Mayer. In the photo, Mayer was lying upside down on a chaise lounge. Her blond hair was neatly fanned out and shiny like white gold. She was wearing a form-fitting blue Michael Kors dress, Yves Saint Laurent heels, and dark red lipstick. Her eyes held the camera, gazing sideways through half-closed lids.

That Thursday in November, Mayer looked like a different person. She looked agitated. Nervous. Her hair was wet. She wore no makeup.

Mayer knew about the confusion and the anger in the room. She'd been reading about it all week.

One of Mayer's first moves after joining Yahoo was to institute a weekly Friday-afternoon meeting of all Yahoo employees, called FYI. The point of the meetings was to bring "radical transparency" to a company where, for many years, employees had to learn about what management was up to by reading the press—mostly reports from a journalist named Kara Swisher.

FYI meetings would begin with a confidentiality reminder. Mayer would announce new hires and work anniversaries. Then she would go over Yahoo's "wins of the week." Mayer or another executive would go into "deep dives," giving presentations on topics like why Yahoo had acquired a certain company or how a new Yahoo product worked. At the end of the meeting, Mayer would take questions from Yahoo employees and either answer them herself or ask one of her direct reports to squirm in the spotlight.

Sometimes the questions would come in live from a Yahoo employee holding a microphone in URLs. More often, the questions were submitted during the week leading up to the FYI through an application called "Yahoo Moderator" on Yahoo's internal network. Everyone in the company could see questions after they were submitted, and employees would vote on which questions they wanted Mayer to answer that week.

Over the next year, employees asked Mayer tough questions on confidential topics, and she—or one of her top executives—would answer them with surprising candor. A popular topic: the status of layoffs and reorganizations reported on by the press. Another: Why was she blocking so many good hires? Whenever Yahoo spent millions of dollars to buy a startup, employees would demand an explanation from Mayer.

Finally, one Friday in October 2013, someone asked Mayer if she would do an FYI where the questions were submitted anonymously. Mayer said yes.

When the questions came in, they were so brutal that Mayer decided not to wait until a Friday to address them.

So now it was a Thursday: November 7, 2013. Everyone in the company was waiting for Mayer to say something to remind them that she was the CEO who was finally going to restore Yahoo to its rightful place in the Internet industry.

Mayer took a breath. She said hello to everyone. She reminded them of the meeting's confidentiality. She said she looked through their questions and she had something she wanted to read. It had been a book in her hands, after all. A children's book.

She began to read.

Bobbie had a nickel all his very own. Should he buy some candy or an ice cream cone?

Mayer held the book up, to show the employees the illustrations.

Should he buy a bubble pipe? Or a boat of wood?

Another illustration.

Maybe, though, a little truck would be the best of all!

Employees in URLs exchanged looks. At their desks, employees in remote offices grew confused.
What was Mayer doing?
She kept reading.

Bobbie sat and wondered, Bobbie sat and thought. What would be the nicest thing a nickel ever bought?

Mayer seemed to skip a few pages. She read, with a slight agitation in her voice:

He might buy a bean bag or a top to spin. He might buy a pin-wheel to give to little Brother. Or should he buy, thought Bobbie, a little pencil box?

Mayer seemed to be reading with real frustration now, as though all of the anger and confusion in the room would just go away if everyone would just understand the story she was reading out loud.

"Bobbie thought—and suddenly a bright idea came," Mayer read, reaching the book's last pages.

He spent his nickel just like this - - - -

Mayer held the book up to show its last illustration. It was a drawing of a little red-haired boy riding a merry-go-round pony.

Hardly anyone could see the page.

No one understood what Mayer was trying to say.

⸻

The irony is, the only reason Marissa Mayer had to explain herself to a roomful of demoralized and confused Yahoos that Thursday in November 2013 was that, a year before, she decided not to fire five thousand of them.

Actually, Mayer had to make that choice three times.

When she joined Yahoo in the summer of 2012, one of the first meetings she took was with a company executive named Jim Heckman. Heckman had been a top dealmaker for the interim management team that had immediately preceded Mayer. In that meeting, Heckman told Mayer that he had deals lined up with Google, Microsoft, and a New York advertising technology company called AppNexus. The plan was to outsource various Yahoo functions to each. Then Yahoo would be able to get rid of as much as a third of its headcount.

Within a day of the meeting, Mayer canceled all the deals and asked Heckman to leave the company.

Then Mayer had to decide what to do about Project Alpha.

Project Alpha was the code name for a massive overhaul of Yahoo begun by another one of Mayer's predecessors, Scott Thompson. Thompson had been Yahoo CEO for only a short time—from January 2012 to May 2012—but Project Alpha was going to leave a mark. It called for Yahoo to reduce its number of data centers from thirty-one to six and its workforce of fifteen thousand employees and three thousand contractors by as much as a third. Thompson initiated Project Alpha on April 4, 2012. When he did that, hundreds of Yahoo employees were told that eventually they were going to be fired, but not just yet. This was called getting put "on transition."

Project Alpha sought to reduce Yahoo's workforce by cutting whole divisions from the company rather than by examining the work of each employee in each group and identifying the poor performers who should go and the high performers who should stay, even if that meant moving to another group. When Mayer heard that, she couldn't believe it. She quickly reduced the scope of Project Alpha and asked her top executives to recruit back into the company high-performing Yahoo employees that Thompson had put on transition. At an FYI on September 28, 2012, Mayer told employees that Thompson's plans had damaged Yahoo's culture and that she wouldn't be using the same kind of cost-cutting tactics.

Finally, Mayer had to deal with the board, which also wanted her to fire lots of Yahoos.

When Yahoo's board of directors hired Mayer in July 2012, the directors made clear to her that they thought she should cut headcount by as much as 35 to 50 percent.

Mayer seemed to get the idea but made no promises in her interviews for the job. She did, however, agree that Yahoo needed to reduce its costs and focus on making fewer products, better. She said that by her first board meeting, in September 2012, she would present a cost-cutting strategy.

The notion that Yahoo needed to fire a lot of its people was conventional wisdom within the industry by the time Mayer took over in summer 2012. The week of her hire, Marc Andreessen, a widely respected startup investor who had been part of a private equity group that looked at buying Yahoo in 2011, told a reporter that Yahoo should fire ten to twelve thousand people.

So when that board meeting came in September, several directors, including hedge fund manager Dan Loeb, the director most responsible for Mayer's hire, expected her to present a plan for layoffs.

That's not what Loeb and the rest of the board got. Mayer told them that layoffs of any kind, let alone 35 to 50 percent cuts, would be too damaging for employee morale. She said that Yahoo's basic infrastructure was so byzantine and jerry-built that it would be unwise to blindly rip whole teams of people out. She said Yahoo was going to need all the talent it could find to turn around, and she didn't want to risk putting good people on the street.

Many of the directors, including Loeb, didn't like what they heard, and there was some tension in the room. But they'd just made a huge bet on Mayer only months before, and there was no choice but to go with her plans.

Mayer was thrilled.

On October 12, 2012, Mayer got the chance to share the good news, when, at an FYI, an employee asked if reports about layoffs were true.

Mayer, standing onstage in front of a giant purple curtain backdrop, said, "So are there secret talks going on about massive layoffs and massive reorganizations?

"No.

"Have I had conversations with people about them?

"No.

"Is this something that weighs on me?

"Yes.

"You probably have heard and seen some of the comments from Marc Andreessen and others about how many people might need to be laid off. Have I heard some of those?

"Yes.

"Do they weigh on me?

"Yes.

"Have I been actively considering plans around them?

"No.

She said that Yahoo would still have to make some changes, but that she wanted them to be "small."

"As of right now, we're not looking at layoffs. We're looking at stabilizing the organization. I can't make a promise that there won't be a change in that in the future, but as of right now, there's no active planning or conversations going on."

Then Mayer said something about how Yahoo would get "fit as a company" by setting goals and then using those goals to measure "who's performing well" and "who's struggling." Few in the room thought much about what she meant by that. What they heard Mayer saying was: I'm not going to fire you, your friends, or ten thousand other people.

The Yahoos started clapping.

Mayer liked the applause.

"You should feel good about that," she said. "That should be a giant round of applause, a big sigh of relief from everybody."

Even as Mayer decided not to fire five or ten thousand people during the fall of 2012, she still wanted to figure out some way to cut costs, or at least control spending, at Yahoo.

She had to.

Since joining, she'd discovered that Yahoo had even more workers than the headcount of fifteen thousand it published in its reporting to the SEC. There were also another three thousand contractors around the globe, working what were essentially full-time jobs, just without the benefits. Meanwhile, Yahoo's actual full-time employees had been getting paid more than the industry average for many years. In the tumultuous years leading up to Mayer's arrival, prior CEOs had given employees fat raises and big bonuses in an effort to keep them from leaving the company.

Mayer knew she needed to tighten the belt in 2013. Mayer also believed that the company's workforce needed to get more talented. That meant recruiting and retaining high performers and flushing the poor performers out.

Mayer believed she had a plan that could achieve both goals at once.

The plan hinged on bringing into Yahoo a management technique Mayer learned at Google.

Starting in 1999, Google management used a system called Objectives and Key Results, or OKRs, to measure the effectiveness of its employees, divisions, and the company overall. The idea for OKRs came from Google investor John Doerr, the famous venture capitalist. Doerr got it from Andy Grove, who developed a similar system called Management by Objective during his successful run at Intel.

In the OKR system, every Google employee would come up with a list of quantifiable goals every quarter. The employee would present this list to a manager for sign-off, then the approved goals would be entered into Google's internal network, where everyone in the entire company could see them. The next quarter, the employee would meet with the manager again, review their performance, and get a score on their OKRs. That score would determine the employee's bonus payment and ability to get a raise, a transfer, or promotion within the company.

Starting in September 2012, Mayer introduced a clone of OKRs to Yahoo. She called them Quarterly Performance Reviews, or QPRs. Employees from Mayer's direct reports on down would get a score every quarter, from one to five. A one meant the employee consistently "misses" goals, a two meant the employee "occasionally misses," a three, "achieves," a four, "exceeds," and a five, "greatly exceeds."

Mayer rolled out her cost-cutting, talent-improving plan in stages. First, she introduced the concept of goals to employees.

Then Mayer announced a "target distribution" for the company.

In effect, a target distribution meant Mayer wanted managers to put a certain percentage of the employees they managed in each of the five buckets. Ten percent would go into "greatly exceeds," 25 percent into "exceeds," 50 percent into "achieves," 10 percent into "occasionally misses," and 5 percent into "misses."

Then Mayer rolled out new policies wherein employee eligibility for bonuses, promotions, and transfers within the company would be based on their average score for the past three quarters. Employees with low enough scores would be asked to leave the company.

Over her first year, the plan seemed to work—or at least accomplish Mayer's two goals for it. Mayer felt Yahoo's talent level was rising. And, without going through any morale-draining layoffs, Mayer was able to move six hundred low-performing employees out of the company.

Unfortunately for Mayer, the plan also produced a few unintended consequences.

In August 2012, *Vanity Fair* published a story by Kurt Eichenwald about the downfall of Microsoft over the prior decade. In the story, Eichenwald attributed Microsoft's woes to all sorts of issues, but he said company insiders blamed one Microsoft management system most of all: a process called stack ranking. Also known as "the performance model," "the bell curve," or "the employee review," the system forced Microsoft managers to rank the people on their teams from best to worst, with a fixed percentage going into each of five buckets: top performers, good performers, average performers, below average, and poor. Employees ranked poorly would see their lives materially turn for the worse as they lost out on raises, promotions, and bonuses.

As if writing an indictment, Eichenwald listed out the negative consequences of the well-intended system. Because someone would have to be ranked worst even on teams full of all-star performers, Microsoft's most talented employees refused to work together. Because employees were not judged on their own work, but on how well they did relative to their peers, they would actively seek to undermine each other.

As employee ratings got passed up the management ladder, individual scores sometimes had to be adjusted at the department level so that the right amount of employees were in each bucket. This led to favor-trading between managers. It also meant employees felt they had to brownnose their boss's peers and their boss's boss.

Stack ranking had come into fashion after GE CEO Jack Welch used a similar system, called rank-and-yank, to turn around that company in the 1980s and 1990s. But by 2012, thanks to stories like Eichenwald's and several studies, the practice's limitations were widely known, even by some at Yahoo.

On December 21, 2012, at the last FYI of the year and shortly after Mayer began rolling out QPRs at Yahoo, an employee named Carl Moyer asked Mayer: "Do you think the new bell curve for review scores has a negative impact on teamwork and morale?

"Knowing that we're stack ranked against our teammates and that someone gets the low score seems to incent lack of cooperation.

"Surely no one wants that."

Mayer told Moyer he misunderstood.

"I want to be clear," she said. "It's not a stack rank. It's sort of a bucket sort. So you end up either in exceeds, meets, strongly exceeds, things like that. But it's not a stack rank. As a result, I don't think it has some of the same characteristics as an actual stack rank."

Mayer would stick to this semantic line of defense for the next year. It irritated employees, and even some of Mayer's direct reports, to no end. The problem was that while "stack rank" and "bucket sort" were different words, the systems those words described had the same effects. Mayer had given the company's senior managers orders for how many of their employees could go into each bucket. These senior managers had then passed down the ratios to the managers below them. And so on.

It was a forced curve. In general, only 75 percent of any group got in the top three buckets. Twenty-five percent of every team had to go into the bottom two—"occasionally misses" and "misses." The result: Teammates directly competed with each other to make sure that they weren't a part of that 25 percent.

Mayer would also say that because her distribution curve called for 50 percent of Yahoo to fit into the "achieves" bucket, it was not as "fine grained" as a stack ranking and therefore wouldn't lead to as many problems of competition between employees.

Fine grained or not, there were serious consequences for employees who got stuck in the wrong bucket. To get significantly ahead in life as a Yahoo employee, you needed to make sure your grade was better than that of 65 percent of your team colleagues. Under the new system, the only way to get a promotion or a raise at Yahoo was to have an average score of three for the past four quarters. You could get an "exceeds" for three quarters and an "achieves" for one, and you'd land below the threshold. No raise for you. Good luck next time.

Lots of Yahoo employees at all levels understood that the company needed to be tighter with its compensation. Anyone who did a little research would find out that Yahoo engineers got higher salaries than counterparts at rival tech companies.

But one thing bothered Yahoo's engineers about the cost-consciousness when it came to take-home pay: It didn't seem to apply to everyone.

The rumor was that Mayer was paying people from her old company, Google, massive salaries to get them to join Yahoo. They'd whisper to each other: Was it true that ex-Googlers were getting paid $300,000 on average?

Also, Yahoo kept acquiring small, failed startups as a way of quickly hiring whole teams into the company. Word was, the mobile engineers on those teams were getting three-year deals worth $1 million.

As 2013 rolled on, Mayer's system made life particularly difficult for Yahoo's middle managers. It was hard to get talented people to work in the same group. Not only did people not want to compete against other talented employees, they also worried that if they transferred in the middle of a quarter, they'd whiff on their goals, get a mere "achieves," and lose out on a chance for a raise anytime in the next twelve months.

Workers would prioritize tasks that got them closer to their personal goals over doing anything else. This made sense. Collaborating and helping out on a project that wasn't going to get you closer to an "exceeds" was just a stupid thing to do.

The worst part was, every quarter, managers would guide their teams toward collective goals, and then, even if all of those goals were met, they had to single out a few people and tell them they had missed expectations. Occasionally, a middle manager would quietly rebel and file a packet of QPRs to Yahoo human resources that listed each employee as an "achieves" or better.

But HR would kick the packet back and tell the manager to get their calibrations right. Somebody always had to "occasionally miss." Even if no one ever missed.

One ugly part of the process every quarter was a series of so-called "calibration meetings."

In calibration meetings, managers would gather with their bosses and review all the employees under their watch. Then the managers and their bosses would adjust the scores of those employees so that the department as a whole had the right amount of people in each bucket—10 percent in "greatly exceeds," 25 percent in "exceeds," and so on.

What went down at these meetings was not what Mayer had intended. Mayer wanted employees to be rated objectively against the goals they'd agreed on with their managers at the beginning of every quarter. What happened instead was that managers would sit there and look at an employee that needed to fit into a particular bucket and try to think up reasons why they fit there.

Sometimes the reason would be a political one. Managers would strike bargains—agreeing to rate certain employees in one another's groups higher and employees in some other manager's group lower, so that the curve fit.

Sometimes the reason would be more superficial. That employee ate lunch with the right people or could hold a conversation with the boss in the hallway? Exceeds. This one shuffled around and kept to himself? Occasionally misses.

Mayer herself attended calibration meetings where these kinds of arbitrary judgments happened.

The senior executives who reported to Mayer, known collectively as her E Staff and called L2s (Level Twos), would join her in a meeting room called Phish Food on the executive floor of building D on Yahoo's Sunnyvale campus. There, they would go over the names and ratings of L3 and L4 executives.

There would be a bunch of people sitting around a table holding spreadsheets of names and ratings. If the name of an L3 that was unfamiliar to Mayer came up, the rating would usually stick. But if she knew the name of a person and could recall an interaction, that person's rating would go up or down based on how that relatively trivial interaction had gone.

At one such meeting on October 26, 2012, the name Vivek

Sharma came up. At that point, Sharma was working with Mayer on a major redesign of Yahoo Mail, a project code-named Quattro.

Several hundred million people use Yahoo Mail every month, and Quattro represented a major turning point for the product, but that's not what finally determined Sharma's rating at the meeting.

An L2, Yahoo chief marketing officer Kathy Savitt, said, "He just annoys me. I don't want to be around him."

Savitt didn't really need to be around Sharma much, as he worked in Yahoo's product organization and had relatively little interaction with marketing.

But Mayer agreed with Savitt.

She docked Sharma's rating, which inevitably decreased his take-home pay for the year. In January 2013, Sharma left Yahoo for a senior position at Disney.

<hr>

Throughout Mayer's first year at Yahoo, QPRs and complaints about the calibration system came up often at Friday FYIs. Even at the otherwise celebratory FYI just preceding Mayer's one-year anniversary, someone asked about the "demotivating" nature of the program.

Then, in October 2013, Mayer agreed to let employees ask questions anonymously. Finally given the chance to vent without fear of repercussions, employees submitted hundreds of angry questions.

One question got 1,531 votes from employees, making it the first one Mayer read.

I was forced to give an employee an occasionally misses, [and] was very uncomfortable with it. Now I have to have a discussion about it when I have my QPR meetings. I feel so uncomfortable because in order to meet the bell curve, I have to tell the employee that they missed when I truly don't believe it to be the case. I understand we want to weed out mis-hires/people not meeting their goals, but this practice is concerning. I don't want to lose the person mentally. How do we justify?

Eight more questions had more than a thousand votes.

Could you please address why managers are forced to have an average rating for their team? If everyone on the team exceeds expectations, the manager is not allowed to rate each member as such.

The salary of many of current Yahoos (joined before Marissa joined as CEO) needs to be normalized with that of new/returning Yahoos. I'm a manager and was asked to give a salary which is at least 20–30 percent high[er] than that of what other employees in my team with similar experience are making, so approval goes through hiring & executive committee. When I asked if there is a way I can increase [the] salary of my current employees, there was no proper answer from management or HR. Can this be addressed?

[Is it] true that we will cut 20 percent of the work force in a silent layoff based on QPR results?

Based on my experience, I don't feel like the process was done correctly nor was I treated fairly. My former manager did not provide feedback or guidance, other than to say that higher-ups decided the numbers and he had no input. Considering how important these ratings are, can we have a legitimate appeals process?

During the QPR process, is it true that the manager of each team has to bucket their team members into 1 of the ratings; below expectations, meets, and exceeds? There has to be a person at each level? Is it also true that if the individual receives below expectations 3–4 quarters in a row that they will be terminated? Is Yahoo using a practice of eliminating the weakest link? But what if the "weakest" are only scored that way because managers are forced to put them there?

More often than I'd like, I'm told we are executing a certain way "because Marissa said so." This explanation leaves out valuable context. There was probably a good reason for the decision, but that's absent from this pat answer. Can we ban the practice of "because [executive] said so" and encourage people to explain why a specific choice was made when relaying those decisions to others?

The latest round of layoffs affected those with "misses expectations" on their QPR. I lost a colleague in this last round of layoffs who had all "meets" from their most current QPR; they got the axe because of PRIOR misses on their QPR. Is this a message we really mean to send? That improving ultimately doesn't matter because you might get sent to the guillotine anyways, because of previous performance? Is it true we force managers to assign some "misses"—thereby forcing layoffs periodically?

The last question with more than a thousand votes called for Mayer to fire some of her executive staff.

Is E Staff subject to the same QPR and calibration process? Should we expect to see one or two of them departing soon, like these people leaving now?

On Yahoo's internal network, called Backyard, the questions went on like that for pages and pages.

On November 7, 2013, the hundreds of people who asked those questions and the thousands more who voted them up filled Yahoo's cafeteria, URLs. In New York and Santa Monica, they waited at their monitors, hoping to finally hear answers from Mayer.

That's when Mayer went onstage, sat at her chair, and read a children's book to them, holding up the illustrations like she was a kindergarten teacher and they were all six years old.

After reading *Bobbie Had a Nickel*, Mayer gave a speech. In a defensive tone, she stressed, like she always had before, that the QPRs were not a stack ranking, that there were no stealth layoffs going on at Yahoo. No one believed her. Her plan had been to cut costs and improve the mix of talent at Yahoo without damaging morale. Her plan had failed.

Not everyone in the room opposed Mayer's QPR system. Some thought it was a tough, perhaps not very transparent, but effective way to get the clock punchers out of the company. If it worked for Jack Welch at GE, it would work for Mayer at Yahoo.

Others looked at the scene around them, reflected on Mayer's terrible performance onstage that day—usually a strong point—and suddenly wondered: Maybe not even Marissa Mayer, with her incredible work ethic, genius sense of what made an Internet product usable, worldwide fame, and talent-attracting charisma, would be enough to save Yahoo.

After all, she wouldn't be the first talented executive to have tried.

And what made her so different?

There is no one in the world like Marissa Mayer. In 2012, she was thirty-seven years old, a wife, an expecting mother, an engineer, and then, suddenly, the CEO of a $30 billion company.

Marissa Mayer is fascinating for her contradictions.

Onstage, in front of hundreds or thousands, she is warm and charming and laughing. But in a room with just a few others, she's cold and direct and impersonal. In a one-on-one she can't hold eye contact.

Mayer calls herself a geek, but she doesn't look the part. With her blond hair, blue eyes, and glamorous style, she has Hollywood-actress good looks. She is the frequent profile subject of fashion magazines, which love her for her Oscar de la Renta obsession, her femininity, and her implicit feminism. But Mayer explicitly rejects feminism—and she has shown up to the most important meetings of her life with wet hair and no makeup on.

Over her decade-plus career at Google and at Yahoo, Mayer alienated several designers who worked for her because those designers were not making enough choices based on hard data. But over and again, Mayer makes her own choices, design and otherwise, based on little more than an intuition.

Her instincts are often right. They are also often wrong. But, when Mayer makes mistakes, she makes mistakes fast.

Like many leaders, she expects her charges to follow her

orders—sometimes just because she said so. And yet, no CEO is more open with employees.

Most CEOs of Mayer's stature—people running multibillion-dollar public companies the size of Yahoo—are gregarious, outgoing types, the kind of person who might have been a politician if the world of business and money hadn't beckoned. Baby-kissers. Backslappers. Schmoozers. Mayer is not that type. Peers from every stage of her life—from her early childhood days to her first years at Yahoo—say Mayer is a shy, socially awkward person. She calls herself "painfully shy."

Mayer runs a company whose brand is strongest in the middle of America, and she sits on the board of Walmart. And yet Mayer, who is also from the heartland and prefers Catalina French dressing for her salad, would rather Yahoo's middlebrow media brands be more like the high-end magazines she loves, such as *Vogue* or *Town & Country*.

Widely admired by the public at large, Mayer has many enemies within her industry. They say she is robotic, stuck up, and absurd in her obsession with detail. They say her fixation with the user experience masks a disdain for the moneymaking side of the technology industry. Then there is her inner circle, full of young, wildly loyal men and women.

To a public casually interested in her career, Mayer's working life before Yahoo—spent entirely at Google—is remembered as one success after another. It wasn't. Mayer started off at Google spectacularly well, designing its home page, creating its product management structure, and becoming a face of the company. She was one of the most powerful people at one of the world's most powerful companies. Then, suddenly, she wasn't. Soon she was leaving.

There is no company in the world like Yahoo.

Back in the 1990s, Yahoo *was* the Internet. It was founded by a kid who'd hardly held a job before and another who grew up on a commune, neither of whom really wanted to make their project into a business. Then it became a $128 billion company within five years, dwarfing media conglomerates and technology giants decades older. But just as quickly as it became the world's most famous Internet company, Yahoo crashed to earth during the dotcom bust. It lost nearly all of its value.

Yet, Yahoo's users remained loyal to the company and its joyful brand. For the next decade, dozens of brilliant, hardworking executives tried to build on that loyalty and restore Yahoo to its early glory. Some succeeded for spans of time, but none stopped Yahoo's slow slide toward irrelevance.

Then, in 2012, came Marissa Mayer—full of contradictions, yes, but also full of fight.

This book is the candid, inside-the-room story of Yahoo—its creation, its sudden success, its slow and painful downfall, and its superstar CEO.

It's about the people who ran Yahoo for its first decade and a half. It goes inside their heads as they make genius moves and giant blunders.

It's about the rise and fall of Marissa Mayer at Google. She joined as a lowly engineer, twenty-four and shy. Within years, she was part of a secret cabal that ran the entire company. But she made enemies along the way and in the end they brought her down.

It's the story of how Mayer came to Yahoo thanks to a cast of international players: a smack-talking New York hedge fund manager, an Internet agitator from Canada, a masterful negotiator in Hong Kong, and a billionaire mogul in Tokyo.

Finally, it's the story of Marissa Mayer's race against the clock at Yahoo. When Mayer joined Yahoo in the summer of 2012, her timing couldn't have been better. She joined Yahoo just before its stock price started soaring due to the company's investment in a booming Chinese startup called Alibaba. Investors piled into Yahoo with little care for how well the core business Mayer was running performed on a quarterly basis. It was a huge advantage for Mayer. Unlike most turnaround CEOs, she would have the luxury of retooling Yahoo without having investors demand immediate results.

But the cover provided by Alibaba would not last forever—just two years, until it went public. Then Yahoo would once again be judged based on the merits of its core business. Would Marissa Mayer be able to get the company into good enough shape for its big reintroduction?

At first, the answer seemed to be an obvious yes. Mayer arrived at Yahoo like a superhero. She was confident and full of ideas, and for all the world looked like the exact right person for the job. But thanks to a series of her own mistakes and Yahoo's inherent problems, she soon realized she was in for a knock-down, drag-out fight.

PART

1

Sparky's Big Machine

Jeff Mallett walked through the stadium tunnel toward the harsh desert sunlight. Then he walked out into it. Squinting, he looked around. It was incredible. Everywhere he looked around the giant U-shaped stadium, he saw Yahoo purple.

It was January 28, 1996. In a couple hours, the Dallas Cowboys were going to play the Pittsburgh Steelers in Super Bowl XXX at Sun Devil Stadium in Tempe, Arizona. But for now, the stadium was still mostly empty. That meant Mallett could see the purple seat cushions on every one of the 76,000 seats in the stadium. He knew that on the back of every cushion there was a pouch. And inside every pouch, there was a CD-ROM. And on that CD-ROM: a web browser, preloaded with Yahoo.com.

Yahoo wasn't even a year old, and yet here it was, playing in the Super Bowl with the big boys: brands like GTE, Miller Lite, and Coca-Cola. Mallett was so thrilled, he couldn't contain himself. Standing there in the stadium, he twitched with excitement.

Then again, twitching with excitement was not very unusual for Jeff Mallett. That's how he got the nickname Sparky. Mallett was a small man, standing five feet five and weighing just 140 pounds, but the amount of energy pumping through him would certainly have been enough to power a much larger human. He was always wired and amped up—especially when it came to building a business.

Mallett grew up in Victoria, British Colombia. His parents ran several businesses out of the family home. Mallett always pitched in. For a while, his mother converted part of the house into a tearoom. Mallett would run around taking orders from large groups without having to write anything down. As a teenager, he opened his own business, selling home insurance. Though small, Mallett was fit, tough, and competitive. He played hockey and baseball. He went to the University of Victoria on a soccer scholarship. During the summers, he'd come home and work two jobs—one in an office during the day and one at a restaurant serving drinks at night.

After college, Mallett ran sales and business development for another company created by his parents, Island Pacific Telephone. In 1988, he moved to San Francisco and joined Reference Software, a small startup that made the algorithms powering spell-checking and grammar-checking in word processor applications. The startup sold to WordPerfect Corporation. Mallett ran the consumer-facing side of that business. Then WordPerfect sold to Novell, which wanted to take on Microsoft. By his midtwenties, Mallett had made his first million dollars. He had a big job at Novell with a big corner office, a big desk, and a really big salary.

But he was bored. He wanted to build a business.

One day, he got a call from Silicon Valley investor Mike Moritz of Sequoia Capital. Moritz had been following Mallett's career since Reference Software turned down Sequoia's investment offer.

Moritz told Mallett he had a job for him at a startup Sequoia was investing in.

Have you heard of the World Wide Web? Moritz asked Mallett.

Yes, Mallett said, he had.

Have you heard of Yahoo? Moritz asked.

Yes, Mallett had, actually. At Novell, he'd formed a partnership with America Online, and the people there talked a lot about Yahoo, a website that seemed to do many of the things America Online's software did, but for free, on the web.

Moritz told Mallett: Well, this startup is like Yahoo.

Mallett lost interest. He'd have been interested in working at Yahoo, sure. It was a phenomenon already. But a company *like* Yahoo? Pass. He never called Moritz back.

A couple weeks later, Moritz called Mallett again.

Moritz asked him: "Are you stupid? You don't even want to come out and talk to Yahoo?"

Mallett said: Wait. What? Yahoo?

Mallett thought: Shit!

He flew out to California right away. He shared a six-pack with the Yahoo cofounders. He signed on as COO in the summer of 1995.

He was immediately thrilled with his choice, and by the Super Bowl in January 1996, he'd become emotionally invested in the company. One reason why: It was looking like he would basically get to run the place.

Mallett wasn't CEO of Yahoo. That was a guy named Tim Koogle. But it was already obvious that Koogle was more into the view from thirty thousand feet than the day-to-day operations of the company. Koogle had long silver hair and a New Age vibe. He looked good in a black turtleneck. He was a force for calm. The board liked him. So did the press. Some found him kind of ornamental.

Then there were Yahoo's cofounders, former Stanford graduate students named David Filo and Jerry Yang. No one wanted them to run the company. Not the investors. Not the other executives. Not even them.

When Yang and Filo started Yahoo, they weren't trying to start a business worth tens of millions of dollars. They weren't trying to start any kind of business. They weren't even trying to create a website lots of people would use. They just wanted to make a handy tool for themselves and have some fun.

All the rest just kind of happened to them. It was like they were a pair of paddleboarders who got lucky and somehow caught a wave and started surfing—and then that wave turned out to be a tsunami.

Truly, the thing that Yahoo was in 1996 could exist only because of technology that had been a long time coming. But at the same time, Yahoo became the multibillion-dollar company it eventually became only because it was built at the exact right moment.

In April 1963, computer scientist J. C. R. Licklider wrote a memo proposing an "Intergalactic Computer Network." That October, he went to work for the US Department of Defense. There, Licklider persuaded two colleagues, Ivan Sutherland and Bob Taylor, to build a prototype network. Sutherland and Taylor had one running by the end of 1969. By 1971, fifteen computers connected to the network, by then called ARPANET.

In 1974, Vinton Cerf, Yogen Dalal, and Carl Sunshine described this growing network as "internetworking," and used the word "Internet" for shorthand.

In 1989, Tim Berners-Lee and Robert Cailliau proposed a system where a user could click on links to "access information of various kinds" on a "web of nodes" that the user could "browse at will." This system became known as the World Wide Web, and the nodes, web pages.

In April 1992, Berkeley student Pei-Yuan Wei released ViolaWWW, an application for browsing the World Wide Web from UNIX computers. At the National Center for Supercomputing Applications in Illinois, a researcher named David Thompson downloaded ViolaWWW and showed it to Marc Andreessen, a student intern. Andreessen and another student, Eric Bina, began working on their own browser in December 1992. In September 1993, Andreessen released Mosaic, a browser that worked on Windows and Macintosh computers.

That fall, two graduate students in Stanford's computer-assisted design program downloaded Mosaic and started telling each other about all the cool web pages they were finding with it. For example, they liked this one site with a lava lamp on it. They liked the site from NERF, the makers of toy guns. They liked a lot of porn sites, and they liked a page called Quadralay's Armadillo Home Page.

Finally, one of those two students, David Filo, made a list of all the sites he liked. He shared it with his friend Jerry Yang. Yang made a list, too. Filo combined the lists, and in early 1994, Yang published the list on a web page hosted for him by Stanford. At first, Yang called the site Jerry's Guide to the World Wide Web. Then, Jerry and David's Guide to the World Wide Web.

In April 1994, the list had a hundred sites on it, and the guide got a thousand visits a week. That seemed like a lot at the time. But that summer, word of the directory spread. By September 1994, the site had two thousand links on its list and was getting fifty thousand visits per day. By then, Yang had begun organizing the links on the site into nineteen different categories, from Computers to Art to Business.

Along with computers to host the site, Stanford gave Filo and Yang a trailer to house their physical operation. Inside, the place was cluttered with pizza boxes, dirty laundry, and golf clubs.

Filo, an extremely shy person, hated having his name on the site. Yang also wanted a new name, something more memorable. One night, the pair sat down with a dictionary. They wanted the name to be an acronym that started with Y and A, for "Yet Another." They flipped to that part of the dictionary. One word in particular leapt out. Its definition: "a boorish, crass, or stupid person." Just the vibe they were looking for.

They figured out a phrase to fit the acronym: Yet Another Hierarchical Officious Oracle. They put the word on their page in a font called Uncle Stinky and stuck an exclamation point at the end. Yahoo, the brand, was born.

Yahoo still wasn't a business, however. Its creators weren't businesspeople. Filo grew up on a commune. He fell in love with engineering constructing toy bridges and cranes as a kid. When his family built its own house when he was in the fifth grade, Filo and his brother hammered on the roof, laid drywall, and installed electrical wiring. Filo became fascinated with tools and solutions. To him, that's what Yahoo was.

Though Yang had a master's degree in electrical engineering, he didn't help Filo much on the technical side. Yang wasn't an entrepreneur yet, either. In fact, he had never held a full-time job before. For him, Yahoo was a good time—a better time than working on his graduate thesis, for sure. Yang's main role was to be magnetic, a spiritual leader and spokesman—at first, on campus, and later, in the press. Filo, an introvert, was happy to see Yang play the front man.

Perhaps the only reason Yahoo ever became a business at all was what happened in October 1994. That's when Marc Andreessen's startup, Netscape, launched an even more consumer-friendly version of the Mosaic browser, called Navigator. Netscape Navigator linked directly to Yahoo.com from a button at the top of the application labeled "directory." As millions of people tried the World Wide Web for the first time, they went straight to Yahoo to figure out where to go. By January 1995, Yahoo listed ten thousand sites and got a million hits per day. Stanford, overwhelmed by all the traffic, told Filo and Yang they needed to find their own servers.

Servers cost money. If the project was going to continue, it was going to need investors. It was going to have to become a business.

This proved to be a simple transition. In fact, the first hard business call Yang and Filo had to make was whether or not to sell the thing and walk away millionaires one year in. In March 1995—just days after Yahoo was officially incorporated—America Online CEO Steve Case offered to buy it for $2 million. He said if Yang and Filo didn't accept his offer, America Online would have to crush them. Yang and Filo said no thanks and, in April, sold 25 percent of Yahoo to venture capital firm Sequoia Capital for $1 million instead.

Sequoia Capital partner Mike Moritz joined Yahoo's board. One of his first moves was to go to Yang and say: Jerry, you have no idea what you're doing. You should be Mr. Feel Good. Shake everyone's hands. Slap a lot of backs. Be the nice guy. Let me hire some adult supervision.

Though Yang had listed himself as Yahoo's chairman and president in the company's first tentative business plan, he said Moritz could go ahead and find someone who would be better at scaling the business. Moritz didn't have to convince Filo to work behind the scenes. That's what Filo wanted. He was the ultimate introvert. As the company staffed up, new employees learned that you could sit in a room with Filo for thirty minutes and he would feel no obligation to say anything to you.

Moritz zeroed in on Mallett for Yahoo's number-two job. He asked a headhunter named Alan Sabourin to find him a CEO. Sabourin suggested Tim Koogle. Koogle went to the University of Virginia and then Stanford, getting degrees in mechanical engineering at both. He started a robotics company in the early 1980s. It failed, and then he joined Motorola. The biggest job he ever had was president of the Litton Industries unit that made bar code scanners. Most recently, he'd made a big push for more investment into his unit and the Litton bosses had said no.

Koogle met with Yang and Filo. They liked how he talked about not caring if Yahoo made him rich. They liked that he described Yahoo as something "with strong organic take-up" when what he meant was that people were using it. He sounded the part. Moritz was impressed that Koogle had doubled bar code scanner sales in three years. He also liked that he'd had a little bit of failure in his career and had something to prove. Moritz was glad Koogle had worked on Motorola's venture capital team and understood startups.

Koogle got the job. He was Yahoo's CEO and chairman.

Mallett had also just signed on as COO and president. To figure out who would do what, the two met for the first time over dinner one night in Palo Alto. Koogle, twelve years Mallett's senior, seemed nice enough to Mallett. He was happy to let the younger man handle most of the day-to-day operations.

Yahoo had its adult supervision.

There was a lot of work to supervise. The company Mallett and Koogle joined was hardly a company at all. It occupied a small, 1,500-square-foot office in a one-story building in Mountain View. The furniture was all secondhand folding tables and chairs.

Even with the Sequoia money, there was only six weeks of cash left. And the core Yahoo operation wasn't exactly sophisticated. With the help of some temporary managers, Filo and Yang had gone out and hired a half-dozen college students to sift the hundreds, then thousands, then tens of thousands of link submissions that were coming in every day from people and businesses setting up pages on the World Wide Web. Each student had to go through a hundred to three hundred sites per day and decide whether or not they would add any value to the Yahoo directory.

Filo and Yang had come up with a business plan in March, prior to fund-raising. It called for Yahoo to become an advertising-supported *TV Guide* for the Internet. It said that Yahoo would only ever sell ads against its five most popular pages, and that it would cycle through just eight advertisers every three months.

Mallett threw the plan out.

August 1995 brought the first big change to Yahoo's core functionality. The company signed a deal with Reuters to publish ten stories per day on Yahoo.com. Then it signed ad deals with six advertisers, including Visa and General Motors, charging them just $20,000 per month.

That fall, Mallett, Koogle, and Yang set out to find more investment funds for Yahoo. They met with Eric Hippeau, the CEO of magazine publishing company Ziff Davis. He wanted to invest. They lined a deal up. But then Ziff Davis itself was acquired by Softbank, a massive Japanese conglomerate headed by an energetic, golf-loving industry titan named Masayoshi Son. Hippeau introduced Masayoshi Son to Jerry Yang and the two hit it off. Together with Reuters, Softbank invested $5 million in Yahoo at a $40 million valuation—just eight months after Sequoia invested at a $4 million valuation.

Masayoshi Son told Yang he wanted him to start thinking about how to expand Yahoo internationally. He thought the company could do well investing in Asia, in particular.

By then, the number of links people were submitting to Yahoo every day had reached the thousands, and Yahoo's coterie of college kids were totally swamped. Softbank's money allowed Filo to hire some serious technical help.

When the Softbank investment hit Yahoo's bank account, the company had only six full-time employees. By the time Jeff Mallett watched Dallas Cowboys wide receiver Kevin Williams field the opening kickoff of Super Bowl XXX in front of 76,000 people sitting on purple seat cushions, Yahoo had fifty people. In the next four months, the headcount would quadruple to two hundred.

That was just the start.

––––

Over the next four years, Yahoo went on the greatest run the world of business had ever seen. When Yahoo began selling ads in 1995, the estimated size of the entire online advertising market was $20 million. By 1997, Yahoo's revenues alone were $70.4 million. The next year, they were $203 million.

Yahoo went from 200 employees in 1996 to 400 at the end of 1997. It had 803 in 1998 and 1,992 in 1999.

Traffic to Yahoo.com went from 6 million daily page views in March 1996 to 14 million by the end of the year. In 1997, they reached 65 million; in 1998, 167 million.

Yahoo held its initial public offering on April 12, 1996. The stock traded up to $43 dollars per share and then came back down to $33. The 151 percent IPO spike was the third-largest in history. At the end of the day, Yahoo's market capitalization was $848 million. That meant the company was worth $808 million more than the valuation at which Masayoshi Son and Softbank bought in three months before. Jerry Yang and David Filo went to bed that Friday night worth $130 million each, a little more than a year after they incorporated the company.

It takes a female elephant twenty-two months to gestate a calf. Filo and Yang made their first $100 million in less than half that time.

But that was nothing. Both were billionaires by the summer of 1998—only four years after they started swapping lists of links with each other.

Here's what happened: All of the media-connected world began to hear about Tim Berners-Lee's World Wide Web, and Yahoo.com was the most user-friendly way to see what was out there.

In 1996, Yahoo ditched the Uncle Stinky logo when, at a trade show in Boston, it looked bad on the booth. Employee number ten, David Shen, came up with a new one. Out went burgundy and lowercase letters. In came bright red capital letters and a boxy exclamation point. The ubiquity of that Yahoo logo by summer of 1998 was stunning. It was on Visa cards, Zamboni machines at NHL games, and Ben & Jerry's ice cream containers. There was a Yahoo magazine. When Hasbro came out with a ".com" version of Monopoly, Yahoo got the Boardwalk slot on the board. By then, too, Wall Street analysts had come up with a term for what Yahoo was: a portal. It was the consumer-friendly interface for the entire web. In many ways, Yahoo *was* the web.

That's because, over his first few years inside Yahoo, Jeff Mallett had built a giant manic machine operating at a tempo matched only by his own. Inside this machine sat Mallett, frenetically manipulating the controls.

Mallett began building his machine after he saw how successful Yahoo's deal with Reuters was in the summer of 1995, when Yahoo started serving ten news stories a day from the wire service. At that moment, Yahoo became more than a directory full of website listings. For Mallett, it became a real-time interactive platform that provided users something they wanted, right when they wanted it.

Mallett and the rest of the company's management team decided Yahoo needed to build out more of those kinds of products and services.

But what kinds of products and services? The next breakthrough for Mallett and Yahoo came with the realization that it had in its possession a live, constantly updating treasure map that could answer this question exactly.

Mallett came from the world of PC software, where you built features and hoped that users liked them and that their appreciation showed up in sales. At Yahoo, he saw that you could actually track which categories and subcategories users were clicking into on the directory as they tried to find a product that they wanted to use. He realized no one was in a better position than Yahoo to use that data to build the products people wanted to find on the web. He called this "click-finding."

And so, in 1997 and 1998, Yahoo rapidly expanded its lineup of products and services. It added chat rooms in January 1997 and classifieds in February. It spent $94 million to acquire an email product in October. It launched a travel section in November. In 1998 came sports, games, movies, real estate, a calendar, file sharing, auctions, shopping, and an address book. By 2000, Yahoo had four hundred different products and services. In 1999, you could open Netscape Navigator and use the Internet all day and never leave Yahoo and never want to. This was by design.

Mallett knew a company with a typical organizational structure would never be able to build, maintain, and update all those products. So he didn't build a typical organizational structure for Yahoo. He decided to hire as many people as possible and group them into product teams, which he called "pods." Then, when Yahoo had more than five hundred employees, he began encouraging employees to join second product groups as part of something called a "virtual seven." Like Mallett during his summers in college, employees would have day jobs and night jobs. How it would work was that Mallett would take someone from one team—say, Yahoo Finance—and tell them to find six other people from around the company to build an entirely new product. It didn't matter if the team all worked in the same place. Maybe you found someone in London who was good at building a real-time feed in HTML. Maybe the best sales person for the team was located in New York and the designer you needed was in Sunnyvale. Fine. Just go. Build it now. And don't forget your day job. Eventually there were hundreds of pods and ad hoc virtual sevens and just a few core corporate functions like HR and legal run out of Sunnyvale.

At the center of it all, keeping tabs on everything, was, of course, Mallett. His goal: Track those server logs and push Yahoo to evolve as fast as the new Internet consumer—hopefully faster. He put a general manager at the head of every pod and told them to act like startup CEOs. He gave them funding and aggressive revenue targets. He staffed the positions with graduates from the country's top MBA programs. It was very easy for him to recruit. Bright young self-starters loved the idea of running their own well-funded business under a brand consumers already loved.

Mallett worked ninety hours a week keeping up with everyone he'd hired and everything they were working on. It wasn't hard for him. He found working gave him energy. He felt like he was on a mission. He believed the key to keeping such a distributed organization pointed in the right direction was to have a clean and simple strategy that everyone knew. By then, Yahoo was in twenty-seven countries, and Mallett would go into every office around the world and ask every employee, What is Yahoo's mission? He wanted a specific answer: to have a branded consumer service that aggregates the best services in content, communications, and commerce, and provides it in a simple easy format to search and find and consume.

That's it, he'd think when someone got it right. Clean and simple.

Because he couldn't be everywhere all the time—though he seemed to try—Mallett set up something called neighborhood watch. Its goal was to flush out of the company poor performers and people who just didn't understand the mission. If an employee or someone they worked with wasn't the perfect person for their job, employees were to let Mallett know. A lot of times, people told on themselves. They'd come to him and say, "I can't scale. I'm in over my head." Mallett took great pride in the fact that he had more people resign than he ever had to fire.

Despite the workload and frenetic pace, Yahoo was not a hellish place to work.

That's because amid Mallett's hyperactivity and Yahoo's hypergrowth, the company managed to retain a vibe to match its brand: friendly, irreverent, and a little anti-corporate. This was because of its cofounders and CEO. In February 1996, Yahoo moved to a new office, relocating from Mountain View to Sunnyvale, another Silicon Valley town south of San Francisco. Though there was room to have private offices for executives, Koogle, Mallett, Yang, and Filo opted to work out of cubicles just like everyone else. Yang and Filo kept driving the same cars to work they always had: a beat-up Toyota Tercel and an Oldsmobile Cutlass. Koogle lived in a small rented apartment. On weekdays, he'd gather the troops and give speeches about Yahoo's incredible successes and the next hills it had to charge. In the hallways, he'd stop to chat with anyone. He'd coach. He'd co-manage. He'd give input when asked. He was calm. He was sexy. In his all-black outfits, his flowing silver hair and deep blue eyes really popped. On weekends, he went glassblowing. At board meetings, he handed the directors a short bullet-pointed list of topics to cover.

Yang remained Yahoo's spiritual leader—a sort of walking, talking embodiment of the brand. He and Filo called themselves "Chief Yahoos." He acted as an advisor to Mallett and Koogle on strategy, specializing in Yahoo's global expansion. He drove the formation of a joint venture with Softbank to launch Yahoo Japan, and he went to Japan to set up that office. He did the same in Korea.

Filo kept to himself, working quietly out of his cubicle, helping a growing team solve technical problems that fascinated him. He did not lead the team. That job went to a man named Farzad

Nazem, an Oracle veteran known to everyone as Zod. Zod had his pick of Silicon Valley's engineering talent, and he would give job applicants brutal exams. He put three complex questions on a whiteboard, started a stopwatch, and told the applicant to solve everything in fifteen minutes. Go. Yahoo developed a reputation for having the best engineers in the Valley. It was the place to work.

By the start of 1999, Yahoo had expanded to China and Germany and Australia. It had an impressive list of partners—huge brands like Visa and MTV. Yahoo was at the table for every mergers and acquisitions (M&A) deal that went through Silicon Valley. It was closing in on some insane milestones: 4,000 employees hired, 250 million users reached, $1 billion in all-time revenues generated. Yahoo had basically created the online advertising industry, inventing ways of serving and tracking ads that had become standards. Competitors of all sorts, from Time Warner to Disney to NBC, had tried and failed to clone Yahoo's model.

The big, older companies failed to take out Yahoo for a number of reasons. The Internet was a side business for them. They couldn't attract talent the way Yahoo was able to with its stock compensation. Yahoo was based in Silicon Valley, where the pool of available engineers was deep. Yahoo had a huge head start, thanks to the early link from Netscape. Yahoo's brand was synonymous with the Internet. Most important of all: Yahoo's web products worked better and faster, thanks to an innovative distributed network of servers.

At the beginning of that year, 1999, Yahoo had a market value of $23 billion. And there was this stat: Yahoo's original product, its directory, accounted for less than 20 percent of the site's total page views. The other 80 percent of traffic went to products developed on Mallett's watch. He rightly felt like he had built a big company.

In the first three months of 1999, Yahoo's market cap jumped from $23 billion to $35 billion. The rest of the year went even better. When Yahoo paid a crazy high price of $5.7 billion for a startup called Broadcast.com, it sent Yahoo's stock up 22 percent the next day.

Over the whole year, Yahoo generated $590 million in revenues. During the fourth quarter alone, sales figures matched all of Yahoo's sales in 1998.

On January 3, 2000, Yahoo's market cap reached $128 billion—up $105 billion from the year before.

Then things started to fall apart.

———

By late 2000, tensions were boiling over inside Yahoo.

One day, Jerry Yang sat down for an interview with Doug Levy, a former journalist who had become well known for his tech-industry coverage in *USA Today*. Levy was no longer a member of the media. He was working as an independent media consultant and he'd figured out a good gig. He would go into a company and interview its executives as though he were going to write an article. Then he'd prepare a critical piece and let them read it. The idea was to show them where the company's holes were.

The meeting started pleasantly enough. Levy told Yang: Look, I'm doing a fake story but it's going to be a real interview. So I'm going to have to ask some tough questions.

Yang seemed to get the idea. But then Levy started asking questions. It had been a difficult year for Yahoo, and Levy had lots of material.

He asked questions like: Was Yahoo's advertising business as dependent on dot-coms as Wall Street analysts alleged?

And: How would Yahoo deal with the reality that web surfers weren't clicking on ads as much as they used to?

Yang answered the questions, but he was getting visibly irritated—red in the face, even. Levy went on:

Was Yahoo management still working well together?

Was it true that management discord had been the reason Yahoo had been unable to acquire eBay?

Yang started fidgeting with a pen on the table in front of him.

Speaking of eBay, what was Yahoo going to do about all these fast-moving startups competing with Yahoo products?

Finally, Yang had enough. He said, "I'm done with this." He stood up. He was still holding the pen he'd been playing with. He flung it down and across the table. It skittered across the surface toward the consultant.

The interview, fake or not, was over. Yang stormed out.

The main problem with Yahoo in 2000 was that, in a way, its advertising business had become too successful over the prior five years.

As Yahoo's popularity surged in 1996, 1997, and 1998, other Internet startups—dot-coms, everyone called them—discovered an incredible reality: Just by announcing a partnership with Yahoo or its rival, America Online, the dot-com's stock price would shoot through the roof. For example, a company called Individual Investor Online announced it would supply content for Yahoo Finance in August 1998. Its stock spiked 36 percent that same day.

Yahoo executives, particularly its chief dealmaker, Ellen Siminoff, quickly realized the company could profit from the phenomenon. Yahoo developed a lucrative business based on squeezing startups for all they were worth.

Siminoff or one of her lieutenants would field a call from a well-funded startup asking to become Yahoo's premier bookseller, online travel agency, or music seller. Siminoff would say, Sure, but it's going to cost you. The startup would say, How much? Siminoff would say, How much do you have?

The answer was "A lot."

In 1998, venture capitalists invested $22.7 billion in startups, many of them dot-coms. In 1999, that number more than doubled to $56.9 billion. Often enough, that money flowed straight from the venture capitalists to the startups in their portfolio to the coffers of Yahoo and its portal rivals.

For a time, the arrangement benefited everyone. By 1999, well-funded dot-coms were paying Yahoo millions of dollars just to be able to mention the deal in their regulatory filing prior to going public. Then, on the day of the IPO, investors—often amateurs wanting in on the action—would bid the dot-coms up to crazy prices.

In July 1999, a company called Drugstore.com was preparing to go public. In terms of revenues and profits, it was a small business. In fact, it was losing a lot of money. In the first quarter of 1999, it had sales of $652,000 and losses of $10.2 million. The next quarter, sales reached $3.5 million, but losses steepened to $18.8 million. The company said it had only 168,000 paying customers. And yet, Drugstore.com went ahead with its plans to go public. Investment bankers at Morgan Stanley Dean Witter advised the company to price its shares between $9 and $11. Then, the day before Drugstore.com's IPO, the bankers changed their minds. They told Drugstore.com to offer its shares at a higher price—$15 to $17 per share. It turns out even that was too low. The next day, Drugstore.com went public and shares traded all the way up to $69 per share before settling at $54.25. The company planned to go public with a market cap of $680 million. It finished the day with a market value of $2.1 billion.

One reason for the spike: In March, Drugstore.com had announced a major advertising partnership with Yahoo and a few other portals. Drugstore.com would be Yahoo's premier online pharmacy partner. For the privilege, Drugstore.com paid Yahoo and the other portals $25 million. No one much cared that Drugstore.com had only $38 million in the bank and was blowing it all on just a couple marketing deals—it had a deal with Yahoo.

The problem with squeezing startups was that, over time, distribution on Yahoo.com proved to be less valuable than dot-coms or their public investors thought. When Yahoo first started showing banner ads—rectangular graphical advertisements on the margins of its sites—about 5 percent of users who saw them would click on them. By the end of 2000, click-throughs were down to 0.5 percent and falling.

During its short life as an independent company, Petstore.com spent $150,000 per month on Yahoo ads, paying about $200 per new customer. Drugstore.com's $25 million spend on portal marketing didn't have a very good return on investment, either. Three years after its IPO, its share price was below $1.

For a time, Jeff Mallett didn't believe the source of funding for his sprawling machine was unsustainable. When Yahoo bought a web publishing startup called GeoCities in 1999, GeoCities CEO Thomas Evans—a veteran of the magazine industry—warned Yahoo executives about aggressive tactics: "Ad sales are a cyclical business. People hate you. You're arrogant and condescending. When there's a downturn in the market, they'll cut you first."

Mallett shouted him down. "You don't get it!" he said. "You're old media!"

But then, in April 2000, Yahoo held a conference for its salespeople in Arizona. Yahoo's top sales executive, Anil Singh, walked onstage in front of hundreds of people. Singh joined the company as its first sales employee in 1995 and had hired everyone in the room.

Singh was famous for rah-rah speeches full of "Anilisms" like "Get with it!" and "We're rockin'!" and the crowd expected more of that. Instead, Singh went onstage and put on-screen behind him a huge picture of a dark, foreboding cloud. Like a frightened prophet, he warned the room: "A storm is coming!" He said Yahoo would have to start selling ads to more traditional companies, that the days of selling ads to dot-coms at exorbitant prices would not last forever. He spent the rest of the conference hammering home the theme.

The rich kids who made up Yahoo's sales force thought it was a real bummer. Many didn't believe Singh. Their paychecks were still heavy with commission fees. Like Mallett, they'd been at Yahoo for a few years now and everything had only gone up and to the right.

Then, in the late spring of 2000, previously bullish Wall Street analysts Holly Becker, from Lehman Brothers, and Henry Blodget, from Merrill Lynch, began openly wondering how much of Yahoo's revenues was coming from unstable dot-com businesses. On July 7, a Friday, Deutsche Banc Alex. Brown analyst Andrea Williams downgraded Yahoo stock from a "strong buy" to a mere "buy." The stock dropped $5.88 to $116.50. Mallett was furious. When the *Wall Street Journal*'s Mylene Mangalindan wrote up Williams's report in a Monday news story, Mallett's PR team declared war on her and forbade any executives from ever talking to her again.

But dot-coms kept failing despite big partnerships with Yahoo, and Wall Street analysts noticed. On August 28, 2000, Becker dropped the hammer. She said that of Yahoo's top 200 advertisers, 61 percent were dot-coms. She downgraded Yahoo. The stock dropped 9 percent in a day.

By October 2000, Mallett got the picture. His glorious machine, his sprawling system of four hundred pods and hundreds more virtual sevens, was in peril. At a retreat in Yosemite National

Park, Mallett told the senior management team that Yahoo needed to change the way it did business. It had to find a more sustainable business than squeezing startups. It had to treat advertisers better.

It was the right thing to say. It was too late.

When Jeff Mallett was twelve years old, he was shorter and smaller than the rest of the kids on his soccer team. But he was so intense and passionate about winning, the coach made him captain anyway. On the field, Mallett's teammates thought he was fearless, the way he'd throw himself around on the field, at and between and around much bigger kids.

On the morning of Tuesday, November 21, 2000, Jeff Mallett sat in his cubicle and tried to draw upon those leadership skills once more. But instead, all he felt was angry.

That morning, Morgan Stanley Dean Witter analyst Mary Meeker, previously an unapologetic Yahoo bull, had published a seriously damning report on the company's business. She wrote that Yahoo had a 30 percent chance of missing its revenue targets over the next few quarters because it depended too much on Internet advertising, which she called "tough and wacky."

"Among Internet leaders," she wrote, "we think Yahoo...is most at risk."

Now, Mallett held a printed-out copy of the report in his hands. For ten minutes, he sat in his cubicle and seethed.

Then the rage passed and a familiar sense of determination set in. Mallett took the report and pinned it to his cubicle wall—just above his children's artwork. He stuck a Post-it note on it.

The note read: "The market's tough, but we're tougher."

Along with Koogle and Yang, Mallett came up with a plan. He called it Yahoo 2.0. The gist was: Yahoo would hire new general managers for key products, move away from selling ads to dot-coms, and begin charging users for some of its products and services.

Meanwhile, Meeker's November 21 report spurred Yahoo's board into action as well. At their meeting in Sunnyvale later that quarter, Yahoo's seven directors discussed whether or not the company needed new management. Mallett and Koogle, who both served on the board, recused themselves from the conversation. That left the call to Jerry Yang, Yahoo's only cofounder on the board; Mike Moritz, Yahoo's original investor; Eric Hippeau, Softbank's representative; Art Kern, an independent director; and a new director, Edward Kozel.

On the one hand, 2000 had been a brutal twelve months for Yahoo's stock. It would finish the year down 87 percent from a January 3 high. But the company had managed to double 1999's revenues. It seemed unfair to fire a CEO after such a strong financial performance. Koogle was safe. Anil Singh, however, was not so lucky. The sales boss who had warned of a coming storm soon found himself leaving Yahoo to spend more time with his family and pursue personal interests.

As Yahoo 2.0 gained traction, Mallett began to wonder if all the turmoil might actually lead to change at the top of the company—change that would put him ultimately in charge. Then he began to believe this would happen. In a January 2001 interview with a top candidate for a sales job, he let it slip that he would soon "move up."

But on January 10, Yahoo 2.0 met its early death. Ten days into the quarter, advertising sales were so bad that management decided it had to warn shareholders. Koogle offered to resign. For two months, Yahoo directors considered whether to accept.

Finally, on February 27, 2001, the Yahoo board met to decide what to do. Yang, growing ever bolder and more confident as a business leader at Yahoo, did most of the talking, along with Moritz, Yahoo's original investor. Koogle, still Yahoo's chairman, reiterated his offer to resign. The board accepted his offer. Yahoo would immediately begin a search for a new CEO.

Mallett expected his fellow directors to tell him he would be a candidate for the job. After all, he'd built the machine that 250 million people used each month and that generated $1.1 billion in revenues in 2000.

But that's not what they told him. They told him he was not a candidate to be CEO. Mallett was shocked and saddened.

In the end, three traits cost Mallett his shot at the job—none of which he could ever have changed.

The first was his age. Moritz and Yang wanted to hire a CEO with gray hair. Someone with experience running a large public company. Someone Wall Street would trust. In February 2001, Mallett was only thirty-five years old. How could a CEO under forty save Yahoo?

The second trait that cost Mallett was his ambition—his thirst for power. In 1999, Yahoo had been close to acquiring online auctions startup eBay. eBay's board and Yahoo's board approved the deal, but it fell apart when Mallett demanded that eBay's CEO, Meg Whitman, report to him and not Koogle. There was also talk that Mallett would target Yahoo executives who seemed to threaten his influence with Yang and Koogle and make their lives hellish until they quit the company. The hard-playing competitiveness that had driven Mallett so far since his youth—to his first million dollars in his midtwenties, to the corner office at a big software company, to the near-top of a $128 billion company—was his tragic flaw.

Sadly, the final trait that cost Mallett his chance at the CEO job was his height. Because of it, high-powered executives visiting Yahoo would sometimes show up for a meeting at Yahoo's headquarters, find Mallett waiting for them in a conference room, and assume he was an intern—someone there to get the coffee. Mallett could see them thinking that. Yahoo's directors never mentioned height as an issue to each other, but they would say things like: Yahoo needs someone with stature. They didn't want to put Sparky in charge.

The night of February 27, Tim Koogle called Jim Citrin of executive recruiting firm Spencer Stuart and asked him to begin finding a replacement.

On March 7, Merrill Lynch analyst Henry Blodget wrote a note wondering if Yahoo was about to get rid of its management team. Merrill was hosting an Internet conference that week and Yahoo's new CFO, Sue Decker, had been scheduled to speak. But suddenly she couldn't make it. There were also rumors that Jerry Yang canceled plans to speak at another event in Utah that week. Yahoo's stock tanked to $20.94 in the first seven minutes the market was open that morning, before the Nasdaq finally halted trading in YHOO. At five in the evening in the Eastern time zone, Yahoo issued a press release announcing a conference call later that day. On the call, Koogle revealed that he was stepping down.

On April 17, Yahoo said it had hired a new CEO: former Warner Bros. chief Terry Semel.

Koogle stepped down from his chairmanship on May 1. He was ready to go. He had a place in Italy and a Mercedes convertible that needed more driving.

Mallett stayed. The board offered him a lot of stock to stick around and help Semel get up to speed. Plus, Mallett wasn't ready to go. He'd built a machine, and he wanted to keep it running.

But soon, Semel hired the former chief of Reader's Digest, Greg Coleman, to run Yahoo's business in North America. He asked Mallett to focus on Yahoo's international business.

One day, Mallett found himself in Zurich, Switzerland. He'd just finished negotiating a deal with FIFA, international soccer's governing body. For some reason, he was in a nostalgic mood, and he started thinking about the first international deal he ever made for Yahoo. Way back in 1996, he went to Canada and partnered with Rogers, the big media company. It had meant a lot for Mallett. Now, in a plane on a tarmac in Zurich five and a half years later, Mallett was satisfied to have completed yet another deal with yet another global brand.

Then something strange happened. Mallett and the rest of the passengers on the plane were told to go back into the terminal. Their flight was canceled. Two airliners had flown into the World Trade Center towers in New York.

Mallett was stuck in Zurich for a week. That week, he thought about his kids. He missed them. He thought about how he hadn't been around to see them growing up. He'd been working too many ninety-hour weeks building a giant sprawling machine called Yahoo. He was proud of what he'd done. Sometimes, like an incantation, he'd recite these figures to himself: $1 billion in revenues, 250 million users, 4,000 employees.

But now, someone else was running that machine. Sometimes, Mallett couldn't bear to watch.

At the end of that week in Zurich, Mallett thought: That's it. I'm done. Within a few months, he was gone from Yahoo forever.

Every so often during the next dozen years, Mallett would wake up and realize he had been dreaming of running Yahoo again.

2

The Mogul

While Jeff Mallett sat in an airport in Zurich on September 11, 2001, a few people were already working at Yahoo headquarters in Sunnyvale, California. It was just after six in the morning, and the place was in a panic.

Yahoo had a new headquarters in Sunnyvale now—a classic corporate campus with sidewalks connecting big, boxy-looking, glass-and-steel buildings.

That morning, the executive team met in building D and decided everyone in the company should go home or stay home. They decided it made the most sense if the email came from Terry Semel, Yahoo's new CEO.

This posed a problem. Semel wasn't much of an emailer. It wasn't clear he actually knew how to use email or his laptop at all.

A solution presented itself: A communications manager named Shannon Stubo had arrived early at the office that day. She was summoned to Semel's office.

Actually, it wasn't Semel's office.

It was a Yahoo conference room.

But it was his office.

When Semel arrived at Yahoo, he was told that Koogle, the company's prior CEO, had worked in a cubicle just like the rest of Yahoo's employees. If Semel wanted to fit in, he'd do the same. This was hard for Semel. At his old job, he'd had a mahogany-paneled office the size of a small apartment. Still, he tried.

Cubicle living didn't take. Within weeks, he took over a nearby conference room, using its big table as his desk and keeping a TV on in the corner. Officially, the room remained a conference room. Unofficially, it was Semel's office.

By ten thirty, Stubo and a couple other people from HR, PR, and the executive team gathered in Semel's conference room. Stubo sat in front of Semel's laptop on the conference table. Semel dictated a note to Yahoo's four thousand employees about that morning's national tragedy. The young woman at the table typed away while the older executive paced and dictated. The whole scene felt very old-fashioned. Not very Yahoo.

Semel put off that kind of vibe a lot. This was natural, considering his background and age.

When Terry Semel joined Yahoo in April 2001, he was fifty-eight years old, twice the age of the average Yahoo employee. With his neatly trimmed gray hair, small, expensive-looking frameless glasses, and nice loafers, Semel looked like a well-dressed great uncle or grandfather.

Semel did not come from the dot-com industry. He was not even particularly familiar with the Internet, which, in his Brooklyn accent, he pronounced "Inna-net."

Semel made his name in the movie business. He started out as an accountant back east. Then, in 1965, his pal Dan Romanelli said he should try a sales-training program put on by Warner Bros., the big movie studio. Semel felt he might be a natural salesman. He went for it.

Semel was right; he turned out to be an ace salesman. He ended up selling movies to theater chains all across the country, from New York City to Cleveland to Los Angeles. He got poached by CBS and then by Disney, running distribution operations for both companies by the time he was thirty-two. In 1975, he got pulled back into Warner Bros. Within five years, he was running the whole studio along with a co-CEO, Bob Daly.

Under the tutelage of Steve Ross, the CEO of Warner Communications, Semel and Daly ran Warner Bros. for the next twenty years.

Over those twenty years, Warner Bros. revenues grew from $750 million to $11 billion. Semel and Daly did it by diversifying the business beyond theater sales. Semel rented out unused lots at Warner's studios to rivals, opening a new revenue stream and starting a trend that all the big studios ended up copying. He went hard into video. Later, when the rest of the industry was worried DVDs would ruin the video-rental business, Semel pushed forward and won big in what turned out to be an expanding market. Semel became known as a shrewd negotiator, a loyal boss, and a talented entertainment executive. Stars like Mel Gibson and Tom Cruise loved him. He bet big on Tim Burton's *Batman*, and Warner Bros. made a ton of money selling action figures and other merchandise. During his time in the movies, Semel did so well they put his handprints in the sidewalk in front of Mann's Chinese Theatre in Hollywood.

In 1998 and 1999, Semel and Daly's hot streak came to an end. While other studios were getting big hits out of small-budget films like *The Wedding Singer* and the *Scream* franchise, Warner Bros. had plowed huge sums of cash into flops like Kevin Costner's *The Postman* and the remake of a British television show called *The Avengers*. Warner's amusement-park and music businesses weren't doing great, either. By mid-1999, Semel was coming to the end of a deal that had paid him $500 million, and he knew the next offer wouldn't be as rich. On July 14, 1999, Semel and Daly went into Time Warner CEO Gerald Levin's office in Rockefeller Center and quit.

Semel wasn't retiring. He didn't feel old yet. He wanted to go out and earn some more; an early divorce meant that $500 million wasn't all his. Semel wanted to write the next chapter, he told colleagues.

A bunch of the other studios in Hollywood called Semel up and asked if he wanted a job. He passed. He'd already done all that. He formed an investment group called Windsor Media. He hired some young people to help him manage his money—kids named Jeff Weiner and Toby Coppel. Windsor made a few investments in Internet companies. None amounted to much.

Then, in March 2001, Yahoo announced it was looking for a new CEO, and a couple days later, Semel got a call from his friend Jerry Yang.

Semel met Yang in 1997 at a retreat put on by boutique investment bank Allen & Co. in Idaho. They stayed in touch, having lunch together every few months. Yang, technically still in his first full-time job—Chief Yahoo—was still learning about business and seeking more mentors like the one he had in Softbank's Masayoshi Son. Semel kept up the relationship because he wanted to know more about the "Inna-net." The more he talked to Yang, the more he realized its promise. It could be the world's best distributor of content—better than videocassettes, better than DVDs, and way better than driving all over the Northeast selling movies to regional theater chains.

In April 2001, Yang offered Semel the job. He wanted Semel to turn Yahoo into a next-generation media company. Semel said yes, and became chairman and CEO on May 1. He wanted to be Hollywood's bridge into the digital era. It was an adventure worthy of being his next chapter.

When news broke of the hire, people in Hollywood couldn't

believe that Semel, of all people, was going to go run a dot-com business. Semel's old boss, Gerald Levin, apparently laughed out loud when he heard the news. That guy? Going there?

Semel did think about whether it was insane for him to join an Internet company when he had no idea how software was made and had never really used the Internet or computers. But, he thought, I don't know how to act, direct, or operate a camera and I was good at running a movie company. And, as a new Internet user, I'll be a lot like all the people we want to use Yahoo. I'll get where they are coming from.

Semel's arrival at Yahoo was a bit of a culture shock. Unlike with Koogle, it didn't feel like you could just walk into Semel's cubicle. Semel didn't walk the halls. There was the conference room that became his office. Word got around that he didn't use email, or Yahoo even. While Koogle had kept a one-bedroom apartment near Yahoo's office, Semel continued to live in a Los Angeles mansion. He commuted to work each week on a Gulfstream. When in town, he spent his nights at the Four Seasons in San Francisco and rode into the office each day in the back of a Range Rover.

Semel didn't make much of a salary at Yahoo: just $310,000 per year, the same as Koogle. He did, however, ask for and receive a lot of stock options. His first grant would allow him to buy ten million shares, 2 percent of the company, at a price between $17.62 and $75. Then Semel upped the ante on his incentives and took $17 million of his own money and bought a million shares of Yahoo on the public markets. He got into Yahoo cheap. This was after the company had shrunk more than 90 percent in a year—from $128 billion to $12.6 billion.

The idea was: If Semel was able to stop Yahoo from shrinking and get it growing at a decent pace again, he would make an unbelievable amount of money.

The flip side was: If Semel couldn't get Yahoo growing again,

he'd walk away poorer, having proven all the doubters in Hollywood and in Yahoo's offices right, that he was an old, out-of-touch
Luddite who should have stuck with an industry he knew something about.

———

For the next five years, Terry Semel and Yahoo proved all the doubters wrong.

In his first year on the job, 2001, Yahoo lost $98 million. In 2005,
it profited $1.2 billion. In 2001, Yahoo's market cap was $12.6 billion. In 2006, it was $50 billion, as much as Disney's or Viacom's.
Revenues between 2001 and 2005 went from $717 million to $5.3
billion. In Semel's first month on the job, Yahoo had four thousand
employees. By 2006, it had more than ten thousand.

Semel's formula for success was simple: He rode the Internet
adoption and Internet advertising waves and didn't panic. Even
though Yahoo's ad business had imploded with the dot-com bubble,
actual web users continued to visit the site more every day. To succeed, Semel just had to take all that attention and build a traditional
advertising business out of it.

He replaced Mallett with Dan Rosensweig, making him Yahoo's
chief operating officer in 2002. Rosensweig made his career at Ziff
Davis, the publishing company that invested in Yahoo in 1995. At
Ziff Davis, Rosensweig worked his way up in sales and eventually
became the publisher of *PC Magazine*. Then he launched a magazine called *Yahoo! Internet Life*, a joint venture between Yahoo and
Ziff Davis. Finally, he took over Ziff Davis's Internet operations, a
spun-out company called ZDNet. He took ZDNet public and then
sold it to CNET in 2001.

For many Yahoo employees, Rosensweig was a far more visible
leader during the Semel era. At all-hands meetings, Semel would
get up and say something in a flat, quiet tone that everyone would

forget. Then Rosensweig would stand up and be the cheerleader guy, inspiring the troops. Rosensweig had dark, close-cropped, curly hair that was thinning up top. He looked jolly, with his shiny cheeks and toothy smile. Rosensweig held Mallett's job at Yahoo, and he was also a more active operator, reporting to a relatively passive CEO. But he was never as bullheaded and pushy with Semel as Mallett had been with Koogle.

Crucially, Semel kept on the chief financial officer he inherited from Tim Koogle. Her name was Sue Decker. She joined Yahoo in 2000 and, for most of the next decade, few people would have as much influence on the company as her. She was tall, with short blond hair and a serious demeanor. She nearly always wore business suits and jackets in a palette heavy with tan, blue, and gray.

Born in 1962, Susan Lynne Decker grew up in Denver. She went to Tufts University, where she double majored in computer science and economics. She got a master's from Harvard Business School.

During her first year in graduate school, Decker interviewed at a small investment bank called Donaldson, Lufkin & Jenrette. Decker hadn't held a full-time job between college and graduate school, so, on her résumé, she listed some of the odd jobs she'd done for money. One of them was "professional magician." It was a stretch. Decker had once performed for a bunch of six-year-olds and made a little money.

Of course, the DLJ interviewers asked her about her magic skills.

Decker was one of those shy people who force themselves to dive into uncomfortable situations because they know that's the only way they are going to get what they want out of life.

Decker dove in. She said to her interviewers: "Would you like to see a trick?"

They took the bait. Decker said she had an invisible deck of cards in her pocket. She made a show of taking it out and handed it to one of the interviewers. She said: "Pick a card, any card."

She said: "What's the card?"

The interviewer played along, made up a card, and said, "It was the eight of hearts."

Decker pulled out a real deck of cards from her pocket. She fanned out the cards—only one was face down. Decker turned it over: the 8 of hearts.

She got the internship.

By the mid-1990s, Decker was working as an analyst for DLJ, covering advertising and newspaper stocks as well as "information" stocks like Reuters. Still naturally shy but full of ideas, Decker made a habit of forcing herself to express big, bold opinions. In the late 1980s, she called a downturn in the newspaper industry when everyone else, including Warren Buffett, was bullish. Decker was proven right. Decker became a star at DLJ, rated number one in her sector for ten consecutive years by *Institutional Investor*.

When businesses built around the Internet started to go public, many investment banks found analysts to cover all Internet stocks. Merrill Lynch hired Henry Blodget; Morgan Stanley had Mary Meeker.

Donaldson, Lufkin & Jenrette decided its analysts would cover Internet companies based on their sector. Its retail analyst covered Amazon. Its software analyst followed Netscape. Its advertising analyst, Sue Decker, reported on Yahoo.

When Yahoo went public in 1996, Decker was one of just three analysts on the deal, and the only one who had covered the advertising industry. Decker followed Yahoo until 1998, when she was made research director at DLJ. In 1999, she called Jerry Yang to brainstorm about the Internet. Did he think there were any companies out there that she could help run? She became the CFO of Yahoo in June 2000.

What Decker found when she got to Yahoo alarmed her. The year prior, 1999, Yahoo had generated about $1 billion in revenues selling ads, which was great. There were two problems. The first was that a huge percentage of the billion dollars came from ads sold to dot-coms—dot-coms that Decker believed did not have defensible business models. The second problem was that Yahoo was not telling its investors how much of its revenues were coming from dot-coms. That meant Yahoo investors were betting big money on the health of some seriously volatile dot-com businesses without knowing that was what they were doing. Decker didn't think that was right.

Her first big decision as Yahoo's chief financial officer was a tough, painful one. In the September quarter of 2000, she told investors, for the first time, that more than half of Yahoo's revenues came from pure-play dot-coms. The disclosure destroyed the stock. On September 26, the stock hit $8.11, bringing Yahoo's market cap down to $5 billion—$123 billion off where it had been in January.

Few investors were upset with Decker. In fact, people were impressed. Yahoo's stock would have ended up tanking anyway in the coming months as dot-coms imploded and Yahoo revenues shrank. Thanks to Decker's disclosures, investors gave her and Yahoo credit for warning them about what was coming. For investors, bad news is always better than surprising bad news. Inside the company, Decker got credit for protecting Yahoo's reputation on Wall Street.

She earned more respect when, at the end of 2000, the Yahoo board told management to cut costs. That meant layoffs. One director looked at Decker and said, "Whatever you think you need to cut, you need to cut some more." Decker didn't falter. Along with Mallett, she retooled Yahoo's cost structure so that in 2001, the company was able to nearly break even on $400 million less in revenues. The cuts were deep. Four hundred people lost their jobs. But the cuts were swift, and once they were over, Yahoo's employees knew they were safe.

Decker's deep cost cutting in early 2001 allowed Semel to invest quickly in a sales force that could grow Yahoo's revenues generated by more traditional advertising sales.

To lead his sales force, he had Greg Coleman. Coleman had actually been Koogle's last big hire, joining Yahoo on March 20, 2001. Coleman was usually in an oxford shirt. He wore glasses on a round face and had thinning hair on top. Like all good salesmen, he would use the name of the person he was talking to. Like all great salesmen, he wouldn't overdo it. He had a direct way of a looking at a person and exuded empathic skills.

Coleman came to Yahoo from Reader's Digest and had been in publishing for twenty-five years. When he got to Yahoo, he would laugh a lot because he believed there were so many simple things he could do to get the business growing.

For starters, he could hire salespeople who actually knew buyers in the companies they were trying to sell ads to. Yahoo didn't have that before.

Even simpler: He could hire reps who knew how to use the phone to sell ads, rather than just take orders over email. Yahoo didn't have that before.

The next easy thing for him to do was to go out and apologize to everyone. In 2001, everyone in the ad agency world was angry at Yahoo because, as the market was crashing and the agencies wanted out of long-term deals they had signed up for in better times, Yahoo had said no.

So Coleman went on an apology tour. To warm the relationship even more, he hired sales leaders who were well known and well liked in the agency world. Then it was just a matter of showing the agencies and big ad-buying companies how big Yahoo was in terms of audience size. This was fun for Coleman to do because Yahoo kept getting bigger. In 1999, Yahoo had 100 million users each month. By 2002, it had 200 million. In 2006, Yahoo would become the most popular website on the planet.

Coleman liked to use a fishing analogy to describe the situation when he arrived. He would say that during Yahoo's first several years, the fish had jumped out of the water and into the boat. So no one inside the company had bothered to learn how to do simple things like bait a hook or throw a line in the water. What was the point? After the crash, the fish stopped jumping in the boat. But they were still in the water. Yahoo just needed someone to teach everyone how to fish. That was him.

In 2002, Yahoo grew its revenues 35 percent, almost to $1 billion again. They took off from there. So did Yahoo's stock price. From a low of $8.11 on September 26, 2001, it reached $43.21 on January 6, 2006.

Semel's gamble on himself and Yahoo paid off wildly. Before 2006 began, he banked more than $400 million, buying Yahoo shares at the low prices guaranteed in his option grants and selling them at higher prices on the public market.

The money was his to keep forever—no matter what came next.

In June 2000, Cindy McCaffrey, the head of marketing at a small startup based in Mountain View, called her counterpart at Yahoo. McCaffrey had to ask for a favor—a favor she wasn't going to get.

It was the height of the Jeff Mallett era, when he was using "click-finding" to decide in which "pods" he wanted to invest to build products and services for users coming to Yahoo.com. When Mallett found an activity Yahoo users liked to do, he would decide whether or not Yahoo should build a product around that activity, buy a company that made that product, or partner with one that made it. For example, in the case of email, Mallett had decided to buy. So Yahoo bought a company called Four11 for $94 million and used its technology to launch Yahoo Mail.

In the case of the small Mountain View startup McCaffrey worked for, Yahoo had decided to partner.

This was huge news for the startup, and McCaffrey and her bosses wanted to make a big deal out of it. So she was calling Yahoo to ask if, on the day of the announcement, Yahoo would be willing to send its cofounders, David Filo and Jerry Yang, over to the startup's offices to make an appearance and give a speech.

The woman from Yahoo that McCaffrey got on the phone was very nice and very polite, but she was also very young. Early- to midtwenties, it sounded like. McCaffrey did not let this put her off. McCaffrey said to the Yahoo woman: Jerry and David are so similar to our founders, who also went to Stanford. We'd really like them to come.

The Yahoo woman said she'd run the request up the flagpole.

Later, on the phone again with McCaffrey, the twenty-five-year-old from Yahoo said sorry, Jerry and David were busy that day, but Yahoo wanted to send its chief technology officer, Zod.

The truth was, the Yahoo woman's bosses thought the partnership was not a very big deal. She was told to give McCaffrey a polite but firm no.

This was an instance of Yahoo, then the Internet's most impressive and valuable company, big-timing a little startup called Google.

It wasn't the first time Yahoo dismissed Google.

Back in 1997, when Google was still a Stanford thesis project called BackRub, its creator, Larry Page, wanted to sell it for a million dollars so he could finish his PhD and become a professor. Page met with Jerry Yang and David Filo. Everyone got along, but Yahoo passed.

It's not that Yahoo management didn't think algorithmic

search was better than a handmade directory. Yang, Filo, Mallett, and Koogle all did. They just thought of Yahoo as a front-end company—a consumer-friendly user interface for the web. A brand. They thought of algorithmic search technology like Google's as commoditized, back-end technology. They believed that in the coming years, they would license search technologies from small, hard-core search companies that worked on nothing else. They liked the idea of being able to swap in better technology from another provider at any time. It was like how Dell and Gateway didn't make the chips inside their computers; Intel and AMD did.

By 2000, Yahoo had four thousand employees and only six of them working on search. This drove a man named Udi Manber nuts. As the head of Yahoo's search group, he wanted to hire a bunch more people and build an algorithmic search product for Yahoo. But management told him no. Instead, his job was to find the best back-end provider. He recommended that Yahoo dump its current search provider, Inktomi, and go with Google. Manber got the green light and finalized a deal. Google would provide Yahoo search, and Yahoo would pay Google every time a search query hit its servers. Yahoo also let Google put its logo on Yahoo search results pages.

It was as this deal neared completion that Cindy McCaffrey called up Yahoo and got big-footed by a twenty-five-year-old on the other end of the phone.

The announcement came on June 26, 2000. Not a lot of reporters came to Google headquarters. Those were the days when the *San Jose Mercury News* wouldn't come to the Googleplex because it was too far north up 101.

━━━━━━

Over the next twenty-four months, everything about search changed.

The first thing that happened was that Yahoo users loved Google search. Search traffic on Yahoo.com increased 50 percent in two months.

The next thing to happen was that Google.com started growing incredibly fast.

Yahoo's dealmakers were partly to blame. The Google logo on every Yahoo search results page was free advertising. It let consumers know why Yahoo search had suddenly gotten better: this thing called Google. Millions of web users went to Google.com and never came back.

In October 2000, Google sought to take advantage of its growing traffic by selling ads. Google called its ad product AdWords.

AdWords quickly proved to be an effective tool for marketers, and this made it lucrative for Google. AdWords ads got a much higher click-through rate than any other ads on the Internet. Unlike Yahoo, which sold banner ads against its search results pages, Google sold text ads that looked a lot like regular search results. That made them clickable. What made them even more clickable for consumers was how relevant the ads were to their search queries. That's because advertisers could pick which search queries would bring their ads up. Ford, if it paid enough, could put a link to its website on the top of every Google search for "cars for sale."

Google had gotten the whole idea for how its ads would work from a company called GoTo.com, a search engine that had been selling paid listings since 1998.

The next huge change to the search industry came in late 2001, when GoTo changed its name to Overture and began offering to provide web search to big websites and portals like Yahoo. The big change was that, instead of asking portals for money, Overture offered to pay them. Overture's deal was that it would serve AdWords-like ads against its search results and split the revenues with the portal.

In November 2001, Yahoo signed a five-month trial deal with Overture. It already had Google providing "organic" or "editorial" search results, so Yahoo told Overture: Just give us your ads and your cash and we'll see how we like it.

Yahoo liked the deal a lot.

The combination of Google search and Overture ads immediately added tens of millions of dollars to Yahoo's bottom line, helping it recover quickly from the loss of all those nonrecurring, startup-squeezing deals from the dot-com era. When the five-month trial was up, Yahoo signed a three-year deal with Overture in April 2002.

The following summer marked two years since Yahoo blew off McCaffrey and Google. The world had changed.

Now, Yahoo knew it needed to own search.

So, in the summer of 2002, Semel reached out to Google and asked if it would ever sell.

The Google people told him the price was $1 billion.

Semel met with his corporate finance team and they went through a process, trying to figure out if that was a fair price. The truth about the models, charts, and graphs developed by corporate finance teams like Yahoo's in 2002 is that they could come up with whatever answer the higher-ups wanted to hear.

The team told Semel $1 billion was more than fair; it was cheap. Semel had the green light. But when he went back to Google, Larry Page said sorry, the price was now $3 billion.

Semel met with his team again. He got the green light again. He went back to Google.

This time the number was $6 billion.

Semel went nuts when he heard that.

"Five billion dollars, seven billion, ten billion. I don't know what they're really worth—and you don't, either," Semel told his staff. "There's no fucking way we're going to do this!"

Actually, Yahoo and Semel might even have done a deal at $10 billion. But by then, they knew Google would never sell. Google cofounders Larry Page and Sergey Brin were willing to entertain Yahoo's offers, but ultimately they wanted to keep the company independent. Google was already insanely profitable, and its board had no problem shooting for an IPO. Yahoo never really had a chance to buy Google in 2002. That moment in 1997 was it.

Fortunately for Semel, when he joined Yahoo in April 2001, he'd given Sue Decker and the two young executives he'd brought over from Windsor, Jeff Weiner and Toby Coppel, a special assignment. He wanted the three of them to look at what Google was doing and what GoTo was doing, and figure out if search was something Yahoo needed to own, and if it was, how. Decker, Weiner, and Coppel spent the summer and fall of 2001 working out a strategy in conference rooms in building D. By the time Google was telling Semel $1 billion, $3 billion, and then $6 billion, they had a plan.

Now it was time to put that plan into action. It was time to go to the mattresses.

At first, they called it Project Godfather.

They called it that because, in the movie *The Godfather*, there's a montage where, as Al Pacino's Michael Corleone has his godson baptized in church, his hit men take out all of his family's enemies at once.

That was the plan Decker, Weiner, and Coppel had come up with for Yahoo. They were going to have Yahoo's M&A team take out the entire search industry—except Google, of course—all at once.

Yahoo's M&A boss, Keith Nilsson, was a tall, thin, high-cheekboned dealmaker in a sport coat. Nilsson loved the "Project

Godfather" code name. Whenever someone said it, he could hear the music from the movie in his head.

Then it dawned on him: Man, if that code name ever leaked to the press, it wouldn't look good. A touch too strong of a connotation.

So okay. Project Godfather became Project Symphony. It was still an aggressive play, and some of the most fun months in Yahoo's history.

Here's how it started: In the spring of 2002, Nilsson and his team took over the Phish Food conference room where Yahoo's board and executive team met in building D. On the whiteboard, Nilsson had the entire search industry mapped out.

Here's how it ended: On Sunday, July 13, 2003, Nilsson came into the office in shorts and a T-shirt to wrap up acquisition negotiations with Overture. There were just a few quick items to tidy up. The Overture team took one conference room and Nilsson and his guys took another. It was going to be easy.

It wasn't. Nilsson didn't get to go home that night. Overture was a public company, and the deal had to be announced before the markets opened Monday. So when talks hit a couple snags, no one left. Finally, it was 5:50 Monday morning, and early risers were starting to come into the office to work. The market opening came and went and still the two companies weren't done. Finally, five minutes after the opening bell, it was finished. The release went out. Somebody popped the champagne and everybody walked around giving handshakes and toasts, still in their weekend wear.

In the end, this was the sequence: In December 2002, Yahoo bought Inktomi for $235 million. In February 2003, Overture bought AltaVista for $140 million. Then, in July 2003, Yahoo bought Overture for $1.63 billion. Bang, bang, double-bang.

With Inktomi and AltaVista's search technology, Yahoo believed it could reach parity with Google in terms of organic search. With Overture, Yahoo believed it could sell ads just as well as Google, too.

There was one puzzling thing about the whole campaign: Microsoft used Inktomi for its algorithmic search and Overture to sell its search ads. Why had Microsoft allowed Yahoo to buy both? Was it planning something drastic?

Meanwhile, at Google, Yahoo's M&A spree had people nervous. Cofounder Sergey Brin moved a bunch of search relevancy engineers into cubicles closer to where he sat. It was time to take the competition seriously.

In the days after the Overture deal, Brin and cofounder Larry Page visited Semel in his office. They told him: What you've just done? This means war.

Semel laughed.

He said: "Are you going to bomb us?"

———

When Semel resigned from Yahoo in 2007, the *New York Times* published an unsigned editorial blaming Yahoo's downfall on Semel's inadequate response to Google.

It read: "Terry Semel failed as Yahoo's chief executive more than any other reason, of course, because he didn't respond properly to the challenge of Google. Mr. Semel passed on many opportunities simply to buy Google. And he was slow to understand Google's key business strategies—the power of search, the money from search advertising, the enormous value in creating a network that sells ads on other Web sites, and the improbable power of running a big company like a collection of dorm room startups. What's galling, of course, is that Yahoo was a leader in offering Web search and online advertising years before Google started."

But that's not how history should read.

History should read: Semel tried to buy Google for billions of dollars. Google said no. So Semel went out and bought a bunch of companies to create a Frankenstein version of Google for much less money. And it worked. For a while.

For eight months, Yahoo search grew much faster than Google search. Then, for a few months in the fall of 2004 and the winter of 2005, Yahoo and Google were essentially tied when it came to how much each owned of the search engine market in the United States. The margin was slimmest in November 2004, when, according to web metrics firm comScore, Yahoo held 32 percent of the market and Google held 34.6 percent.

Search was an incredibly valuable market for Yahoo to colead. It turned out that a search ad is the perfect ad. It shows up exactly when a consumer is looking for it. Marketers couldn't pour money into search ads fast enough, and Yahoo profited wildly from it. In 2002, Yahoo's first full year monetizing search with Overture ads, its revenues were $953 million. In 2003, the year Yahoo bought Overture, revenues grew 67 percent to $1.6 billion. In 2004, they grew 118 percent to $3.5 billion.

Those would be Yahoo's last winning years. In 2005, Yahoo's revenue growth began to slow and Google started to widen its lead in search market share.

From there, Google would go on to become the richest, most powerful Internet company in the world, reaching a market cap of $400 billion by 2014. Yahoo would live through a decade of decline and turmoil. All because Google won the search market and Yahoo lost it.

There are a million reasons why Yahoo lost to Google in search, but there's also just one reason why: Yahoo put the ads on its search results pages in the wrong order. Google put the ads on its pages in the right order.

At the beginning of the Internet, the main way Yahoo and other web publishers would charge advertisers was by how many times web users saw their ads. Ads were typically sold on an "impressions" basis—actually, on a per-one-thousand-impressions basis, also known as a CPM (cost per mille). They were sold that way because TV, radio, and print ads were sold that way. Yahoo and publishers would measure how often users clicked on ads, but mostly as a way of showing the advertisers how much attention their ads were getting.

Then, in 1998, an entrepreneur named Bill Gross created GoTo.com, which would become Overture. Instead of charging advertisers on a per-impression basis, he thought it would be a better idea to charge them on a cost-per-click (CPC) basis. He was right. By March 2002, when Google launched a cost-per-click version of AdWords, CPC was the main way search ads were sold.

Every time a user searched for a term like "flower delivery" and then clicked on an ad from 1-800-Flowers, Google, Overture, and eventually Yahoo would get a small amount of money from 1-800-Flowers, or whoever's ad it was. And the ad buyer was happy, because that meant they were getting someone onto their website who had been looking to make a transaction. The model worked.

But it worked better for Google.

Overture, and then Yahoo, would arrange the ads on the search results page from top to bottom in the order of which advertisers were willing to pay the most per click. It was a straight auction for every keyword. To the highest bidder went the top, most valuable slot.

Google's system for determining the arrangement was more complicated. It optimized the order for yield. Sometimes, it would put an ad at the very top of a page from an advertiser with a lower bid, because the ad was much more likely to be clicked on by users. Google's logic was sound: An ad that pays $0.55 per click is more valuable than an ad that gets $1.00 per click if it gets clicked on twice as much. Google would also do things like award the top slot to advertisers who bid the second-highest amount. That encouraged advertisers to bid high, knowing that they would never be caught far outbidding the marketplace. Google also played around with which ads it would show against which queries, never being as basic as Overture's strict auctions.

Essentially: Overture ran its monetization system from a spreadsheet, while Google used algorithms as sophisticated as the ones it used to crawl the web.

One reason for this was that, as an independent company, Overture had not made algorithms. When it was GoTo.com, it actually ordered all search results based on cost-per-click, not just its ads. Overture never needed the kind of PhDs and researchers working at Google.

Ironically, Yahoo did have top algorithmic talent inside its company. Part of Project Godfather had been to acquire Inktomi, which was full of brilliant search scientists just as good as anyone at Google. But Yahoo was reluctant to move those people into Overture because it was trying to run Overture as an independent, wholly owned subsidiary. The reason: Overture's biggest client was MSN.com, owned by Microsoft. MSN, a portal, was a direct competitor to Yahoo. Yahoo executives worried that Microsoft would pull MSN's business from Overture if it looked like Overture was too closely held by Yahoo. So Inktomi's engineers stayed put and Google ate Overture's lunch.

By 2005, Google's yield was much higher than Yahoo's on a per-search basis. Google took that extra cash and used it to outbid Yahoo on huge distribution deals that added chunks of market share. Google became the default home page and default search engine for the Firefox browser in 2004. In December 2005, Google paid Time Warner $1 billion to provide AOL's search results and search ads. In 2006, Google agreed to pay News Corp $900 million to provide search and search ads for MySpace. In 2007, Google agreed to pay IAC $3.5 billion to display search ads on Ask.com, a search engine with less than 5 percent share.

By then, Google had figured out that it was in an "increasing-returns business"—the more it spent, the more it made.

One reason that happened was that as Google added market share, search marketers decided to quit splitting their budgets between Yahoo and Google and concentrate all their bidding power in one market—Google's. That further drove yield, further enabling Google to buy market share, and on it went.

Inside Yahoo, Decker scrambled to find a way to match Google's massive bids for distribution deals. But she could never make the math work.

Finally, Yahoo launched a huge effort to improve its search ad yield. The project was code-named Panama. It was a multiyear project with the goal of bringing algorithmic expertise into Overture. Panama was led by a longtime Yahoo executive named Rich Riley and a search scientist named Qi Lu. And thanks to Panama, Yahoo caught up some. It quit ordering ads by highest bidder. It started taking the second-highest bids. The problem was, by the time all that happened, Google had ten thousand people working on search ads optimization, and it had countless more insights on how to juice yield. It was using that extra yield to invest in future products like Android and Chrome, which, like distribution deals, would put Google search directly in front of the consumer—but in an even more permanent fashion.

By then, it was too late for Yahoo to win search. Terry Semel was going to have to find another way into the future for Yahoo.

The more Terry Semel thought about it, the more he was sure he had Mark Zuckerberg in the palm of his hand.

It was July 2006. Semel was at Yahoo headquarters, waiting to be called into a conference room in building D. Joining him there would be Keith Nilsson, the lean Yahoo dealmaker who'd orchestrated Project Godfather a couple years before.

Nilsson and Semel were going to enter the room after Mark Zuckerberg arrived. Then Semel was going to deliver some tough news. After that, Semel believed, they were all going to shake hands and celebrate Yahoo's acquisition of Facebook.

Ever since his days of driving up and down the Northeast Corridor selling movies to theater chains, Semel considered himself a master negotiator. During his two-decade career in Hollywood, he earned the reputation as one. In fact, he was so good at it, there was an industry term for what he did to people: "getting Semelized." Producer Arnon Milchan, who made forty films with Semel, including 1997's *L.A. Confidential* and 1993's *Free Willy*, once described the process to a reporter. "First he doesn't return your calls for a while, so you get desperate. Then, when he finally agrees to see you, he makes you wait two hours. By the time you are ushered into his office, and he's given you a big hug and asked you about your life, you're so emotionally drained that you've almost forgotten why you came. He, however, has not."

During Yahoo's Project Godfather M&A spree of 2002 and 2003, Semel put his bargain-driving skills to use on Overture CEO Ted Meisel. Overture was based in LA, and during negotiations, Semel would have Meisel come over to his house on Sundays. They'd meet in Semel's lush home office. The two would catch up. It was friendly. But Semel would have Yahoo CFO Sue Decker there, too. And after a while, she'd show Meisel a series of financial models, demonstrating that, over time, Overture's margins were going to narrow and that really, the company wasn't worth as much as he thought. Meisel would hold firm on his asking price. But then the three of them would meet again the next Sunday, and the next. Finally, when Overture sold to Yahoo, it was for about 15 percent less than Meisel originally asked—a savings of $300 million. That's more than the amount Yahoo had paid for Inktomi, the other key acquisition in Project Godfather.

Now Semel was going to "Semelize" Zuckerberg. He was going to tell Zuckerberg, Look, $1 billion is too much. We can do $850 million. Zuckerberg, of course, was going to accept the lower offer. He was twenty-two. His board wanted him to sell. Even a slightly reduced offer was going to make him very, very rich. Rich enough to buy an island.

This wasn't Yahoo's first look at Facebook. Lots of people inside Yahoo had thought about buying Facebook since Zuckerberg created it in a Harvard dorm room in 2004. That year, a Yahoo M&A executive named Mike Marquez met with Zuckerberg and Facebook president Sean Parker about a possible deal. Later, Yahoo even put in an offer to buy Facebook right before it took its second big round of venture capital funding.

This effort was more serious. The idea to buy Facebook in 2006 came to Semel from the ranks below. The head of Yahoo's music group, David Goldberg, sent an email about it to his boss, COO Dan Rosensweig. Rosensweig had one of the guys on his team, Brad Garlinghouse, make a case for the acquisition in a pitch deck. They called it Project Fraternity. Garlinghouse pitched Project Fraternity to Semel and the rest of his executive team in the spring of 2006. Garlinghouse said there was a case to be made that Yahoo should buy Facebook for as much as $1.6 billion.

At the time, Facebook was a college-only social network. Rosensweig argued that if you opened it up to the rest of the world, Facebook could become one of the Internet's most valuable properties. Yahoo's top sales executive under Greg Coleman, Wenda Harris Millard, loved the deal. She didn't care if Facebook ever opened up beyond college kids. She thought she could easily sell enough ads to justify a big offer from Yahoo. College kids were a hard demographic for marketers to reach.

Semel decided to meet with Zuckerberg, Facebook's twenty-two-year-old CEO and cofounder. So one day late in June 2006, he flew up from LA and drove to the Palo Alto home of Facebook's COO, Owen Van Natta, to see Zuckerberg. The three got along okay, and the process went forward.

Semel put Yahoo M&A executives Toby Coppel and Keith Nilsson out front on the deal.

At first, Zuckerberg seemed very reluctant. He'd show up late to meetings, and then he'd act bored and irritated. But when he met Rosensweig, the two hit it off. Over a series of dinners, they talked about how, if Yahoo were to buy Facebook, it would run as a wholly owned but independent subsidiary, with Zuckerberg at the top. Rosensweig told Zuckerberg Facebook could stay in its Palo Alto headquarters and keep its culture. It would just have the backing of Yahoo when it needed it.

Zuckerberg said he thought Rosensweig could be the mentor he'd long been seeking to help him build out Facebook. Zuckerberg wanted to focus on developing Facebook's product. He didn't want to worry about operating a company, building out server infrastructure, and hiring an executive team.

Even so, Zuckerberg was still reluctant to do the deal. He wanted to see how big Facebook could get once it was open to the world beyond college users.

Zuckerberg's board of directors and senior management team thought this was nuts. Van Natta was especially vocal. Facebook's first outside investor, Peter Thiel, thought Zuckerberg would be insane to walk away from Yahoo. Zuckerberg eventually said he would do the deal—but only if Yahoo offered $1 billion.

Van Natta got the message to Yahoo: The kid will do it, but the offer has to be $1 billion.

From there, it seemed like only a matter of time till the deal got done. Zuckerberg and Van Natta met with Semel, Coppel, Decker, and Rosensweig at the Four Seasons in San Francisco. Zuckerberg said he wanted $1 billion. Semel said Yahoo could get there. They shook hands. Facebook was going to become a Yahoo company.

Semel took the deal to Yahoo's board, and it approved an acquisition price as high as $1.2 billion. Semel said he thought he could probably get the deal for less than that. A couple directors pulled Semel aside and said to him: Be careful about negotiating too hard. Just get this deal done.

Semel told Mike Marquez, still on Yahoo's corporate development team, to negotiate the deal to the end, and to let him know when there were no more open points.

About three weeks after Semel's first meeting with Van Natta and Zuckerberg in Palo Alto, the moment had come. Marquez let Semel know the deal was all but done. Semel reached out to Zuckerberg and asked him to come to Yahoo.

And now, Zuckerberg was on Yahoo's campus.

Semel headed toward the conference room. When he got there, he saw that Yahoo's best ally inside Facebook, Van Natta, wasn't there. Zuckerberg was alone, dressed like a college kid as usual.

Semel and Nilsson went in. Zuckerberg wasn't much for pleasantries, so Nilsson and Semel started talking about the deal. Then Semel started talking about the state of Yahoo's business. It had just reported earnings. Unfortunately, they were a little disappointing and Wall Street wasn't happy. It was going to be hard, Semel said, for Yahoo to sell a billion-dollar acquisition right now.

We're going to have to do this deal at $850 million, not the billion you wanted, Semel told Zuckerberg.

Zuckerberg was quiet. He looked disappointed.

Nilsson felt the tension rise in the room. It felt awkward. No one on his team—no one at Yahoo that he knew of—wanted to retrade the deal like this. It felt like reneging.

Zuckerberg stayed quiet. The mood was somber. The meeting didn't last thirty minutes, and then Zuckerberg left the building and Yahoo's campus. He stayed radio silent for the next twenty-four hours.

Back at Facebook headquarters, Zuckerberg walked over to his cofounder, a fellow Harvard dropout named Dustin Moscovitz, and gave him a high five. He'd promised his board he would take a billion-dollar offer. Now there was no billion-dollar offer to take. Facebook would stay independent.

The next day, Zuckerberg got in touch with Yahoo just to say he didn't want to take the process forward.

There was some disappointment at Yahoo, but no one was crushed. Not even Rosensweig. Facebook was still just a college-only social network, and its growth was starting to slow. Who knew if it was going to become a big thing once it opened up? A billion dollars was a lot of money. Maybe Yahoo had dodged a bullet. Ad sales executive Wenda Harris Millard was the most bummed.

The fact was, at the time, Yahoo had no problem attracting users to its site. Its 1998 deal to buy Four11 and launch Yahoo Mail had proven to be a huge winner. Hundreds of millions of people would visit Yahoo.com to check their mail each month, and then they'd bounce around other Yahoo properties like search and Yahoo Finance, driving up ad revenues. No one saw that dynamic going away anytime soon. The Facebook acquisition would have been additive. It wasn't viewed as a lifeline.

Word got out about the talks between Yahoo and Facebook months later. The *New York Times* quoted an analyst, Jordan Rohan of RBC Capital Markets, who did not support Yahoo spending $1 billion on Facebook. "Facebook is a nice small business," he said.

Rohan was wrong. Less than a year later, Facebook would take an investment from Microsoft valuing it at $15 billion. In 2011, Facebook surpassed Yahoo's share of the display advertising market. In 2014, Facebook's market capitalization reached $190 billion while Yahoo hovered around $35 billion.

Facebook was hardly the only startup Yahoo nearly acquired during the Semel years, didn't, and then watched grow into a giant. It looked at LinkedIn and Twitter, two companies worth $25 billion in 2014. Yahoo probably could have had YouTube. The cofounders wanted to sell in 2006, and they thought Yahoo was a better buyer than Google because of Terry Semel's Hollywood connections. Maybe he would be able to help them set up content licensing deals and fend off copyright lawsuits. Semel didn't bite. Nilsson was sure Yahoo was being used as a stalking horse. Yahoo put in a halfhearted effort, and YouTube went to Google for $1.65 billion. By 2013, YouTube was generating $5 billion in revenues every year.

It's easy to look at these missed deals and wonder what Semel and his team were thinking. It's true that sometimes they misunderstood the binary nature of Internet acquisitions. If buying Facebook was a bad idea, it was bound to be a bad idea at $850 million, too. If it was a good idea, $2 billion would end up looking as cheap as $1 billion.

But the thing to remember is that Yahoo was, for a time, *the* big Internet company. Semel and his team saw every deal that went through Silicon Valley. If they were ever going to say no, they were inevitably going to say no to companies that would go on to success. Meanwhile, they did acquire dozens of companies, including some massive hits, like Overture and Inktomi.

The truth is, Yahoo's sometimes poor M&A decision-making, and even its loss to Google in search, were actually just the symptoms of a disease rotting Yahoo from the inside out.

On the morning of October 11, 2006, the *New York Times* technology writer Saul Hansell published a story headlined "Yahoo's Growth Being Eroded by New Rivals."

The story hammered Yahoo. It pointed out the stock was down 38 percent so far that year. It suggested Yahoo had failed to acquire YouTube when it could have, losing out to Google because it was too slow. Hansell said Google also beat Yahoo to ad deals with AOL and MySpace. The article said that Yahoo moved too slowly and that its divisions blocked each other. Hansell wondered: "Yahoo may well be slipping because of the sheer scope of its ambitions. It competes in news with CNN, in sports with ESPN, in e-mail with Microsoft, in instant messaging with AOL, in social networking with MySpace, and of course in searching with Google. And it does so in dozens of countries."

That afternoon in building D on Yahoo's Sunnyvale campus, COO Dan Rosensweig held his usual Thursday staff meeting. The room was Phish Food, the same conference room where Yahoo dealmakers mapped out Project Godfather years before.

Among the people in the room was Jeff Weiner, who'd been a kid when he followed Semel from Windsor to Yahoo but was now an executive vice president. There was Mike Marquez, the dealmaker who, with Nilsson, had gotten Yahoo to the brink of acquiring Facebook before Semel had blown it. And there was Brad Garlinghouse, who had pitched Project Fraternity.

Everyone was griping about the *Times* article. The *Times* was biased against Yahoo. The *Times* was in love with Google. Saul Hansell didn't understand Yahoo's strategy.

Finally, Garlinghouse spoke up.

"You guys, everything Saul said was true."

He said that Yahoo was unfocused and was getting beat by Google.

The moment was tense, because Garlinghouse was, in effect, dumping on his boss, Dan Rosensweig, who was sitting right there in front of him.

Rosensweig defused the situation.

"Hey listen, Brad. Fair enough," he said, "why don't you put a pen to paper on some of your ideas for how you think we should fix things." The meeting moved on.

Garlinghouse wasn't sure if the assignment was serious or if it was meant just to shut him up, but he decided to take it on.

Garlinghouse had a boyish face with full cheeks and small, squinty eyes. Prior to Yahoo, he'd been a venture capitalist and the CEO of a startup. He started his career in business development at @Home Network, the big joint venture between a bunch of cable companies during the dot-com era. Garlinghouse liked action and he liked the idea of stirring things up.

The next day, Garlinghouse and two guys from his staff, Sean Flynn and Eric van Miltenburg, grabbed a conference room and spent the next few hours calling out what was wrong with Yahoo and writing it on the board. The day after, they reordered their thoughts into an outline. Then Garlinghouse went home for the weekend and wrote a memo.

He wanted to say that there wasn't enough accountability or sense of ownership at Yahoo. He thought it was too hard to figure out who was in charge of big decisions at the company. Most of all, he thought that Yahoo was spreading itself too thin. It had acquired a photo-sharing site called Flickr—and yet it was still investing in a product called Yahoo Photos. Why?

As he wrote the memo, Garlinghouse thought about a game he'd played with his coworkers at a management retreat the prior summer. There were thirty people in the room, and he told them to write down one word in response to what he said. He said "PayPal." People wrote down "payments." He said "Google." People wrote down "search." He said "eBay" and they wrote "auctions." After a few more companies, he said "Yahoo." He collected the thirty pieces of paper on Yahoo. Everybody had a different word. What was Yahoo trying to be? No one inside the company knew anymore.

Finally, on Sunday, Garlinghouse finished the memo and reread what he had written. He wondered if it would get him fired—if he should send it at all. It was a serious indictment of Rosensweig.

He sent it to Yahoo's cofounders, Jerry Yang and David Filo. Both still worked at the company. Yang was an advisor to Semel, with only two direct reports of his own. He was more like an executive chairman than anything else. Filo still worked in his cubicle, helping other Yahoo employees find technical solutions. Garlinghouse knew both cared a lot about the company, and he felt they were above politics.

Filo wrote back first, within two hours. He asked: Have you shared this with Dan?

Garlinghouse took a breath. He emailed the memo to his boss.

Rosensweig didn't get mad. In fact, he forwarded the memo to a dozen or so people. On Monday, he set up a committee with leaders from across the company. He told them, Let's figure out a reorg to put these ideas into effect.

But then the committee met a couple times and nothing happened. The committee stopped meeting. Garlinghouse thought: Oh well. That's the end of that.

It was not.

On the Saturday before Thanksgiving—November 18, 2006— the *Wall Street Journal* printed Garlinghouse's memo and a stippled portrait of his face on the front page of the newspaper.

The *Journal* called the memo the "Peanut Butter Manifesto," because in it, Garlinghouse complains, "We lack a focused, cohesive vision for our company. We want to do everything and be everything—to everyone. We've known this for years, talk about it incessantly, but do nothing to fundamentally address it. We are scared to be left out. We are reactive instead of charting an unwavering course. We are separated into silos that far too frequently don't talk to each other. And when we do talk, it isn't to collaborate on a clearly focused strategy, but rather to argue and fight about ownership, strategies and tactics. . . .

"I've heard our strategy described as spreading peanut butter across the myriad opportunities that continue to evolve in the online world. The result: a thin layer of investment spread across everything we do and thus we focus on nothing in particular.

"I hate peanut butter. We all should."

The memo said that Yahoo lacked "clarity of ownership and accountability. The most painful manifestation of this is the massive redundancy that exists throughout the organization. We now operate in an organizational structure—admittedly created with the best of intentions—that has become overly bureaucratic. For far too many employees, there is another person with dramatically similar and overlapping responsibilities. This slows us down and burdens the company with unnecessary costs. . . .

"Product, marketing, engineering, corporate strategy, financial operations . . . there are so many people in charge (or believe that they are in charge) that it's not clear if anyone is in charge. This forces decisions to be pushed up—rather than down. It forces decisions by committee or consensus and discourages the innovators from breaking the mold . . . thinking outside the box."

The memo said that Yahoo lacked "decisiveness," that "we lack a macro perspective to guide our decisions and visibility into who should make those decisions. We are repeatedly stymied by challenging and hairy decisions. We are held hostage by our analysis paralysis."

Finally, the memo said that Yahoo was full of employees who were "lacking the passion and commitment to be a part of the solution. We sit idly by while—at all levels—employees are enabled to 'hang around.' Where is the accountability? Moreover, our compensation systems don't align to our overall success. Weak performers that have been around for years are rewarded. And many of our top performers aren't adequately recognized for their efforts."

As for solutions, the memo suggested Yahoo needed to "boldly and definitively declare what we are and what we are not," and that "the direction needs to come decisively from the top." Garlinghouse said that Yahoo needed to fire the heads of failing business units and shrink the company by 15 percent.

Monday was a weird day at the office for Garlinghouse. By then, everyone had read the memo. People he didn't know came up to him. Others just looked his way. Hundreds of emails from Yahoo employees up and down the ranks filled his inbox, mostly with congratulations and attaboys. That night, reporters started calling Garlinghouse and showing up at his home.

Clearly, he'd struck a nerve inside and outside of Yahoo. This is what's wrong with Yahoo, people thought as they read the manifesto.

Garlinghouse was wrong about one thing. His memo didn't read as an indictment of Dan Rosensweig.

To the memo's most powerful audience, big institutional holders of Yahoo stock, it read as an indictment of Terry Semel.

It was the beginning of his end at Yahoo.

On Sunday morning, January 7, 2007, a man in Naples, Florida, sat on a sofa in his condo, pointed a $30 webcam at his face, and pressed record.

Then, for the next seven and a half minutes, he talked about Yahoo. He talked quietly, so as not to wake his wife, who was sleeping in the next room.

He talked about how, over the prior three years, Yahoo stock was down 30 percent while the S&P 500 was up 27 percent and Google was up 343 percent.

He listed off some things Yahoo needed to do to fix itself. He said that Yahoo needed to restructure its board to include more independent directors, hopefully investors who had put their own capital into the company. He said that Yahoo needed to fire Terry Semel.

The man on the couch was Eric Jackson. His video would turn out ugly: low-def and tinny-sounding. It would also turn out to be the start of a movement.

With his thick eyebrows and side-parted dark brown hair, Eric Jackson looked like Coach Taylor from the TV show *Friday Night Lights*. He had that same flat, calm tone, as well—except Jackson, from Canada, doesn't sound Texan.

Jackson started paying close attention to Yahoo in October 2006. At the time, he was running a blog called *Breakout Performance*. The blog existed to market Jackson Leadership Systems, a consulting business started by Jackson's father. Since July of that year, he'd been writing on topics such as "Why Smart Executives Fail" and "What Best-in-Class Companies Do to Grow Leaders." It was boring stuff, and no one was reading it.

Then, on October 13, Jackson wrote a post titled "Terry Semel: Cause of Yahoo's Success or Along for the Ride?" This one actually got some attention. There were comments on the post. He got emails from readers.

Jackson realized he was on to something. He wondered if he'd finally found an opportunity to get into the career he really wanted. When Jackson was at Columbia Business School, working on his

PhD in strategy and management, he did a bunch of research on corporate governance, basically analyzing what kinds of directors, chairmen, and CEOs best lead to long-term increases in the share price of public companies.

A couple years later, Jackson met a professor who told him there was a type of investment style where people used their knowledge of corporate governance to decide whether or not to invest in companies. It was called activist investing. The investor takes a big stake in a public company and then approaches management with advice on how they could do better. If management doesn't listen, the investor takes his message to the company's other shareholders and tries to persuade them to elect new directors to the company's board, who could then hire new management.

Jackson had always thought of investing as something you did passively, judging companies from behind a screen. The activist approach seemed to depend on the strength of your research and analysis and your ability to persuade. It intrigued him. The professor told Jackson to go talk to an activist investor based in San Diego named Ralph Whitworth. Jackson did. He was impressed with Whitworth's methods. While some activist investors started out hostile toward management, Whitworth worked quietly behind the scenes. After their meeting in San Diego, Jackson secretly hoped Whitworth would hire him as an analyst.

Whitworth did not.

So Jackson moved back to Canada to launch a startup. It didn't pan out.

Jackson relocated to Naples, Florida, and began working for his father's consulting firm. Eventually he started the blog. Then he wrote the Yahoo blog post and got a big reaction. Jackson decided to do more research into Yahoo.

He dug up reports about how Semel had failed to acquire Google when he had the chance. He learned that Semel had a handshake deal with Mark Zuckerberg and then blew it. Jackson read about how Semel would have his secretary print out his emails. Then Jackson started digging into Semel's compensation. He went through all the filings and drew up a simple Excel sheet to show how much cash and stock Semel had received over his years at Yahoo. Semel's total compensation stunned Jackson: $600 million.

Then the *Wall Street Journal* published Brad Garlinghouse's Peanut Butter manifesto.

Jackson decided he had to launch some sort of campaign.

First, he tried pitching Yahoo as an activist target to established investors. Whitworth said no, because he wasn't really interested in Internet companies. He preferred companies like Waste Management—it was easier to evaluate assets like landfills. Then Jackson took his idea to Carl Icahn's firm in New York. Jackson met with Icahn's COO. She passed.

Jackson decided to launch a campaign all by himself. He thought about how former Vermont governor Howard Dean had mounted a surprisingly serious presidential bid through grassroots fundraising over the Internet, and how in Connecticut an antiwar candidate named Ned Lamont beat Senator Joe Lieberman in a primary doing the same. Jackson figured the press might like a story about a guy using social media to go after a technology company. He also thought about how the press loved to hate Yahoo. The cranks on Yahoo Finance's message boards would be supportive, too.

Jackson drafted a plan for Yahoo called Plan B and posted it to his site. Then, that Sunday morning in January, he got up early and read the blog post into a camera from a couch in his guest bedroom.

While many activist investors control hedge funds worth billions and hold stakes worth hundreds of millions in public companies, Jackson owned only forty-five shares of Yahoo stock, worth less than $1,300. He represented a tiny fraction of Yahoo's shareholder votes—less than 1 percent of 1 percent of 1 percent.

The press paid attention anyway. Within days, the *New York Times*, the Associated Press, and technology industry site Red Herring reported on an activist campaign against Yahoo. Thousands of people watched his video. Jackson started hearing from Yahoo employees. Soon, small shareholders from all over the country started emailing Jackson, telling him they were in. Eventually, Jackson would come to represent $55 million worth of Yahoo stock.

As the campaign wore on, Jackson wrote to Yahoo and asked if he could speak to management—just the way someone like Whitworth would. He got a meeting with Yahoo's general counsel, Mike Callahan, in April. Jackson hoped he would go into the meeting and Callahan would say Yahoo planned to act on two of the nine points Jackson made in his Plan B. Then Jackson could declare victory and move on. But Callahan and a more junior Yahoo lawyer just sat there and politely listened.

The next step for an activist investor with millions or billions of dollars to spend would have been to launch a campaign to convince the rest of Yahoo's shareholders to vote new directors onto the board—a "proxy contest." Jackson didn't have the time or the money for that. What he could do, however, was ask shareholders to officially "withhold" their votes for certain directors. If any director got more than 50 percent "withhold" votes, the director would have to step down immediately.

In a May 2 blog post, Jackson asked for shareholders to vote "withhold" at the Yahoo shareholder meeting on June 12, 2007. Later, he'd suggest Yahoo shareholders specifically target Semel and the three directors on Yahoo's compensation committee.

As impressive as his coalition of shareholders sounded, representing $55 million, it was still only a tiny sliver of Yahoo's shareholder base. Jackson knew that if his campaign was going to get any results, it needed support from the large mutual funds that were Yahoo's biggest shareholders.

So, Jackson had phone calls or meetings with eight of Yahoo's ten top shareholders—mutual funds such as Vanguard, State Street, and Capital Research Global Investors. Each of the fund managers told Jackson they could never come out and publicly support what he was doing, but that they wanted him to please keep banging the drum. Each said they would likely vote "withhold."

Jackson wondered if he might actually pull this thing off.

Then, on June 12, 2007, at Yahoo's annual shareholder meeting, the results were announced.

Semel and the three directors on the Yahoo board's compensation committee each got more than 50 percent "yes" votes. None of them would be forced to resign.

But here's the thing: Public companies hold these kinds of elections every year. Typically, board-sitting CEOs and other directors get about 1 percent or 2 percent "withhold" votes.

Semel and the three directors on the comp committee each got around 40 percent.

It was a stunning embarrassment.

At the shareholder meeting itself, Jackson stood up and told Semel he should have apologized to Yahoo shareholders for his performance over the past two and a half years.

Jackson asked Semel: "So, you are happy being number two in search?"

Semel said: "I think you're being cute about that."

Jackson asked: "Do you have fire in the belly for this job?"

Semel: "Absolutely."

But the truth was, Semel did not. Not anymore.

Inside Yahoo, the drumbeat of shareholder disappointment had been loud and constant since around the time of the Peanut Butter manifesto. In December 2006, Semel reorganized his management team. Dan Rosensweig, the chief operating officer who had pushed so hard for the acquisition of Facebook, was out. Semel elevated CFO Sue Decker into an operational role, with responsibility over Yahoo's ad business. Her title changed to president.

But even with the changes, Yahoo's first board meetings of 2007 had been brutal. After the rebound during Semel's first few years, powered by Project Godfather and Greg Coleman's display advertising business, Yahoo stock had done very poorly over the past several quarters. There was a lot of pressure.

It was becoming obvious to everyone: Terry Semel was failing.

The truth was, Terry Semel was always going to fail at Yahoo.

When he joined the company in 2001, he inherited a flawed, spray-and-pray product strategy and an equally sprawling and unwieldy organization. For all his strengths in sales and success in Hollywood, Semel was never the right person to fix either problem.

When Semel joined Yahoo, it had four hundred different products and services. It was an indefensible position that made Yahoo vulnerable to the eBays and Googles of the world—well-funded startups that did just one thing well.

Yahoo needed someone who could pick one product—or even just a dozen—to bet the future on. But Semel had no sense of the web, not from an engineer's perspective and not from a user's.

When Terry Semel got to Yahoo, he would call Mallett up and ask him what things were.

"What's a buddy list?"

"A server?"

"A protocol?"

One night, he called up Mallett to ask him how to log in to Yahoo.

Meetings between engineers and Semel would always start very slowly, because it took him a long time to figure out what everyone was talking about. After the acquisition of Four11 in 1998,

Yahoo Mail became one of Yahoo's most important products. But Semel never got much better at email than he was on the morning of 9/11. Years in, Rosensweig had to explain to Semel the sequence of screens Yahoo Mail users would go through to send and receive messages.

For a time, it seemed Semel had picked one area for Yahoo to invest in: original content. He brought in Hollywood executives like Lloyd Braun, the former ABC programmer. Yahoo staffed up in Santa Monica and became the leading sports news site on the web. But Yahoo never fully committed to becoming a media business first, mostly because search advertising revenues dwarfed traditional display advertising revenues.

Semel's tech ignorance hurt Yahoo in other ways, too. As much as he couldn't play offense—come up with the good ideas—he couldn't play defense against the bad ones, either. For far too many years during the Semel era, Yahoo would show a confirmation screen after a user sent an email. There was no reason for this screen to exist other than that it was a place for an ad. When Google launched Gmail, there was no such screen—and consumers began to switch.

The other problem Semel inherited when he joined Yahoo was the organizational structure left to him by Jeff Mallett.

When Semel arrived, the company had forty-four business units, with the leaders of all forty-four acting like CEOs with their own profit-and-loss statements. This was an easy way for Mallett to grow Yahoo fast, but it made the company hard to sustain later. Executives and teams didn't collaborate. Sometimes they would outright compete. Semel reduced the number of Yahoo's business units to four, but problems with overlap and competition remained. Yahoo's popular sports news sites linked to Yahoo's movie news pages but not its regular Yahoo News section. The reason was that Yahoo Sports and Yahoo Entertainment profits and losses accrued to one manager and Yahoo News to another. Yahoo's network effects suffered.

Meanwhile, one division would launch and run Yahoo Photos, and another would own Flickr, a photo-sharing website. While Facebook rose to power, Yahoo funded a social network called Yahoo 360 and another called Yahoo Groups—but neither reported to the head of Yahoo social media. Yahoo was slow to launch a YouTube competitor in 2006 because two different divisions wanted to build one. Yahoo Classifieds, HotJobs, Yahoo Personals, and Yahoo Autos were all listings businesses, but each had its own back-end listings technology.

Mallett also left Semel and Yahoo in an awkward position overseas. The company was impressively global for a five-year-old startup, but it had gotten that way through a series of joint ventures with foreign partners. Often, Yahoo had not successfully shared its technology with those companies. Yahoo Mail wasn't a globally unified product until well after Semel's departure in 2008. Search wasn't globally unified until 2009.

As with Yahoo's flawed product strategy, Semel was the wrong person to step in to operate or fix Yahoo's unscalable org structure.

The only reason Mallett's organizational structure worked at all, when it did, was that he was at the center of it, pulling the levers and running the hamster wheel at a million miles per hour.

Mallett was a high-energy, hands-on leader. Semel was not.

Mallett was also a dictator. Semel was not.

Perhaps because he knew his own limitations, Semel ruled Yahoo by consensus. He had an ability to bring up a contentious issue at a meeting with all his lieutenants, have them debate, and come out the other side with everyone feeling good and on board. This meant his direct reports loved working for him. But it also meant Yahoo usually made decisions very slowly and with great aversion to risk.

This put Yahoo into contrast with more successful technology companies with more dictatorial people at the top. Apple had Steve Jobs. Facebook had Mark Zuckerberg. Amazon had Jeff Bezos. Tesla had Elon Musk. Larry Page always had the final say at Google.

The reason tech dictatorships work isn't because the dictators are perfect. Steve Jobs didn't want to put iTunes on Windows machines, and he didn't see the point of apps on the iPhone. Mark Zuckerberg pushed several products on Facebook users that invaded their privacy and caused huge uproars. It's that dictators make mistakes quickly, and the good ones learn from them and move on.

After the embarrassment at the shareholder meeting on June 12, and in the days leading up to Yahoo's June board meeting that same week, Semel went out to dinner with Jerry Yang. They talked about Yahoo, Semel's role going forward, and Yang's, too. They made a plan.

At the board meeting that week, Yang asked Semel if he was willing to commit to Yahoo for the long term.

Semel said he wasn't, and that he understood that meant he should resign. He would do so, effective immediately. His great next chapter was complete.

Then Yang said that he would like to be CEO.

Yang was at once an odd and an obvious choice.

Odd, because though it had been thirteen years since he and David Filo began posting links, and twelve years since they incorporated Yahoo, Yang still did not have much operational experience. He had only two people reporting to him. His job under Koogle and then Semel had been to be a consigliere—a cheerleading number-two partner. He would give advice and then fall in line after the CEO made a choice.

He was an obvious choice because it was plain to see that Yang was a visionary when it came to the web. He had cocreated Yahoo, which for all its ups and downs as a business was still a website that nearly a billion people used every month. Yang was also a clever strategic thinker. He had driven the company's relationship with Masayoshi Son and advocated for Yahoo Japan, a joint venture with Softbank.

In 2005, Yang's strategic thinking and vision led Yahoo to sign a deal that would one day save the company and make possible the hire of Marissa Mayer.

That year, Yang met a Chinese entrepreneur named Jack Ma at Pebble Beach, the famous golf course. Like Yang, Ma had taken investment from Masayoshi Son. Soon, Yang was flying Yahoo's executive team to Hong Kong, hammering out a big, billion-dollar investment in Ma's company, which was called Alibaba. By 2007, Alibaba was showing some real progress with its e-commerce site, a thing called Taobao.

The other reason Yang was an obvious choice was that he was a cofounder. He was passionate about Yahoo. He was Chief Yahoo. He bled purple. Everyone knew that, whatever might come Yahoo's way in the next few years, no one would work harder to keep it strong and growing.

And independent.

3

Bear Hugs and Poison Pills

Shortly after five p.m. on January 31, 2008, a fax machine whirred to life on the third floor of building D at Yahoo's Sunnyvale headquarters. Out came a piece of paper.

That paper might as well have been a bomb, because what was written on it was going to blow apart everything Jerry Yang and Sue Decker had been working on for the past six months.

After his last board meeting as CEO, in June 2007, Terry Semel called Sue Decker and told her that he was stepping down. He said that Jerry Yang was going to become Yahoo's next CEO.

This was bad news for Decker. Ever since a reorg the December before, people inside and outside Yahoo had begun predicting that she would be the company's next CEO.

Now what was going to happen to her?

Decker didn't have much time to wonder, because a few minutes later, she got a call from Yang.

Yang said, "I'd like to make you president, and we're going to do this together."

She asked: "How long do I have to decide?"

"Tomorrow morning."

The next morning, Decker told Yang she was in.

Decker always had two goals for her career. The first was, she wanted to have the power to make changes that would positively impact the places where she worked. The second was, she wanted to be continuously learning—peeling the onion, she would say. Decker's career as an analyst had provided lots of learning. So had being CFO. By 2007, Decker believed she understood Yahoo and the Internet industry as well as anyone. Now, Decker was ready to take action, to shape an organization around that knowledge—to have an impact. Taking the job was scary. But two decades after her magic trick during an interview at DLJ, Decker was used to pushing herself into uncomfortable situations. In fact, it was now her favorite thing to do.

Yang wanted to prove he was finally ready to run the company he'd cocreated. Back in 1994, he was a kid who had never held a real job. He was still perfecting his English. Now he was a seasoned executive on the other side of a dozen-plus years of apprenticeship under impressive mentors like Semel, Koogle, and Masayoshi Son.

On June 18, 2007, Yahoo announced Yang as its new CEO. Yang said he would take the next hundred days to reexamine the company and come up with a plan.

"No sacred cows," he promised.

For the next three months, Yang and Decker met with Yahoo's top executives and reconsidered what Yahoo could be. It had this huge audience of users. Should it focus on just growing that? It had all this advertising technology. Should it just be a company that provided that technology to others? Then there was search, and competing with Google. Was it worth trying to stay in that fight?

One quick change came in August 2007. Greg Coleman was out. The sales executive who had taught Yahoo how to sell ads after the dot-com bubble didn't like Decker, and Decker didn't like him. Not anymore, anyway. Along with everyone else, Coleman admired Decker for the job she'd done in 2000 and 2001, boldly communicating the depth of Yahoo's woes to Wall Street and then slashing headcount deep enough for the company to get growing again as fast as possible. But he considered her lost when it came to online advertising and sales strategy. He thought she was too wound up in abstract formulas rather than the reality of Yahoo's business.

When Semel gave Decker operational authority over Yahoo's ad business in December 2006, Decker called Coleman into a conference room for an ad sales strategy session. She stood at the whiteboard and outlined while he sat at the table and listened. Finally, she could see how agitated he was becoming.

"What is it, Greg?"

He said, "You've never spent any time with our clients!"

He asked her where she was getting her ideas about sales strategy. "Are you getting it from a book? Or Google?"

The meeting ended abruptly. So did Coleman's time with Yahoo after Decker's ascent.

"I decided it was time for me to do something else," he told a reporter after the news broke.

As Yang and Decker continued to home in on what they wanted to do with Yahoo's assets in the fall, they sought help from outside the company. Yang reached out to Steve Jobs, who had famously returned to Apple to save the company after years away. Yang hadn't ever been exiled the way Jobs had, but he saw parallels in their stories. So did Jobs. Plus, Jobs knew and liked Decker from Pixar, where she sat on the board of directors.

At an off-site with Yahoo's top 200 executives that fall, Jobs gave a speech. He talked about how companies will often make a list of the ten things they want to get done in a year. He said the smart companies will take that list and shrink it to three or four items. Then he said, "This is how I do it. I take a sheet of paper and I say, 'If my company can only do one thing next year, what is it?' Literally, we shut everything else down."

Decker and Yang never reached that kind of focus with Yahoo. But by the end of that year, from a world of possibilities, they did narrow down the company's aims to just three. Aim one: Yahoo would be the "starting point for web users," just like it had been in its earliest days. Aim two: Yahoo would be a "must buy" for online advertisers. It would be a "must buy" because it would sell ads shown on Yahoo.com and on the websites of partners, such as a consortium of newspapers. It would be a "must buy" due to its ability to target those ads to the exact right users, based on their demographics, location, and countless other variables. Aim three: Yahoo would work to create "platforms" for which developers would want to build applications, just as there were applications that used Windows and Google Maps.

These were Sue Decker's long-held ideas for what Yahoo should be. They were more hers than Yang's or any other Yahoo executive's, and they were about to be brought to life.

As 2007 ended, Decker and Yang planned for two big meetings at the beginning of 2008. One would be with Yahoo's board, on January 31. At that meeting, Decker and Yang would pitch their plan to Yahoo's directors—including the company's new chairman, Roy Bostock. Then, the next week, Yang and Decker were set to go on another retreat with Yahoo's top executives, this time to begin putting their plan in action.

The February meeting never happened.

As the January 31 board meeting reached its conclusion, an assistant stepped into the room to interrupt. She slipped a note to Jerry Yang.

He had a phone call.

It was Microsoft CEO Steve Ballmer on the line. He wanted to talk about a fax he just sent through.

Ballmer told Yang that Microsoft wanted to buy Yahoo.

Ballmer's tone was friendly, but his words were threatening—the term for the situation was: "hostile."

Ballmer said that Microsoft had been trying to do a friendly deal with Yahoo for a couple years now and it had gone nowhere. This time would be different. He was faxing over the offer now.

Ballmer said to Yang: If you and Roy tell me that Yahoo has a price and you are willing to sell the business, we'll keep our offer private and work out the details over the coming days. But if you guys just don't want to sell the business, then we are going to go public with the offer and see what investors think.

Yang pleaded with him. He said: You don't lose anything by waiting a week.

Ballmer said: If you really don't want to sell the business, then I don't want to wait.

Yang told Ballmer he wouldn't have a response for two days.

Then Yang went back to the boardroom and told the other directors what was happening. The board read the faxed letter from Ballmer.

Microsoft was willing to pay $31 per share for Yahoo, valuing Yahoo at $45 billion. Microsoft would pay half the price in cash and make up the other half with Microsoft stock.

Ballmer said Yahoo and Microsoft had to combine to battle Google. "Today, the market is increasingly dominated by one player who is consolidating its dominance through acquisition. Together, Microsoft and Yahoo can offer a credible alternative for consumers, advertisers, and publishers."

Then, at the bottom of the letter, Ballmer laid out his threat. He wrote, "In light of the significance of this proposal to your share-holders and ours, as well as the potential for selective disclosures, our intention is to publicly release the text of this letter tomorrow morning....

"Depending on the nature of your response, Microsoft reserves the right to pursue all necessary steps to ensure that Yahoo's shareholders are provided with the opportunity to realize the value inherent in our proposal."

When the markets closed earlier that day, Yahoo's stock price was $19.18. Microsoft's $31-per-share offer was a 62 percent premium. It was a huge offer.

In Phish Food, the Yahoo boardroom, the directors and executives scrambled into action.

Within minutes, Yahoo's bankers at Goldman Sachs were on the line. The bankers' message was: This is a marathon, not a sprint. Do not react quickly. Gather your facts. Figure out Yahoo's stand-alone value. Because Microsoft's offer is half stock, figure out what the value of the combined companies would be.

Decker started thinking about process. She thought: Okay. We're either selling to Microsoft or we're not. And if we're not, we have to really validate why in a very public way.

Yang knew dealing with this offer was his job now. Internal plans and projects were going to have to give way to external posturing and negotiating.

And then there was Yahoo chairman Roy Bostock. Bostock was mostly bald, with a crown of salt-and-pepper hair around the sides of his head. He wore big, circular, gold-rim glasses on his face. In corporate head shots, he smiled broadly or with a smirk. In person, he often looked stern. He bore a resemblance to Dick Cheney.

The board meeting that day had been Bostock's first as Yahoo's new chairman, replacing Terry Semel. Before, Bostock had been a longstanding director at Yahoo—and a good one, everyone thought. He'd built his career in advertising, and he had always been helpful connecting Yahoo to advertising customers.

Bostock was proud of his new job and fiercely loyal to Jerry Yang.

When Bostock thought about the way Steve Ballmer was behaving, it made him angry. It made him want to fight.

The man behind Microsoft's big offer was an executive named Hank Vigil.

Vigil was a strategist who had been with Microsoft for two decades. He was one of Ballmer's most trusted confidants.

Vigil was round-faced. His olive skin contrasted with thick and bright silver hair. Vigil wore stylish glasses and expensive suits with dress shirts open at the neck. Vigil was brusque in his manner. He was prone to exasperation—especially with people who didn't understand basic ideas.

For example: In the months and years leading up to January 31, 2008, Vigil had grown very exasperated with the people running Yahoo. Somehow, they didn't understand that they needed to get on board with Microsoft or Yahoo was going out of business. Somehow, they didn't understand a simple truth: If Microsoft and Yahoo didn't combine, Google was going to own the Internet—forever.

Vigil and Microsoft considered acquiring Yahoo many times during Yahoo's run from startup to giant public company. But the day Vigil became determined that Microsoft had to buy Yahoo was December 19, 2005.

That's the day Google announced it would pay Time Warner $1 billion to provide search and search ads for AOL.

The deal was supposed to have been Microsoft's—Vigil's, specifically. Microsoft and Time Warner would create a new company that would sell search ads and banner ads on AOL.com, MSN.com, and other sites owned by other companies. As late as December 5, the deal was good to go.

But then Google stepped in with its billion dollars, and it was all over in two weeks.

The amount of money Google was able to offer AOL confirmed Vigil's worst fear: that Google had stumbled into an increasing-returns business, where the more it spent, the more it made. Google was making so much more from search ads than anyone else, it could far outbid rivals like Microsoft and Yahoo to distribute them across the web. Vigil feared that soon, Google's market share would grow so large that search marketers would decide they couldn't afford to waste money buying ads with other search engines. They would decide to use that budget only on Google ads, to make sure they could bid as high as possible. Google would own an effective monopoly on the Internet's only real business model. It would be game over.

Secretly, Vigil worried that Google was already a monopoly. He realized the only way to prevent Google from owning the search market would be for its competitors to team up. Microsoft, he knew, needed to buy Yahoo. Yahoo needed Microsoft to buy Yahoo. He set out to spread the word and get the deal done.

A month after the December 2005 AOL-Google deal, in January 2006, Vigil was in Las Vegas at the Consumer Electronics Show when he spotted Jerry Yang. Later at the conference, Vigil button-holed Yang. He told him: I know we've talked about merging Yahoo into Microsoft before, but now it's for real. Let's do this.

Yang wasn't interested. Though Yahoo's search share had already begun to decline, Project Godfather was still juicing Yahoo's revenues. The search war didn't seem lost yet to Yang. Besides, Microsoft did not seem like a cultural fit for Yahoo. Yang admired Bill Gates, but he did not admire Microsoft's corporate style. Yahoos wore jeans and sandals. Microsoft executives wore suits and wing tips. The deal went nowhere.

Vigil tried again in 2007. At the beginning of the year, Ballmer sent a friendly letter to Terry Semel that signaled Microsoft might be willing to offer something around or even above $40 per share for Yahoo. Semel called Ballmer and said it wasn't a deal he wanted to pursue at the moment. Ballmer withdrew the tentative offer.

Then Semel resigned in June 2007. Ballmer kept in touch with Yang through the following fall. Yang rebuffed him.

Finally, Vigil convinced Ballmer that Microsoft faced an existential threat in Google and that it needed to own Yahoo, whether Yahoo management liked it or not.

The pair set about planning a bear hug. They picked January 31, the day Google would report its earnings for 2005. They believed Wall Street's anticipation of huge numbers from Google would drive Yahoo's stock price below $20. That day, Yahoo closed at $19.12. Ballmer called Yang, and away the fax went. It was on.

Time to come to Daddy, Vigil thought.

Brad Garlinghouse, the Peanut Butter manifesto writer, was with his wife on a ski trip in Tahoe when, as he was getting ready for bed, he saw a note from management alerting Yahoo's top 200 executives to be ready for a conference call the next morning.

Garlinghouse emailed around with other senior executives. Did anyone know what's up? No one did.

By the time Garlinghouse woke up the next morning, on February 1, 2008, the news was everywhere.

Ballmer had made good on his threat. Microsoft published a press release and his letter to the board at 7:30 a.m. Eastern.

The release's headline: "Microsoft Proposes Acquisition of Yahoo for $31 per Share."

The *Wall Street Journal* quickly followed with a long story featuring an interview with Ballmer. The lede: "The battle for supremacy in the Internet era is entering a tumultuous new phase."

When the press release went out, it was already twelve thirty in the afternoon at Yahoo's London office.

The leader of Yahoo's European operations, Rich Riley, a tall blond man, was sitting on the sales floor when the news crossed the wires.

Suddenly, he felt all the eyes in the room looking at him, to see if he, the most senior Yahoo executive within five thousand miles, had any idea what was going on.

Riley thought: Fuck, I don't know.

Garlinghouse, Riley, and about fifty other senior executives at Yahoo—from Decker to Yang to Semel's guy Jeff Weiner to deal-makers Marquez and Nilsson—finally got on a conference call around nine in the morning, Pacific time.

Many of the executives on the call thought they were dialing into one of the last calls Yahoo management would hold as an independent concern. By then, Yahoo was a twelve-year-old company. It wasn't a fast-growing startup anymore. It had seen epic highs, reaching a market cap of $128 billion in 2000. Then, after a crash down to $5 billion, Yahoo had managed to rebound to a $50 billion market cap after Project Godfather. Yahoo had serious momentum back then. No way would it have made sense to sell to anyone, especially Microsoft. But now, Yahoo's market cap was below $30 billion. Microsoft's offer was $45 billion. It seemed like a good deal, especially since many of the executives on the line had been paid in stock over the years. Accepting Microsoft's offer wouldn't bring the riches they might have once thought were coming their way, but it would be better than nothing. A 62 percent premium wasn't nothing.

Others on the call thought Yahoo should take the offer because they shared Hank Vigil's view: Yahoo would be in a much stronger position to compete with Google if it combined with Microsoft.

So it was fairly stunning when Roy Bostock, a chairman many

of the Yahoo executives on the line had not yet met, pronounced Yahoo's initial stance toward Microsoft's offer: "Our attitude is going to be combative."

Riley, in London, heard that and thought: Did he just say "combative"?

Usually, when big mergers are announced, the stock price of the company being bought rises to the buyer's offering price. Sometimes, investors bid the stock up even more, because they expect the acquisition target to hold out for a higher price, get it, and then accept the deal.

But at the end of the trading day in New York on February 1, 2008, Yahoo's stock price closed at $28.38, three dollars below Microsoft's offer.

The market didn't think Yahoo was going to be able to accept Microsoft's humongous bid.

───────

The Yahoo board formally rejected Microsoft's offer on February 11, 2008—arguing that it substantially undervalued the company.

Then, on February 12, the board took a drastic step to make a hostile bid more difficult and expensive for Microsoft. It voted to adopt a new severance plan for Yahoo employees where, if the company were to be acquired, any Yahoo employee who quit "for good reason" would get a large cash payout and a bunch of stock they would have otherwise had to stay in their jobs for years to get. A "good reason" would be "any substantial adverse alteration" in the employee's job over the two years following the change in control. Given that many Yahoos had very specific responsibilities and qualifications, many of them would have been able to walk with cash and stock after the deal.

In the world of mergers and acquisitions, the adoption of that kind of severance plan in the face of a hostile takeover is known as a "poison pill"—as in the suicide pills spies take when they are captured by the enemy.

With the plan's passage, Yahoo's board sent a message to Microsoft: You'll never take us alive!

It set negotiations off on a bad footing.

First, Microsoft's lawyers met with Yahoo's lawyers at a law firm near Sunnyvale. The room was crowded and noisy, and nothing got done. Microsoft's lawyers left the Bay Area wondering who was the decision maker at Yahoo. They wondered why the meeting had happened.

Ballmer—tall, bald, big-nosed, and imposing—finally met with Yang, Filo, and Yahoo lawyers in person about a month after the offer hit. The meeting did not go well. Yang and Filo were standoffish and defensive. They had not warmed up to Ballmer's bear hug.

The truth was, Yang was actively exploring all possible alternatives. The day the offer was made public, he was on the phone with Google CEO Eric Schmidt. Schmidt said he'd help in any way he could to fend off Ballmer. Over in Europe, Yahoo had outsourced its search engine and search advertising to Google, and it was going very well. Maybe it was time for Yahoo to do that globally. Riley, who'd engineered the European deal, was flown back to California and put to work on the possibility.

Yang talked to Time Warner CEO Jeff Bewkes. Did it make sense to trade Yahoo stock for AOL? Yang talked to News Corp CEO Rupert Murdoch. Did it make sense to combine Yahoo and MySpace?

On March 18, Yahoo published a presentation for shareholders arguing that, following the plan Yang and Decker had come up with the prior fall, Yahoo would be able to double free cash flow within two years, from $1.9 billion to $3.7 billion. They projected 2010 revenues would be $8.8 billion, up from $7 billion in 2007.

Yang said that the strength of the business would be display advertising, a business in which Yahoo was still a leader over Google.

On April 5, a frustrated Ballmer sent the Yahoo board a letter.

He wrote, "It has now been more than two months since we made our proposal to acquire Yahoo at a 62 percent premium to its closing price on January 31, 2008, the day prior to our announcement. Our goal in making such a generous offer was to create the basis for a speedy and ultimately friendly transaction. Despite this, the pace of the last two months has been anything but speedy."

Ballmer wrote that Yahoo's search business had continued to decline and that the overall macroeconomic market was looking suddenly weaker as well. He noted Yahoo's attempt to strike an alternative deal had so far failed.

Then Ballmer hit the board with a threat: "If we have not concluded an agreement within the next three weeks, we will be compelled to take our case directly to your shareholders, including the initiation of a proxy contest to elect an alternative slate of directors for the Yahoo board."

Two days later, Yang and Bostock wrote a letter back saying: We'll sell the company, but only at a higher price.

Then, as if to respond to a threat with a threat, Yahoo announced it would begin experimenting with Google search ads. Riley had managed to move that deal forward—and was in fact getting close to securing a payment that would make the billion dollars AOL got from Google in 2005 look small.

Yang and Ballmer met again, this time at a law office in Portland, Oregon. Again, the meeting went poorly. Yang went through a long PowerPoint presentation that concluded with a slide saying that Microsoft's price substantially undervalued Yahoo.

Ballmer said: Okay, what price would properly value Yahoo?

Yang didn't have an answer.

Leaving the contentious meeting, Ballmer wondered if Microsoft was going to have to go straight to Yahoo shareholders and get them to vote Yahoo's directors out. A Microsoft executive said: "They are going to burn the furniture if we go hostile. They are going to destroy the place."

But then, suddenly, Yahoo seemed to warm to Microsoft's bear hug.

On April 26, the day of Ballmer's three-week deadline, the Yahoo board sent Microsoft another letter, emphasizing that it was open to a deal, just not at $31 per share. Ballmer called Yang and said that Microsoft could offer more.

On Friday, May 2, Microsoft's top lawyer, Brad Smith, called Ron Olson, an outside lawyer for Yahoo, and told him Microsoft's board had approved an offer of $33 per share.

That was a 72 percent premium over Yahoo's share price on January 31, 2008. It valued Yahoo at $47 billion—$2 billion more than Microsoft's original offer.

Later, Smith filled Hank Vigil in on the call. He told him that, according to Olson, Microsoft and Yahoo weren't so far apart anymore.

When Vigil heard that, he thought for the first time in almost three months that the deal might actually happen.

Vigil wouldn't have to wait long to find out. Yang and Filo were planning to fly up to Seattle to finish negotiations the very next day—Saturday, May 3.

Late that Friday night, Sue Decker got on a plane to Nebraska. She sat on the board of Warren Buffett's company, Berkshire Hathaway, and it was time for the company's big annual meeting.

It was funny; Decker was going to see Microsoft cofounder Bill Gates at the meeting. He also sat on the Berkshire Hathaway board. She did not plan to bring up the merger talks with him.

Decker had no idea what was about to happen to Yahoo. Earlier that day, Yahoo's board had met to discuss what price Jerry Yang should bring to Ballmer when he flew up to Washington on Saturday.

It sounded like if Microsoft could get to $36 or maybe just $34, the deal would happen. Decker didn't know.

Although 2008 had started with big plans and lots of excitement, the Microsoft offer had become a huge distraction. It was all people wanted to talk about at every level of management.

Decker also worried that Yang was too determined to prove that Yahoo had a better course on its own, without Microsoft. And then there was the new chairman, Bostock. His attitude the whole way through had been huffy and aggressive. It seemed like he and Yang were back-channeling a lot. They weren't including the whole board in big decisions.

Decker was sure the two of them had a plan for the next day. She just had no idea what.

———

Jerry Yang and David Filo had been working together for more than fourteen years by the time they got on a private jet to fly up to Seattle on the morning of Saturday, May 3, 2008.

They'd seen their project grow from a silly website called Jerry and David's Guide to the World Wide Web into a tiny startup. It grew into the most powerful brand on the Internet. It almost died. But then, because real people really loved what they had made, their project grew into influence and power again.

Now, for the first time, one of them was actually running the show.

Now, for the first time, the two of them were seriously considering selling the thing to a giant corporation where everyone wore suits. Filo, the kid from the commune, hated the idea.

Yang tried to be objective. He knew, as CEO and a board member, it was his fiduciary duty to leave emotions and pride out of it. It was hard. He believed he could do it.

There were no independent board directors on the plane. There wasn't anyone there whose only job was to look out for the common Yahoo shareholder. Just two cofounders and a Yahoo lawyer named Mike Gupta.

When Yang and Filo landed at Boeing Field, a small airport for cargo planes and private jets four miles south of downtown Seattle, it was cold and breezy on the tarmac. Mount Rainier soared in the background.

The reception inside the Galvin Flying Services executive terminal hangar, a corrugated steel–sided building just off the airstrip, was warmer. Microsoft CEO Steve Ballmer had built his career in sales, and he was naturally gregarious. With Ballmer was Kevin Johnson, the head of Microsoft's online division.

The group settled into a conference room. Because of the conversation Microsoft's lawyer had with Olson, the outside lawyer for Yahoo's independent board directors, Ballmer thought Yang and Filo would ask him to offer something like $34.50 per share, a smidge above the price Microsoft had indicated it would pay—around $34. This was an increase of billions of dollars on Microsoft's initial offer, which to Ballmer's mind had already been plenty generous for a company that seemed to be eroding.

Ballmer was wrong. Yang and Filo had a much bigger number in mind. They brought up the letter Ballmer had sent to Terry Semel in early 2007. That letter had indicated Microsoft was willing to buy Yahoo at a price per share in the $40 range. Yang said Yahoo wanted $37 per share.

Something clicked for Ballmer.

He said to Yang: Let's leave all the price stuff aside. Assuming we agreed on the price, are you and David in? Do you want to do this? Are your oars pulling in the same direction to help us make this thing succeed?

Whatever Yang and Filo said next, what Ballmer heard was: No.

When, on that same Saturday, Decker saw Microsoft chairman Bill Gates at the Berkshire Hathaway annual meeting in Omaha, she walked up to him and said, "We shouldn't sit near each other."

Gates's handlers made sure of that.

During Berkshire's annual meeting, held in front of 35,000 shareholders, Gates sat at one end of the stage and Decker sat all the way on the other.

Throughout the long meeting, Decker kept getting up to sneak around back so she could check her phone for new information on what was going on in Seattle. Gates never budged. He seemed unconcerned.

On a conference call with Decker and the rest of Yahoo's senior leadership that night, Yang broke the news: He and Filo had carried the Yahoo board's message on an acceptable price and had been rejected. Ballmer was about to put out a press release announcing that Microsoft was walking away from the deal.

As news spread around Yahoo, there was a mixed reaction. Some executives were disappointed. Many were not. There were high fives.

The reaction from Yahoo shareholders was simpler: pure fury. On Monday, May 5, the first day of trading after Ballmer walked, Yahoo shares dropped 20 percent, to $24.37.

On May 6, Gordon Crawford, whose funds, Capital Research, controlled 16 percent of Yahoo stock, said, "I'm extremely disappointed in Jerry Yang. I think he overplayed a weak hand. And I'm even more disappointed in the independent directors who were not responsive to the needs of independent shareholders."

On May 15, Carl Icahn, the activist investor whose firm Eric Jackson had pitched on a Yahoo activist campaign a year and a half before, announced he had acquired 59 million shares of Yahoo. He wanted Yahoo to sell to Microsoft at its offer of $33 per share. Otherwise, he'd rally Yahoo's shareholders to vote in a new board of directors.

Feeling the lash, some of Yahoo's directors reached out to Microsoft on May 17 to see if the deal was really dead.

Yes, it was. Microsoft said maybe it would want to buy Yahoo's search business, but that's it.

Vigil thought: We were serious, and you were not. Now you're paying the price. Sorry, but that's how life works.

Throughout the summer, Microsoft and Yahoo talked about a new "hybrid" deal. Yahoo proposed merging MSN into Yahoo and giving Microsoft 40 percent of the new company. Ballmer wanted Yahoo's search business.

In July, Yahoo settled with Icahn and brought him and two other directors onto the board. At his first board meeting, and at every meeting thereafter, Icahn pushed for Yahoo to do a search deal with Microsoft.

Talks continued, haltingly—too slowly for investors. By September, Yahoo stock was below $19.12, its price the day Microsoft made its original bear-hug offer.

Then the last best hope for the Jerry Yang era at Yahoo died.

Amid all the negotiations with Microsoft, Rich Riley had continued to talk with Google about a search deal. Finally, Google agreed to pay Yahoo billions of dollars in guarantees over the next several years. The deal was signed. The day was saved. Yahoo was out of the search business, but it suddenly had a huge new source of revenue that it could invest in new ventures.

Then, in November, the Department of Justice filed a lawsuit against Google, alleging the Yahoo deal violated antitrust laws. Google backed out of the agreement.

By the middle of the month, Yahoo stock was below $10 per share. Jerry Yang had insisted that Microsoft's $45 billion offer "substantially undervalued" Yahoo. Now the company was worth $14 billion.

Rarely has anyone ever been proven so wrong so quickly and with such expensive consequences.

Yang felt the weight of it, immensely. He thought, I'm just not a very good CEO.

In October, he walked into Sue Decker's office. It was only sixteen months after Yang had called her to say he was going to become CEO and he wanted her to be his number two. Now, he wanted to tell her that he was stepping down as CEO. He and Roy Bostock had talked about it, and the company needed someone new. Yang said Decker would be the inside candidate for the job.

Decker knew the odds of getting the job were slim. She had been around Yahoo forever, and right now that wasn't a good thing. But Decker didn't want to say no, because that would mean leaving with Jerry. It would look like she'd been fired, when she had actually been asked to interview for the top job.

Besides, Decker still had ideas. She still wanted to prove she could rebuild Yahoo around them. She felt that the Microsoft ordeal had nuked any chance of that so far.

She decided to go for the job. Once again, she dug into the models and examined Yahoo's business and the marketplace from top to bottom—like she had been doing since way back in 1996. It was fun to think about what the company should do, without worrying about whether it fit into the vision of some other CEO.

Decker never stood a chance. Besides Yang, no one on the board considered her a serious candidate, least of all Bostock.

When Decker told Bostock her ideas about what Yahoo should do with regards to Microsoft—she wanted to combine the display and search ad business of both companies into one joint venture—Bostock told her, Please don't share that idea with any other board members.

On Monday, January 12, 2009, Yang called Decker and told her the board was going to hire a woman named Carol Bartz to be CEO.

Decker was tired. She said, "That's cool. I would like to resign."

―――――

The year 2008 was a disaster for Yahoo. It began 2008 with a market cap of $34 billion and ended at $17.5 billion. From the week after Microsoft made its offer to December, Yahoo shrank 55 percent.

In some ways, 2008 was a worse year for Yahoo than 2000, when the company shrank 80 percent. In 2000, there was almost nothing Yahoo could have done to prevent its collapse. In 2008, all Yahoo had to do was pick up the phone.

For almost the entire first half of the year, Yahoo sat on an offer to sell at a $45 billion valuation. For a short time, Yahoo sat on an even higher offer.

Then that offer went away and Yahoo imploded.

So whose fault was it that Yahoo bungled the Microsoft offer so badly?

Who was to blame?

Sue Decker, at least partly. When the Microsoft offer came in, Yang asked Decker and her team to establish Yahoo's stand-alone value. Decker reported back a valuation well above the Microsoft offer. But this valuation incorporated huge projections for Yahoo's ad business—that it would grow from $7 billion in annual revenues in 2006 to almost $9 billion in 2010, and that free cash flow would almost double in the same years. When they looked back at those projections, Yahoo executives and investors believed Decker relied too much on projections from overly optimistic Yahoo salespeople.

But then, Decker's projections may have proven correct if the housing market hadn't begun to collapse in 2007 and marketers hadn't begun to rein in their budgets as the Great Recession hit in 2008. Also, Decker had just spent the prior fall and summer coming up with plans to start growing Yahoo again. Of course, she was optimistic about those plans. That's why she had just finished pitching them to Yahoo's board.

Jerry Yang mishandled the deal from the start. He brought in too many advisors and lawyers. At one point, an army of thirty advisors, bankers, and lawyers took over a conference room at the offices of Munger, Tolles & Olson, Yahoo's outside law firm. Everyone had a PowerPoint presentation to show. Everyone had arguments. No one was making decisions. Yang was also prideful about Yahoo's independence. A more objective CEO would have sat across from Ballmer in that airport hangar conference and said, Sure we can row in your direction at $37 per share. Yang was unable to do that.

As much as he honestly tried, Yang wasn't impartial. He knew Yahoo wasn't his company—it belonged to Yahoo's shareholders—but it felt like it was his and Filo's. They had so much emotion invested in the place. So much history. Almost fifteen years. It was always going to be hard for him to get excited about selling Yahoo to Microsoft. Yang believed Microsoft made ugly, bad products. Its besuited culture was so the opposite of Yahoo's.

What Yang really needed, what Yahoo shareholders had really needed, was an impartial, independent voice on the Yahoo side of the table in that conference room in Seattle.

That voice was supposed to have been Yahoo chairman Roy Bostock's.

But Bostock is the one who, from the start, said Yahoo's stance toward Microsoft would be "combative."

One group of angry shareholders would, in a lawsuit, posit that Bostock did not want Yahoo to accept the Microsoft offer because it would have cost him his board seat and chairmanship—which had netted him $1.4 million in stock and salary from 2006 to 2008. Selling to Microsoft would have netted Bostock maybe $90,000.

Bostock had another bad habit during the whole process. Instead of acting like the head of a committee and facilitating discussions with the rest of the board, he acted like an executive—like a little dictator.

Specifically, to other directors and Yahoo executives, it seemed like Bostock and Yang were in constant, behind-the-scenes communication, and that they would make decisions the board should have made together.

A technology company needs a fast-acting decision maker at its top. But that person should be an executive—a COO or CEO, maybe an executive chairman. Bostock held none of those titles.

Bostock's style and title wouldn't have mattered if he had led Yahoo through the offer process to a good result. But he didn't.

The whole thing was a massive screwup and it cost Yahoo shareholders billions of dollars.

The only way for Bostock to redeem himself now was for his pick as Yahoo CEO to prove that she was the perfect hire.

4

F-Bombs Away

On January 13, 2009, Yahoo's new CEO met with a bunch of Yahoo executives for an introductory meeting in building D.

The topic on everyone's mind was: What was she planning to do about Microsoft? Would she try to restart negotiations? Would she sell Yahoo's search business?

Finally, someone asked her directly.

The new CEO's answer: "Steve Ballmer can go fuck himself."

This was Carol Bartz, dropping her very first f-bomb as Yahoo's chief executive.

Bartz was blond-haired and brassy. She often wore a bright red blazer. She made exaggerated faces when she talked. She was an energetic gesticulator, pointing and making fists and waving off ideas and people. She seemed tough.

Bartz grew up in tough circumstances. Her father left the family when she was very young. Then, when Bartz was eight, her mother died. At twelve, she moved to her grandparents' farm in rural Wisconsin.

Once, Bartz and her brother were playing in the barn when

they heard, and then saw, a huge rattlesnake in the rafters. They ran for their grandmother.

Grandma took a shovel and knocked the snake out from above. It hit the dirt hissing. Then grandma chopped its head off with the shovel.

Grandma looked at Bartz and said, "You could've done that."

In high school, Bartz worked at the local bank as a teller and assistant to the president. She earned 75 cents per hour.

She went to college in Missouri and then transferred to the University of Wisconsin in Madison, where she got a degree in computer science in 1971. There was only one other female computer science graduate that year.

During school, Bartz worked as a cocktail waitress in Madison. She memorized the names, hometowns, and favorite drinks of her regulars. After school, she used the same people skills in a series of sales jobs, including one selling bank automation software for Digital Equipment Corporation out of Atlanta.

There, Bartz got her first management job—a promotion from sales rep to sales manager. One of her former peers, a man, said to her, "I have no intention of working for a plug-compatible boss"—by which he meant, in nerd-speak, a woman.

Bartz said, "Well, I'm not going anywhere."

Eventually she was hired by Sun Microsystems in Santa Clara, California. She got her first promotion there when, while her boss was on vacation, she convinced his bosses she could do a better job.

Bartz excelled, climbing all the way to the top of worldwide field operations. Then, in 1992, she became the CEO of a company called Autodesk. Autodesk made AutoCAD, a software application for architects and other designers. It was a huge success in the 1980s, but by 1992 product development was lagging; AutoCAD wasn't even available on Windows yet.

On Bartz's second day at Autodesk, she learned she had breast cancer. Bartz had her breast removed. Within hours after her surgery, she was awake in her hospital bed, hiring her executive team.

Bartz restarted innovation at Autodesk, pushing it into 3D design.

She also won a war with Autodesk's revered founder, John Walker. After making his fortune, Walker had moved to Switzerland and abdicated all his boring management responsibilities to a CEO he promoted from the company's accounting group. The accountant failed, and Walker backed the hire of Bartz. But soon enough, Walker turned on her, too. Therefore, so did a cadre of loyal engineers inside the company. Bartz had the board throw Walker out of the company and made sure that his loyalists followed.

It took her a while, but Bartz was able to turn Autodesk into a lean, revenue-rich, profitable, and fast-growing company.

Between 2002 and 2004, Autodesk tripled in value. It was the top performer in the S&P 500. Sales passed $1 billion in 2004 and $1.5 billion in 2006. Profits grew from $47 million in 2003 to $315 million in 2005.

After fourteen years, Bartz stepped down from Autodesk in 2006, a massive success. She became executive chairman. She spent more time with her daughter. She taught a class at Stanford. She sat on the boards of Intel and Cisco. Her colleagues assumed she would soon be running one of Silicon Valley's big tech companies.

In November 2008, she went to a Cisco board meeting. After, one of her fellow directors, Jerry Yang, came up to her. He asked her if she would be interested in taking the CEO job he had just resigned.

She made a face like Yang was crazy.

She said, "No way. I'm not the right person. I'm not even remotely the right person."

But Yang pressed and Bartz agreed to meet with Yahoo chairman Bostock.

Bostock told her that what Yahoo really needed was structure. He talked about how it was a sprawling mess and had been since its founding.

Bartz thought about how messy Autodesk had been when she got there. She thought: Actually, I might be perfect for this.

She said she was interested.

Bostock was thrilled. He was looking for someone seasoned and savvy—adult supervision. He was blown away by Bartz's track record at Autodesk. Seconded by Jerry Yang, he pushed his fellow Yahoo directors to hire Bartz quickly.

Bostock said Yahoo was lucky to get her, and that her kind of leadership was needed immediately. The place was falling apart. In 2008, revenues had hardly grown over 2007, and search market share was still sinking. The Microsoft saga had cost Yahoo not only its top two executives, but a whole year of executing.

Other directors, including Softbank's representative on the board, Eric Hippeau, asked if it mattered that Bartz didn't have any experience working for an Internet company, any experience marketing to consumers, or any experience in the advertising industry.

Bostock said: She'll learn on the job. It'll be fine.

Bartz was hired without any further interviews.

Bartz couldn't believe what she found at Yahoo.

The place wasn't a mess, as Bostock had described it.

It was complete chaos.

A couple weeks in, she requested a product preview of the Yahoo home page and the company's other big properties—Finance, Sports, etc. Her new staff showed her everything. Bartz noticed the sites weren't all designed the same way. The headers, the fonts, the styles of each page looked different. She said, Let's fix that. She got major pushback from the executives presenting to her. They said what she was asking for wouldn't be easy and would take a lot of time. All the sites ran on different code—thirty-three different types of code.

There were technical mismatches like that all over the place. She learned that Yahoo's two most important products—search and email—worked differently depending on which country you were in.

Then there was Yahoo's bizarre business unit structure. Bartz learned that the people who ran Yahoo's home page didn't want to drive traffic to the Yahoo Finance page because the people running each had separate goals and responsibilities.

It all reminded Bartz of the Winchester Mystery House, that famously weird mansion in San Jose, California. Built in the 1880s by a widow with huge, constant income from the sale of Winchester rifles, it's a massive house that was once seven stories tall. It has secret passageways, stairs that lead nowhere, and doors that open onto walls. The house is said to be haunted.

To Bartz, Yahoo seemed just the same: a complex monstrosity, built without a plan.

Indeed, Yahoo was haunted by the vestiges of Jeff Mallett's spindly, sprawling system of pods and virtual sevens—thrown together in a hurry a decade before. Sue Decker and Jerry Yang had tried to fix the organization, but their answer was an equally distributed "matrix" system. In late February, Bartz exorcised the past once and for all, grouping business units into larger organizations and centralizing functions like marketing and product development under senior executives.

In many ways, Yahoo did not turn into a real, traditionally organized big company until Bartz's quick reorg in the beginning of 2009. The organizational clarity was energizing for everyone inside the company.

That was simple stuff, thought Bartz when it was done.

Next she had to deal with Microsoft. The week she arrived at Yahoo, Bartz charged a group of senior executives with figuring out what to do.

Several senior executives argued that it was insanity for Yahoo to outsource search to Microsoft. They argued that search was the Internet's best business to be in, and that Yahoo was lucky to be number two to Google. They said that having search made it easier for Yahoo to recruit top talent.

These executives were overruled. Bartz told Microsoft CEO Steve Ballmer that if he could promise Yahoo a "boatload" of cash and Yahoo would be able to retain the data on what its users were searching for and the ads and links they were clicking on, he could have Yahoo's search business.

Bartz's thinking was: Yahoo cannot win the search war. It had been an arms race, and Yahoo lost. Any fight now would be Cuba versus the United States, with Yahoo being Cuba. Bartz would be able to take Microsoft's money and invest it into Yahoo's personalization technologies, media businesses, and display advertising technology.

The ten-year deal was struck on July 29, 2009.

The deal and the reorganization made Bartz very popular inside and outside Yahoo after her first six months on the job.

So did a series of brash public appearances where Bartz became known for dropping the f-bomb.

During a call with analysts in April, she said Yahoo laid off seven hundred middle managers because "We had a lot of people telling engineers what to do but nobody fucking doing anything."

Then, during a keynote interview onstage at the D: All Things Digital conference, Bartz asked her interviewer, All Things Digital editor Kara Swisher, "Are we leading up to: I'm both too old and too stupid to know what the Internet is?"

Bartz, sixty, was sensitive to the idea she was too old for the Yahoo job.

Swisher said, "Nope, I'm not going to say that."

Bartz, referring to Swisher's business partner, Walt Mossberg, said, "Because, by the way, Walt is sixty-one and I'm only sixty."

Then Bartz leaned in toward Swisher and, in a stage whisper, said, "Fuck you!"

The crowd whistled and cheered.

After her first six months on the job, Carol Bartz had momentum. The reorg went over well with employees. The board was happy with the search deal. The stock was up from $11.59 when she joined to $16.84 at the end of July and rising.

But then, over the next two years, Bartz was walloped by six global trends.

The first was the continued decline of Yahoo's search market share. Yahoo had 21 percent share when Bartz joined. A year later, in January 2010, it had 17 percent. Search was the best business to be in on the Internet, and Yahoo's presence was shrinking. Sure, Microsoft had made revenue guarantees to Yahoo, but for the most part these guaranteed only the amount Microsoft would pay Yahoo for the traffic Yahoo provided. If Yahoo provided less traffic, Microsoft's payments would be smaller. And Yahoo kept providing less traffic.

During Bartz's first year at Yahoo, the company was also rapidly overtaken by Facebook in the business of selling the Internet's other kind of ads: display ads, also known as brand advertising and sometimes called banner advertising. In the first quarter of 2009, when Bartz joined, Yahoo's share of display advertising impressions in the

United States was just under 15 percent, according to comScore. Yahoo was number one in the market, with MySpace owner Fox Interactive Media following with more than 10 percent share, and Facebook third with around 7 percent share. By the first quarter of 2010, Yahoo's share was down just a little, to around 13 percent. But Facebook had exploded to number one with more than 15 percent share. Mostly, Facebook had eaten into MySpace's share, which had plummeted to below 5 percent. By the third quarter of 2010, Facebook was above 20 percent share and Yahoo was teetering toward 10 percent. Between the third quarter of 2009 and the third quarter of 2010, Facebook's share had grown by 14 percentage points—a full Yahoo-sized slice of the pie.

Market share isn't everything, and through 2010 Yahoo still maintained one big advantage over Facebook: Yahoo was able to charge advertisers more per ad impression. But even this pricing advantage was eroding. Facebook was getting incredibly popular with users around the globe—it had a half billion of them by mid-2010. All those users clicking around Facebook meant Facebook had a ton of display advertising inventory to sell. Facebook's growth flooded the display advertising market with inventory. In the third quarter of 2010, comScore reported that online publishers delivered 1.3 trillion display advertising impressions—a 22 percent increase over the year prior. Demand from marketers could not keep up with all the new supply—budgets were not increasing at the pace of Facebook's growth—and the average price the industry, including Yahoo, was able to charge declined steeply.

Also during Bartz's first year, Yahoo's most important product, Yahoo Mail, began to show signs of weakness. Probably the best acquisition Yahoo ever made was Four11, the maker of RocketMail, in 1997 for under $100 million. By the time Bartz got to Yahoo, hundreds of millions of people around the world and over a hundred million people in the United States were going to Yahoo.com to check their email and, incidentally, click around the rest of Yahoo for news and whatever else, looking at ads the whole way. Thirty billion emails were hitting the company's servers every single day. Yahoo Mail had become the company's "engagement engine." The best part was, Yahoo utterly dominated the other big companies in the market, with more than double the share of Microsoft's Hotmail, Google's Gmail, and AOL Mail.

The problem was, the entire web-based email market began to decline in 2010. The reason was the rise of the iPhone and Android-powered smartphones. Adults stopped checking their email on their computers because they had already seen it on their phones in the default apps provided by Google and Apple. Teenagers weren't emailing at all; they preferred to text or send messages through Facebook. According to web metrics firm Compete, US Internet traffic to web-based email providers peaked in December 2009 at 140 million-plus unique visitors, and quickly declined from there. By September 2010, it was down to 125 million. It kept shrinking, and Yahoo took the brunt of the damage. Between 2011 and 2012, Yahoo email usage declined 25 percent, while iOS email usage increased 74 percent and Android email usage increased 90 percent.

Yahoo's engagement engine started breaking down right as Bartz arrived, and it was dooming. For a long time, Yahoo had been a flailing company because it was not as good at monetizing its huge, fast-growing traffic as Google. Now, Yahoo had an entirely worse problem: It still had huge traffic, but it wasn't growing anymore. It was shrinking. Through the dot-com bust, through the search wars with Google, and through the Microsoft saga, the problem with Yahoo had always been: Users love us so much, and we aren't doing enough with it. Now the problem was: Users are loving us less, and we still aren't doing enough with their attention.

Another reality Bartz could not address was that Yahoo was now an old company by Internet standards. Its age had two nasty side effects. The first was that the talented executives who made Yahoo what it was had all started to leave. Dealmaker Mike Marquez left in 2006. Technical wizard Zod Nazem left in May 2007. Terry Semel's lieutenant from Windsor, Yahoo EVP Jeff Weiner, bolted in June 2008. Qi Lu, a widely respected search scientist, left the same month. So did Brad Garlinghouse, the author of the Peanut Butter manifesto. Sue Decker, with her deep analytical understanding of Yahoo's business, was gone. Jerry Yang remained Chief Yahoo, but his relationship with Bartz was not as close as his relationship with Koogle or Semel had been, and he stopped coming around the campus as much. David Filo continued to solve problems at Yahoo from his cubicle, but Bartz did her best to ignore him, worried that he might be like that interfering founder she had to deal with at Autodesk.

The other side effect of Yahoo's age was that it wasn't cool anymore. In 2011, two years into Bartz's tenure, a company called Hunch did a study comparing Gmail and Yahoo Mail users. It found that Yahoo Mail users were overweight women aged eighteen to forty-nine who lived in the Midwest and had never traveled outside their own country. They owned CDs. They had high school degrees. Gmail users were typically thin men aged eighteen to thirty-four with college degrees. They lived in cities and had traveled to five or more countries. They had MP3s. Yahoo users liked magazines; Gmail users liked blogs. By the time Bartz reached Yahoo, it was becoming unwise to send a résumé from an email address with an "@yahoo.com" at the end.

All of these negative trends around Yahoo had been years in the making. The responsibility for their start lay at the feet of people like Jeff Mallett, Terry Semel, and Jerry Yang—not Bartz.

Nevertheless, the negative momentum existed, and Bartz was unable to reverse it. She would pay the price.

———————

At Yahoo's annual meeting on June 24, 2011, a Yahoo shareholder stood up and, for five minutes, tore into Carol Bartz and the job she had done so far running Yahoo.

"The tone of this meeting is as if the stock is at a fifty-two-week high, not languishing for three years," he said. "I'm going to address the elephants in the room. I think this is a lot of what shareholders are talking about but won't say."

The shareholder complained about Yahoo's share of the display advertising market, where it was quickly becoming dominated by Facebook. He complained about Yahoo's search deal with Microsoft, which had failed to stop Yahoo's decline in that business.

He called for the board to fire Bartz.

"Yahoo cannot afford another exodus of talent, and I think this is likely if Carol remains for the duration of her contract."

At the meeting, Roy Bostock defended Bartz.

"The hard-won progress that we have made is why this board is very supportive of Carol and the management team," he said. "I want to make it very clear about that support. We are confident that Yahoo is headed in the right direction."

Then, in July, Yahoo reported its second-quarter earnings for 2011. They were awful. Yahoo missed Wall Street expectations on sales by $300 million.

On an earnings call, Bartz blamed the miss on a reorganization of the Yahoo sales team that had resulted in more-than-expected turnover, leaving too many clients unattended to.

But within days, Bartz went to Bostock and the Yahoo board

with much worse news: The rest of 2011 was going to be a disaster. Only in May, Bartz had been incredibly optimistic about Yahoo's advertising prospects for the rest of the year. So the sudden change was very alarming.

Bostock decided it was time to rethink Bartz. He considered the revenue problems and how she didn't seem to have a vision for where to take Yahoo next. He reflected on how she had seemed to mishandle Yahoo's relationship with its investments in Asia. He thought about all the M&A interest Yahoo was getting from industry rivals and others. He decided it might be time to let her go.

Jerry Yang, who had first approached Bartz about the job, did not stand in Bostock's way. He felt alienated by her.

On September 6, 2011, Bartz was in New York. Her itinerary that week was to give a keynote interview at the Quadrangle Conference and to meet with hedge fund manager Dan Loeb. But before all that, Bartz looked at her phone and saw that Bostock had called her.

She dialed him back.

He answered and began reading from a fire-the-CEO script, clearly written by a lawyer.

Bartz interrupted Bostock before he could finish reading it.

"Roy," she said, "I think that's a script. Why don't you have the balls to tell me yourself? I thought you were classier."

The next day, Bartz called *Fortune*'s Patricia Sellers, unloaded on the board, and dropped the final f-bomb of her Yahoo era.

Bartz said the board was full of "doofuses." She said, "These people fucked me over" because they were "so spooked by being cast as the worst board in the country."

Right after Bartz hung up on Bostock, she reached for her iPad and sent a note to all fifteen thousand Yahoo employees.

It read:

To all,

I am very sad to tell you that I've just been fired over the phone by Yahoo's Chairman of the Board. It has been my pleasure to work with all of you and I wish you only the best going forward.

Carol
Sent from my iPad

The news made many of Yahoo's top executives melancholy. To them, Bartz was a say-it-like-it-is, call-a-spade-a-spade kind of person. She had balls. She was also a kind, good lady. If you went to her house, she'd take you to her garden and show off her veggie garden, orchids, and talk about the giant squash she once unearthed.

That said, the news wasn't very surprising.

Everyone knew what kind of shape the company was in and all the forces of nature going against it. Most everyone believed that Bartz, despite her heart and her fight, was probably not the CEO Yahoo needed to combat those forces.

Her lack of experience with the consumer Internet, or the Internet at all, proved to be as much of a problem as board member Eric Hippeau and others had worried it would be from the beginning.

Yahoo's top designer, Tim Parsey, once showed a bunch of mock-ups of design ideas he had for some Yahoo products. They were nice mock-ups, maybe even beautiful. They had a little bit of animation to them. Parsey presented them to Bartz with a great amount of storyteller's flair. He liked the word "delicious."

But they were mock-ups—just pie-in-the-sky concepts that didn't answer important questions such as how feasible it would be to launch the products, how they would even really work, and how they would actually get made. They were like concept cars that looked cool but didn't have airbags, bumpers, side mirrors, or even engines. Great-looking product mock-ups are a dime a dozen in the Internet industry. For executives who see them all the time, it can be hard to get excited about them.

So it was surprising to the other, more experienced Internet executives in the room when Bartz appeared to be totally blown away by what Parsey had shown her. She stood up and started clapping—like a total newbie.

In 2011, a Yahoo executive named Scott Burke gave a lengthy presentation to Bartz and the Yahoo board on the state of Yahoo Mail. Burke was a very professorial, intelligent executive who was great at whiteboarding in front of a boss. That day, he came off smart and utterly convincing when he said that what Yahoo Mail needed was a lot more investment—four hundred more people, if possible.

After the presentation, Yahoo executive Ross Levinsohn, a veteran of Fox Interactive Media, turned to chief product officer Blake Irving, a veteran of Microsoft's online group, and said, "What the fuck is he talking about? Mail is over. We should (a) clean up what we have, and (b) just try to keep it going and focus on other things."

But Bartz bought Burke's pitch. She poured more investment into a market that was shrinking by the day.

In an industry where the most successful companies are run by visionaries who see a future improved by their company's products, Bartz was, like Terry Semel before her, a CEO who depended on people she hired to tell her what to do.

In early 2011, Bartz gathered her top executives in Phish Food and said, "Okay, we're fighting about priorities. We're not coming out of this room until we've agreed on a set of key priorities."

She had everyone put their ideas for what Yahoo should be on a whiteboard. Then each executive pitched their plan to the entire room. Bartz handed out poker chips. She told the executives to use the chips to bet on whatever plan they thought Yahoo should bet on. At the end, she counted out the votes and set the direction for Yahoo.

Bartz was also done in by her 2009 deal with Microsoft. The primary theory driving the deal was that combining Microsoft's market share with Yahoo's market share would cause advertisers to hold back some of the money they were spending on Google auctions in order to bid more on Yahoo-Microsoft auctions, thereby driving up Yahoo and Microsoft's revenue per search. That didn't happen—in part because Microsoft's search engine did not work very well in non-Latin-based character sets. It was terrible in Japanese and terrible in Mandarin. So it was not a truly global search technology. In Asia, where Yahoo previously had impressive share, its numbers shrank.

In truth, for the first several years of the deal, Microsoft was forced to pay Yahoo revenue guarantees. These payments weren't much more than Yahoo could have earned on its own, without Microsoft. And then it would have still owned a storefront in the web's best business—search. Instead, for the first five years of the deal, Yahoo lost share and Microsoft gained it.

Finally, Bartz got fired because the same impetus that drove her to drop feisty and humorous f-bombs in public made her a combative presence with the Yahoo board, Yahoo's partners, and Yahoo's cofounders. She wasn't afraid to piss any of them off, and at the end, they were so pissed off at her, they let her go.

———

The first thing Carol Bartz said to Jerry Yang about the Yahoo CEO job was: "I'm not the right person. I'm not even remotely the right person."

Events proved Bartz was right.

The question now was: Who *was* the right person?

The other question was: Who would be willing to try?

After its first early years as a mere directory, Yahoo had always been a sprawling enterprise—sprawling in its headcount, in its product offerings, and in its audience size.

That sprawl, that scale, made Yahoo at once incredibly valuable and incredibly dangerous to those who tried to capture that value.

Before his turn at the top of Yahoo, Terry Semel had been a widely admired media executive. Before hers, Carol Bartz had been a slam-dunk, shoo-in hire because of her impressive run at Sun Microsystems and Autodesk. Before taking the CEO job, Jerry Yang had been a beloved cofounder. Before her promotion, Sue Decker was considered a hero for her boldness with Wall Street and prudence in the boardroom.

After, they were industry pariahs, widely and often unfairly mocked for failing to restore Yahoo to its once-great heights.

Who in the world would ever imagine they could do better?

PART

II

5

Painfully Shy

Marissa Mayer was trying not to cry.

It was 2010 and she was back in her hometown. She was being inducted into the Wausau School District's Alumni Hall of Fame.

Mayer was giving a speech at a luncheon held in honor of her and twenty-five teachers retiring that year.

She stood at a podium in a blue designer dress with a yellow corsage pinned on. She began the speech by thanking her teachers, "each of whom changed my life forever."

Then she started to list her teachers by name. As she did so—"...Mr. Freedly, Mrs. Stay, Mr. Flanagan..."—her face scrunched in a way that made it obvious how important these people were to her growing up.

About six names in, the timbre of Mayer's voice actually broke toward a sob, and she had to catch herself with a breath and a small gulp.

She couldn't stop her eyes from swelling with held-back tears.

Marissa Ann Mayer was born on May 30, 1975, to parents Margaret Mayer, an art teacher and homemaker, and Michael Mayer, an environmental engineer.

Mayer grew up in Wausau, Wisconsin, with a sports-playing brother, Mason Mayer. It was a middle-class upbringing. She had a big doll collection. She went to public schools and worked summer jobs at a movie theater, a grocery store, and a window factory. Her family had enough time and money to enroll her in countless activities.

In the fifth grade, Mayer refused to leave the classroom at the end of the year. She told her Stettin Elementary teacher Wayne Flanagan that she did not want to go to middle school. She was worried she wouldn't make it there, with all the new kids and teachers she'd have to meet.

Flanagan told Mayer, "Oh, I think you're going to make it fine." All year, she had been a star student.

Still, Mayer wouldn't go. Eventually, Flanagan called Mayer's mother to let her know where her daughter was.

In eighth grade, a classmate from Advanced Math called the local radio station and told them it was Mayer's birthday on a day when it was not. The kid, named Brian Jojade, did it because he had a crush on Mayer. He liked the way she sat in the front of the classroom and "always worked hard and made sure no matter what she was going to do, it was going to get done right."

When the DJ read her name out on the air, Mayer hated the prank and let Jojade know.

In high school, Mayer's style was T-shirts, sweaters, and jeans—nice clothes but nothing flashy. And while Mayer always presented well in front of an audience, her peers didn't think of her as particularly extroverted. She wasn't the kid everyone at school thought might be president someday.

Carol Bartz had been her Wisconsin high school's prom queen. Mayer was the one who announced the names of the more popular kids who had been elected to homecoming court.

Mayer's Wausau West High School classmate Elize Bazter says she best remembers Mayer as the girl who was "kind to everyone" but would dodge conversations on her way to go study somewhere else.

Wausau West had a class schedule system where, instead of periods, the day was broken up into twenty-minute "mods." Classes lasted for forty minutes or an hour. That meant there were twenty-minute breaks during everyone's day. Most upperclassmen would use the time to congregate in the school's commons, talking and eating with their friends.

Not Marissa. Mayer would be the person to come down to the commons, get something to eat from the kitchen or the vending machines, then go to the library or the science lab to study. She wouldn't be the one to stay and sit there and converse for twenty minutes.

Growing up, Mayer was not close to many of her peers. The people Mayer spent most of her childhood with were a particular kind of nurturing, mentoring adult: coaches, teachers, counselors, and instructors.

She was in Brownies. She took piano lessons. She played volleyball and basketball. She went to swimming and skiing lessons. She took ballet for as many as thirty-five hours a week during middle school and high school. Her mother says ballet taught her "criticism and discipline, poise and confidence."

She was a pompom girl and a debater. She was on the precision dance team.

Perhaps because she was around all these teachers, mentors, and coaches all the time, Mayer started acting like one of them very early on.

Mayer's childhood piano teacher, Joanne Beckman, remembers Mayer being very different from other children in that she was someone who "watched people" in order to "figure out why they were doing what they were doing.

"A lot of kids that age are very interested in themselves," Beckman says. "She was looking at other people."

Even when she was in fifth grade, Wayne Flanagan could see the pedagogical side of Mayer developing. He thought she would become a teacher someday.

In high school, Mayer felt more comfortable talking to her peers from the front of the room. She took a leadership position in every club she joined. She became president of the Spanish club, treasurer of Key Club, and captain of the debate team.

One of her closest friends from Wausau, Abigail Garvey Wilson, later told a reporter, "When Marissa became captain of the pompom squad, she wasn't in with that clique of girls, but she won them over in three ways.

"First: sheer talent. Marissa could choreograph a great routine. Second: hard work. She scheduled practices lasting hours to make sure everyone was synchronized. And third: fairness. With Marissa in charge, the best dancers made the team."

In 1993, Mayer applied to, and was accepted into, ten schools, including Harvard, Yale, Duke, and Northwestern.

To decide which one she would go to, Mayer created a spreadsheet, weighing variables for each.

She picked Stanford. Her plan was to become a brain doctor—a good profession for a brilliant but introverted person.

The summer before Marissa Mayer went to Stanford in 1994, she began asking herself a question that would guide her through college and for the rest of her life.

What does Zune think?

That summer, Mayer attended the National Youth Science Camp in West Virginia. It was nerd heaven. Picture science labs housed in wooden cabins shaded by trees. Mayer especially loved one experiment where they mixed water and cornstarch to make a sloppy goo-like substance that seemed to defy gravity.

One day, a postdoctoral student from Yale named Zune Nguyen spoke to the campers as a guest lecturer. He stunned all the smart kids in the room with puzzles and brainteasers. For days, the campers couldn't stop talking about his visit.

Finally, one of Mayer's counselors had enough.

"You know, you have it all wrong," the counselor said to Mayer and the campers. "It's not what Zune knows, it's how Zune thinks."

The counselor said that what made Nguyen so amazing wasn't the facts that he knew, but rather how he approached the world and how he thought about problems. The counselor said the most remarkable thing about Nguyen was that you could put him in an entirely new environment or present him with an entirely new problem, and within a matter of minutes he would be asking the right questions and making the right observations.

From that moment on, the phrase: "It's not what Zune knows, but how Zune thinks," stuck with Mayer as a sort of personal guiding proverb.

In the fall, Mayer went to Stanford and began taking premed classes. She planned to become a doctor. But by the end of her freshman year, she was sick of it.

I'm just doing flash cards, she thought. This is easy. Too easy. It's just a lot of memorization.

Mayer wanted to find a major that would train her to think critically and become a great problem-solver. She also wanted to study how people think, how they reason, how they express themselves.

She had a nagging voice in her head saying, It's not what Zune knows, but how Zune thinks.

Mayer began to answer the voice in her head—and find a course of study that helped her learn how to think—when she took an introductory computer science class: CS105.

During the semester, she entered a classwide design contest for extra credit. Calling on the same part of her brain that made her such an excellent pompom choreographer, Mayer made a screen saver featuring exploding fireworks. In a class of three hundred, Mayer came in second.

The design was so good that Mayer's CS105 professor, Eric Roberts, would use an adaptation of her screen saver as an assignment for the next several years.

Roberts was impressed enough with Mayer's exploding fireworks that he invited her and a few other top finishers over for dinner at his house. He became her mentor as, once again, Mayer bonded with a teacher.

Mayer had also found her major.

Mayer opted for symbolic systems—a combination of disciplines straight out of Zune Nguyen's head: linguistics, philosophy, cognitive psychology, and computer science classes.

Symbolic systems has become a famous major at Stanford. Besides Mayer, other alumni include LinkedIn cofounder Reid Hoffman; former senior vice president of iOS software at Apple, Scott Forstall; and Instagram cofounder Mike Krieger.

Mayer's pedagogical streak came out in a big way when she took Philosophy 160A, then considered a "weed-out course" for prospective symbolic systems majors.

For Philosophy 160A, the students break into study groups of a half dozen or so, and the groups are assigned problem sets. Mayer's group—just like all the others—put off their problem sets until the day before they were due.

So that semester at Stanford was full of all-nighters for Mayer and her Philosophy 160A group. During those study sessions, the kids in Mayer's group would get chatty and start to procrastinate. Mayer would always be the one to say: "Okay, back to work. Let's get this done."

The social dynamic of the group was typical for Mayer. As usual, she commanded the room—organized the group's work in an all-business fashion—but was otherwise shy and somewhat reclusive.

In the years ahead, this combination—Mayer's willingness to be authoritative and demanding in the way a teacher would be, and her to reluctance to connect with peers on a personal level—would cause problems for Mayer.

One Stanford classmate interpreted Mayer's shyness as being "kind of stuck up.

"She would do her work and then leave. When other people would stay and hang out and have pizza, she'd just be out of there because the work is done."

Indeed, Mayer doesn't seem to have had a very active social life in college.

One person who lived in Mayer's dorm said she was always "down to business" and "not much for socializing. She wasn't one of those people into making new friends around the dorm. She was always doing something more important than just chilling."

Later at Stanford, Mayer found herself in a group setting that was less social, more comfortable, and more familiar for her. As an upperclassman in symbolic systems, she was tapped to teach a class.

She took to it naturally.

Professor Roberts supervised her teaching. After Mayer taught a course in the spring, Roberts took a survey of her students. The results were astounding: They loved her—even if she did sometimes talk "a mile a minute."

Roberts asked Mayer to stick around Stanford to teach another class over the summer; she readily agreed.

Mayer excelled the rest of her years as an undergraduate at Stanford. After she got her bachelor's degree, she stayed at the school to get a master's in computer science, with a specialty in artificial intelligence.

As graduate school drew to a close, word got out about Mayer's teaching ability.

She soon faced a choice.

Should she become a teacher and step full time into a role that had always suited her so well?

Or should she challenge herself and work somewhere in the technology industry?

———

When people ask Mayer why she joined Google after getting her masters in symbolic systems at Stanford, she likes to tell them her "Laura Beckman story." It's about the daughter of her middle school piano teacher, Joanne Beckman.

Mayer begins: "Laura tried out for the volleyball team her junior year at high school. At the end of the tryouts, she was given a hard choice: bench on varsity, or start on JV.

"Most people, when they're faced with this choice, would choose to play—and they'll pick JV. Laura did the opposite. She chose varsity, and she benched the whole season.

"But then an amazing thing happened. Senior year she tried out and she made varsity as a starter, and all the JV starters from the previous year were benched their whole senior year.

"I remember asking her: 'How did you know to choose varsity?'

"And she said, 'I just knew that if I got to practice with the better players every day, I would become a much better player, even if I didn't get to play in any of the games.'"

The moral of Mayer's story was that it's always better to surround yourself with the best people so that they will challenge you and you will grow.

"My quest to find, and be surrounded by, smart people is what brought me to Google," she says.

And that's the overriding reason why Mayer joined Google.

But she almost didn't get the chance.

Late on a Friday in mid-April of her last year at Stanford, Mayer sat at her computer, eating pasta and reading emails. She already had twelve job offers to choose from and wasn't looking for any more hard choices. So when yet another pitch from a recruiter popped up in her inbox, she tapped on her keyboard's delete key to get rid of it.

Only she missed.

Instead of hitting the delete key, Mayer hit the space bar. It opened the email.

That email's subject line: "Work at Google?"

Mayer read the email and remembered a conversation she had with Eric Roberts, who was still a mentor years after she took his computer science class for nonmajors. The prior fall, Roberts listened to Mayer talk about the recommendation engine she'd built, and then told her she should meet with a pair of PhD students who were working on similar stuff. Their names: Sergey Brin and Larry Page.

Realizing the email she meant to delete was from Brin and Page's startup, Mayer replied, writing that she wanted an interview.

She got one, and met with engineer Craig Silverstein. Silverstein blew her away with his smarts. In the Laura Beckman analogy, he was varsity.

Google offered Mayer a job—an internship, actually.

She didn't say yes right away. Mayer already had a good offer from consulting firm McKinsey. There, her clients would be Silicon Valley companies. She would learn a lot. It would be a steady job.

Google was a much riskier choice.

Mayer decided to figure out how risky.

She looked up historical data on startups in Google's situation. She crunched a bunch of numbers and came up with a figure she believed represented the chances Google would succeed.

She calculated that there was a 98 percent chance Google would go bust.

She went for it anyway.

6

User Friendly

In July 1999, Google was in terrible shape. In the two months since Marissa Mayer, she and her colleagues were regularly working hundred-hour weeks just to keep the search engine running.

On Mayer's second day on the job, she went to the kitchen for a snack at around eleven a.m. There, she bumped into Larry Page, Google's cofounder and CEO. He was standing in a corner.

"I'm hiding," said Page. "The site is down. It's all gone horribly awry."

Google had just signed a deal with Netscape to handle search queries from Netscape.com. Google had only three hundred computers serving search results, and it had asked Netscape to send just a fraction of its traffic. Netscape ignored the request and sent all of its users.

Down went Google.com.

Mayer walked back to her desk. She worked through lunch and then through dinner. Then she worked till well after three in the morning—not for the last time in her first weeks at the company.

The whole thing should have been awful for Mayer.

It wasn't.

It was amazing.

After her awkward grade school and high school years, and the somewhat better but still imperfect college and graduate school years, Marissa Mayer finally felt at home. She had found her people. She had found her place. Google was like a boarding school for super geniuses. Everyone ate all their meals together. They went to movies together. Often, people slept in the office.

One very late night that July, Mayer and her Google colleagues finally ran out of steam and stopped coding. Instead of going home, however, they stuck around the office because a colleague, Harry, was still running Google's web-crawling algorithm. It was a three- to five-day process of five hundred steps, and if Harry screwed up any one step, he'd have to go back to the beginning. So everyone was hanging around to keep Harry properly motivated and caffeinated. They nicknamed him "Spiderman."

As the night wore on, the whole group gathered in a circle in an open space between cubicles. Some sat on the floor, some sat on brightly colored exercise balls. They talked about the future, about what Google could be someday. It was like one of those conversations Mayer used to observe around the Stanford dorms, especially during the fall when new groups of friends were forming. Freshmen would sit around and swap stories and talk about what they hoped to get out of Stanford—what they hoped to do with their lives. Now Mayer was a part of one of those conversations. Everyone was coming up with all kinds of crazy ideas. Someone even suggested the insane idea that Google should scan all the libraries in the world and put every book ever written online. But no one laughed the idea off. They started to think about how it could be done.

It was a magical moment. Finally, an engineer named Georges Harik jumped up from his exercise ball and stood in the center of the circle.

He said, "I just want everyone to stop and remember this moment because whatever happens from this moment on, it will never be as good as it is right now." Everyone took the moment in—Mayer especially.

She was falling in love with Google. The people, the culture, the ideas. She imagined she was feeling how Laura Beckman felt like that first year on the varsity team. Her shyness was evaporating. Mayer felt a powerful drive to prove she belonged on this amazing team, to help any way she could.

And so, twenty-four-year-old Marissa Mayer went after it. Mayer had been hired into Google as a coder. She threw herself into a big project: building a system for Google that would allow it to serve the right ads with the right searches.

But then a funny thing happened. After Mayer had been working on the project for weeks, another Google engineer, Jeff Dean, offered to help. In a relative snap, Dean built a better system than the one Mayer had been working on for weeks.

This made sense. Dean had a reputation in the industry for being among the world's greatest coders. When Google poached him from a company called DEC, several of his colleagues couldn't believe a startup had managed to hire such a talent. Impressed, many of them followed him to Google.

There was no shame in Mayer getting outcoded by Dean. But for her, the experience provided a truth. She realized that she was never going to be as good at programming as Dean—or even in his class. Eventually, Google was going to be full of people who were at his level. If she was going to prove she belonged at Google, she was going to have to find other ways.

Google was still a very small company, and at that point, it needed people who were willing to take on any challenge—from helping out with HR to pitching in on marketing to installing new servers over the weekend. Mayer filled that need.

Her life was: Spend four hours a day sleeping at whatever odd hours; rollerblade and bike around the Stanford campus on the weekend; otherwise, work.

People noticed Mayer. She stuck out because she was a blond woman among mostly male engineers. They took note of her nervous aspect, especially the "nnn" laugh she would quietly make to punctuate an unyielding, opinionated conversational style. They remarked on her smarts, focus, and commitment. They talked about how she would launch herself full force into whatever problems Google needed solving.

Sometimes, Mayer would attack problems someone else was already working on. This irritated other Googlers, but Mayer didn't let it slow her down—possibly because she wasn't aware of the irritation.

One early project Mayer took on was to figure out whether or not the text on Google's search results pages should be serif or sans serif. Serif fonts, like Times New Roman, have those little flags hanging off the ends of some letters. Sans-serif fonts, like Helvetica, have no flags, just letters in their most basic linear forms. Mayer dug into the research. What she found amused her: Serif fonts were more "readable," but sans-serif fonts were more "legible."

Well, that didn't make the answer very obvious, Mayer thought.

But actually, it did, she realized. Because what "readable" meant in this context was that serifs create a horizontal rule across the page that guides the eye, making serif fonts much better for reading long pieces of text. Sans-serif fonts are more "legible" because when the serifs are gone, your eyes can read and recognize a character much more quickly. On a search results page, all you're doing is spot reading. So actually the choice really was obvious. Nnn.

Mayer took the research to Larry Page and argued they needed to make a change. Page agreed. The letters on Google's search results pages lost their serifs.

Mayer had found her niche, an area where she could prove she belonged: improving and guiding the development of Google's user interface, or UI. It perfectly suited her degree in human-computer interaction.

At first, Mayer was just a part-time member of the UI team, a delegate sent from Google's engineering organization. She would work on the look and feel of search results pages while a pair of Googlers from the marketing department oversaw the design of the rest of Google's pages. Then the three of them would pitch their designs to Page, and he'd make a call.

But quickly, Mayer went from part-time team member to group leader. She set up a "UI team" email list to schedule meetings and address issues on the fly. She began leading the weekly UI review meetings. In a darkened conference room with a projector pointed at a white wall, twenty-four-year-old Mayer would lead the team through long sessions reviewing every pixel of design on every page—the width of columns, the margins of pages, the padding between cells. Mayer insisted every decision had to be based on facts and research. The team grew. Mayer became its primary representative to Page.

Then, in March 2000, Larry Page took on a new role in addition to CEO. He became "chief of products." He decided that he would meet once a week with senior leadership from across Google for a product review. Mayer seized the chance to run the meetings for him. Soon, she was setting the agenda for every meeting—determining which Google products would get discussed and who was invited to the meeting.

Less than a year after being hired as a junior coder, Mayer was in charge of the meetings that determined how Google.com would look, and she was literally setting the agenda on the products Google would make. More important, she had proven to be a crucial part of the team.

Mayer could already tell that Georges Harik was wrong about one thing: That night in July 1999 was not going to be the best it ever got at Google. It was getting better all the time.

Mayer's already intense feelings for Google deepened that spring and summer when, quietly, she began to see more of Larry Page outside the office. They went on dates like teenagers. Page had dark brown, almost black hair. He had a big, earnest smile without a hint of cynicism in it. Page had gone to a leadership camp when he was in college and he'd internalized the camp's motto, that one ought "to have healthy disregard for the impossible." Mayer found that mind-set very attractive to be around. She and Page played board games together. They liked Settlers of Catan, especially.

Other Googlers began to hear about the relationship. There was a rumor that Page and his cofounder, Sergey Brin, had been invited to have dinner with the queen of England, and that Page had brought Mayer as his date. People in HR were clueless. Page hadn't told them a thing.

Slowly, everyone started to figure it out. During Google's weekly all-employee meetings, called TGIF, Page would mention attending an event with Mayer. People saw them at a party together, clearly acting like a couple. They would arrive at the office together.

The relationship was very discreet. There were absolutely zero displays of affection between Mayer and Page at the office.

When Heather Cairns, Google's HR boss, finally heard about the relationship, she thought, Huh. Okay. Two quiet people dating each other quietly.

Then she thought, That's a nice couple. They have a lot in common.

The only one little thing that bothered anybody was that between the UI review, product review, and now the relationship, Mayer seemed to have more influence over what Page thought about Google than anybody—except for Brin, of course, and Page's best friend, Salar Kamangar.

But Mayer worked so hard and contributed so much for the next few years that almost no one begrudged her anything.

Not yet.

Marissa Mayer was willing to do almost anything for Google. But in early 2001, she did not want to do what Cindy McCaffrey was asking her to do.

Walt Mossberg, the famous personal technology columnist for the *Wall Street Journal*, was coming to the Googleplex and McCaffrey, Google's head of marketing, needed someone to sit down with him and tell him what the company was up to.

There was no one better to do it than Marissa Mayer.

Since joining in 1999, Mayer had quickly risen up the ranks to become one of the most important people at the company. First, she had taken over the UI meetings, where every new Google product had to survive her judgment. Then she took control over Larry Page's product review meetings. Then Mayer created and started running a new process called the launch calendar. Each week, Mayer would gather the heads of every constituency within Google—marketing, legal, engineering, PR, etc.—and go over the products that were supposed to be launched that week. Each representative would have to green-light every product for launch. But the way Mayer ran things—at a breakneck pace—anyone who wanted to hold up the launch of a product had to have a good reason why. And woe be unto those actually developing the product scheduled for launch if their work was not ready.

McCaffrey believed that, other than maybe Larry Page and Sergey Brin, no one was more knowledgeable about Google's product road map than Mayer.

So McCaffrey went to Mayer and asked her if she would handle the briefing. Mayer said no. She said she was too busy that day. She had too many meetings. Sorry, please try someone else.

The truth was, Mayer wasn't just busy, she was also feeling shy. It would be her first media interview.

Finally, McCaffrey said: If you do it, I'll give you a gift certificate to Watercourse Way, the spa in downtown Palo Alto.

Mayer said fine. She agreed to sit down with Mossberg when he swung through Mountain View.

When they met in Mayer's office, Mossberg got the full Mayer. On came a flood of statistics and anecdotes and arguments, peppered with her elliptical "nnn" laughs, all at a sprinter's pace. Mossberg found Mayer to be impressively articulate, thoughtful, and very proud of her work and her company.

As far as McCaffrey could tell, Mayer knocked the meeting out of the park.

There were three reasons Mayer did so well.

One was that Mayer had an incredible ability to recall the smallest details about Google users. For example, in a UI meeting, Mayer wouldn't just tell a product manager to use one blue over another. She would quote the statistics for which blues generated the best click-through rates among various demographics. With Mossberg, she was able to go deep on Google's technology.

The second reason was that, since she was a kid, Mayer had always been a world-class preparer. No one would ever outhustle her before the big meeting, presentation, or interview.

The third was that Mayer was proud of and passionate about Google to her core, and this made her staccato verbosity charming and charismatic, rather than obnoxious.

A short while after his visit, Mossberg published a column declaring "Google is everything a search engine should be: thorough, smart, speedy and honest."

McCaffrey put Mayer on a list of executives she could trust to handle media.

———

In 2002, Marissa Mayer noticed her new boss was having a problem hiring the right kind of people into Google.

Her boss's name was Jonathan Rosenberg. He'd joined Google earlier that year as vice president of products. His biggest job prior to that had been at Excite@Home, a heavily funded, failed startup.

Rosenberg was a hard-working executive, and throughout his career he had been talented at getting his bosses to like him. He wasn't having much success at that at Google. Google's new "adult supervision" chief executive, Eric Schmidt, seemed to like Rosenberg fine, but Larry Page—the cofounder calling all the shots behind the scenes—was acting like he couldn't stand Rosenberg.

Rosenberg would come into meetings with Page and flash his big-company skill set: structured agendas, market research, and product road maps. Page laughed it all off. That's not how we do it around here, he'd say.

What Mayer noticed was that Rosenberg kept failing at his main job. Rosenberg was supposed to be hiring product managers who could come into Google and shepherd all the projects the company was working on.

Rosenberg would go out and recruit top graduates from Harvard's and Stanford's MBA programs. Then he'd bring them to Page, and Page would reject them.

Finally, Mayer clued Rosenberg in.

She told him: Stop trying to hire MBAs to be product managers, and start hiring computer science graduates with an interest in business. Mayer said: That's the kind of person I am, and look how well I'm doing at Google. That's the kind of person Larry is, too.

She told Rosenberg about a Stanford computer science class

where all the teaching assistants were undergrads who had just taken the class. She said that Google should start a program where it hires those kinds of people right out of school. That way, it could mold its executives to be "Google-y" in the way they thought about the Internet, technology, and business.

She thought maybe Google could call these people "associate product managers."

Rosenberg knew that Mayer was close to Page—that she understood him as well as anyone at Google, and that her idea would fly with the boss.

He said: Okay. Let's do it. You run the program.

Run it, she did.

Within months, Mayer hired her first associate product manager, or APM, a kid from Stanford named Brian Rakowski. She parachuted him into a big secret project Google was working on: a web-based email product called Gmail. There were already a bunch of engineers on the project, and they resented having a twenty-two-year-old dropped in on them like some kind of boss.

So Mayer told Rakowski: Don't be their boss. You are not their boss. They have way too much experience for that to work. If you ever need to get them to do something, the only way they'll do it is if you show them enough data to back up your case. Rakowski and the engineers gelled.

Mayer got permission to expand the APM experiment.

Mayer hired more recent college graduates like Rakowski and started shoving them into engineering groups all over Google. She would meet with her APMs every week to see how they were doing and how the products they were managing were coming along.

Eventually, the APM program turned into an institution—a two-year program for forty or so APMs. Between their first and second years in the program, Mayer would take the APMs on an around-the-world trip to see how real people were interacting with Google products.

The program was good for Google, which gained an energetic and technical product organization, and very good for Mayer. By hiring a bunch of kids, putting them in charge of products being built all over the company, and having those kids report to her, Mayer began to consolidate power at Google. She became the de facto boss of Google's consumer products division.

Sometimes, Google's engineers resisted the APM invasion. In 2003, an APM named Bret Taylor showed up to his first day of work on a new team, and the engineering manager told him, "You're worthless. I don't work with product managers."

But the APM program had backing from the very top of Google, and Taylor stuck around.

Mayer knew she was fighting a turf war, but she didn't think about it in terms of power. She was just taking on as much as she could take on, and assumed everyone who mattered agreed it was for the best. It was part of the same desire that had motivated her before: to prove that she was useful and that she belonged on such an impressive team.

Mayer loved the APM program. She used to be shy around people, but she wasn't shy with her APMs. On trips to faraway countries, she was their leader and spokesman. In the office, they would come to her for advice on topics personal and professional.

Not all APMs loved Mayer. Some did, for sure. If an APM was one of her favorites and could get over her awkward style, that APM would start to like her. Mayer would even grow close to that person. She would talk about her personal life with Larry, make jokes, and even listen.

But if an APM wasn't one of her favorites, Mayer could become especially icy in the way she criticized work. For APMs unused to failure of any kind, Mayer's style was especially jarring. Over her first three years or so running the program, maybe a dozen APMs fled her office in tears.

In 2003, CEO Eric Schmidt made official what was already fact. He put Marissa Mayer in charge of the look and feel of Google's consumer products, including search. In 2005, he made her a vice president. Her face and bio went up on Google's website.

From the time she took over Google's UI meetings in 2000 until several years after her promotion in 2005, Mayer went on an incredible run.

Google search dominated the industry. Consumers flocked to Gmail, Google News, and Google Maps.

Those products succeed in no small part because Mayer lived obsessed with simplifying their "user pathways"—the screens and processes a normal web user would click through to use them.

It was a triumph of empathy.

Which is remarkable, considering that, ever since she was a child, Marissa Mayer had difficulty appearing empathetic. People called her robotic or stuck up. She had a hard time looking people in the eye. She insulted associate product managers with a cold manner.

And yet, despite this trouble with relating, Mayer's job all those years was, basically, to relate with Google's hundreds of millions of users.

How did she pull it off?

With the help of mental scaffolding: process, rules, and mimicry.

One time, an APM brought a product to her for review, and she told him, "This page is too busy. What you need to do is look at every font on the page, every font size. And every time you see a new color or a new font size, you add up a point. I want this page below five points."

The comment about "five points" ended up in the meeting notes, and then it became a rule. No pages with more than five points.

Another rule was: Design a product for the "98 percent use" case. For Mayer, the best example of a product that followed this rule was the Xerox copy machine. It could do all kinds of fancy things: staple, collate, copy, and fax. But if you walked up to one and pressed the giant green button, the right thing just happened. Mayer believed on every good product there should be a big button like that for the 98 percent use case, where if the user clicks it or taps it, they get a delightful, fluid, simple experience.

During a product review, Mayer would count the number of keystrokes it took to get every job done. Too many, and it was back to work.

Mayer learned another rule the hard way. In 2001, Mayer and an engineer named Krishna Bharat launched Google News. It struggled to get adoption. Mayer looked at the user data. People were scrolling up and down a lot, skipping over whole sections of links. Clearly, Google News wasn't surfacing relevant enough stories. So she added a widget that asked users to manually select what they wanted to see and what they did not.

When Larry Page heard about the widget, he got angry. That's not what we do! he said. Google products are machine driven. The rule was: Google products learn what the human wants and give it to them without any human effort.

For Mayer, a subsidiary design rule was: Google products must look like they were created by machines. Don't do any more design than you have to. Keep it clean. Don't let it look editorialized.

There was one way Mayer would allow a rule to be broken: if the product manager was able to present testing data to suggest it should be. Mayer learned the power of testing data early on, when she launched Google News. Prior to launch, the team had to decide which of two possible features to add. Should they add a feature that would allow users to sort news stories by date, or should they include one that would let users sort stories by location? The team was split down the middle. Debate was deadlocked and heated. Finally, Mayer said: Let's pick one and launch it. They picked sort by location. They launched the product on a Monday morning. By five p.m., Mayer was reading three hundred messages from users—almost all of them asking Google to please include a sort-by-date function.

The other way Mayer taught herself to relate to users was by mimicking their circumstances. Mayer went without broadband in her home for years, resisting until it was installed in the majority of American homes. Well after she'd made millions of dollars in Google's IPO, she found herself driving to work on Saturdays just to use her work computer to do Internet shopping because the web was so much faster there. She carried an iPhone at Google, which made Android phones, because so did most mobile web users.

In UI reviews, Mayer would frequently bring up her mother, still living in Wisconsin, and demand that whatever product the team was working on be as usable for her as it was for anyone in the room.

Mayer's priorities worked. With users clicking through Mayer-approved pathways, Google search became the most profitable Internet business ever, Google Maps ate MapQuest's lunch, and Gmail steadily lured users away from Hotmail and Yahoo Mail.

Around 2005, Mayer came into her office visibly upset. She and Larry had broken up. For a few days, she was eager to talk it through with some of her closest colleagues. But then, a short while later, it was like it never happened.

In 2007, Page married a Stanford graduate student named Lucy Southworth. The ceremony was on Richard Branson's private island, Necker Island in the Caribbean Sea.

That same year, a Google colleague emailed Mayer to say, "I'm bringing a boy I think you'd be interested in. Be cool."

The "boy" was Zachary Bogue. Tall and dark-haired, Bogue looks like he could be the star of *The Bachelor*. He had played football at Harvard and was now a banker in San Francisco. When Mayer and Bogue married, there were two ceremonies: One was in California. It was covered by *Vogue* and attended by Silicon Valley's billionaire elite. A second ceremony was held at Mayer's childhood church, Immanuel Lutheran in Wausau.

Of their married life, Bogue once told a reporter: "We continue to do work in the evening. There's never a distinct line between work and home. Marissa's work is such a natural extension of her. It's not something she needs to shed at the end of the day."

As much as Mayer gave to her work, her work gave back to her a hundredfold.

As an early employee, she had received more money from Google's IPO than she had ever dreamed of—hundreds of millions of dollars. She bought a $5 million penthouse suite at the Four Seasons in San Francisco and another home closer to Google's Mountain View campus. She started throwing fabulous parties at both, jumping feetfirst into San Francisco's high-end social scene. Guests at her homes would see expensive original artwork from famous artists, like a four-hundred-piece glass installation by Dale Chihuly.

Mayer continued to have real influence at Google. Her APMs were spread throughout the company, loyal as ever. And, despite the breakup with Page, she remained in a small group of executives with outsized influence over him and the rest of the company. In his book on Google, *Wired* reporter Steven Levy would call the group a "secret cabal."

Marissa Mayer had money and power. Thanks to a relatively recent Google hire, next would come fame.

Starting around 2007, a rumor started going around Google: Marissa Mayer loved press attention so much she had assembled her own PR team within Google to promote her.

How else could you explain the *Vogue* profile?

Or the *Today* show appearances?

Or the *New York Times* profile headlined "Putting a Bolder Face on Google"?

The rumor that Mayer had her own PR team fit into a growing, perhaps sexist narrative about Mayer inside some Google circles: that she was an attention- and credit-seeking master manipulator who got the attention she sought only because of her looks, her gender, and her age, not because she was a great technologist or product maker.

In fact, Mayer did not have her own PR team inside Google. She did, however, have a group of people inside Google's PR organization devoted to promoting her career. They were led by a communications executive named Gabriel Stricker.

Stricker joined Google in September 2006. Stricker was soft-spoken, trim, and bald, with a close-cropped beard. He wore dark jeans and sport coats over plaid shirts. He was hired to help launch Google Books but he spent most of his time getting reporters to write about Google's search products.

In 2006 and 2007, Google was quickly becoming one of the world's most beloved technologies. The company was generating billions of dollars in revenues every quarter, and growing fast. Stricker was inundated with pitches from editors and TV producers wanting to do stories.

But like McCaffrey before him, Stricker had a hard time getting Google cofounders Sergey Brin and Larry Page to do any interviews. Even Google CEO Eric Schmidt was less available than he used to be. Stricker realized that, as far as publicity went, Google had a weak bench behind its top three executives. It needed someone who could plausibly fill in. It needed a star.

Stricker wasn't worried about his ability to make a star. He came to Google from the world of campaign politics, where he was trained to use the press to promote people. But he was worried about the talent at Google. It was all executives like Android boss Andy Rubin, who shared Brin and Page's distaste for the media, or schlumpy engineers who bored reporters just by looking at them.

Then Stricker started working with Google's product leader for search, Marissa Mayer. Reporters seemed to know who she was.

From his cubicle at Google headquarters, Stricker would sometimes hear his colleagues try to pitch reporters with stories.

They'd go: Hey, you should really do a piece about Gmail.

The reporter would say: Awesome, can we talk to an executive?

The PR person would say: Yeah, there's this engineer . . .

And the story wouldn't happen.

Meanwhile, Stricker would call a reporter and say: Hey, you should do a piece about this really interesting thing in search. Do you know that you could type a flight number into search and it actually shows you a result?

And the reporter would say: That's sort of interesting.

Then Stricker would hit them with: This is something that Marissa's been working on.

The reporter's tone would change: Oh, I've heard of her. She's that blond-haired blue-eyed computer scientist lady!

And the story would happen.

The day Stricker fully realized how potent Mayer could be with the media was May 16, 2007. That's when Google held an event for the press called Searchology. At the event, three middle-aged male engineers got onstage and gave presentations on the state of Google search. The media in attendance politely paid attention.

Then came Mayer, and the audience woke up. They laughed at her jokes. For the first two minutes, her talk was punctuated with flash photography.

What Stricker was witnessing, of course, was Mayer in her comfort zone: at the front of the classroom, facing an adoring class.

He began to pitch her more, and the uptake was incredible. Soon, reporters started calling Google and asking for Mayer by name. The media responds to the curiosity of consumers, and consumers were fascinated by the idea that a twenty-something, photogenic, blond woman could be such a technologist—such a geek. They were also curious about Mayer's expensive and stylish tastes. Mayer checked all the boxes.

The bookers on the *Today* show were particularly in love with Mayer. She came on whenever Google had a new product to show off. *Vogue* profiled her. So did *San Francisco* magazine, which dubbed her Googirl. A long *New York Times* profile came in 2008. *Newsweek* called her one of the "10 Tech Leaders of the Future." *Business 2.0* named her to the "Silicon Valley Dream Team." Now-defunct technology news site Red Herring said Mayer was one of "15 Women to Watch."

Mayer's ease with media and the media's attraction to her impressed Stricker—but not as much as Mayer's willingness to deal with it all. Lots of lower-profile Google executives wanted to be higher profile, but few were able to make time for it while still working hard at their day jobs. Mayer was a machine. Her routine for the *Today* show was especially nuts. If her appearance was on a Thursday morning in New York, Mayer would work a full day at Google's offices in California on Wednesday. Then she would take a red-eye flight that night. She would go straight to the *Today* show studios, do her interview, and head to Google's New York office for a full day's work. Then she would fly home. After airliners got Wi-Fi, she would work the whole flight home. And Mayer didn't do any of this in a drag-ass fashion. She was her typical, high-velocity self.

Mayer never asked Stricker to build a PR team to handle all the inbound requests and seek more coverage. But thanks to all the coverage, Stricker was doing well, and, over time, he was given authority to build his own team. He started poaching talent from other teams. One of his team's missions was to elevate the profiles of a number of executives, such as Sundar Pichai, the likable leader of Google's Chrome division. But none got the uptake that Mayer got. So the team spent a lot of time doing what worked: making Marissa Mayer into a world-famous technology executive.

That's how the rumors of her having her own press team started.

They spread, because inside Google, Mayer had a growing number of resentful, jealous, and powerful enemies.

Marissa Mayer's working style at Google earned her fame, power, riches—and, from the very start, enemies.

Mayer's way of flinging herself at whatever problems Google needed solving, even if someone was already working on a solution, especially irritated an early Google employee named Douglas Edwards.

Edwards was hired into Google from the *San Jose Mercury News* as a marketer. Edwards had it rough from the start, as Google's cofounders, Sergey Brin and Larry Page, believed that any investment in marketing tiptoed dangerously close to violating the company's famous rule: "Don't be evil." Eventually, Edwards found a niche at Google. He was put in charge of the written copy that went onto the site, especially the home page. Google's lucrative search advertising product, AdWords, is named after him—because he named it.

Edwards quit Google not long after its 2004 IPO for two reasons. One: He made a ton of money and didn't have to work anymore. Two: He was tired of fighting with Marissa Mayer over the home page. Edwards thought it was his realm, but over and over Edwards would find that Mayer had changed its text without consulting him, because she had an idea, talked to Larry Page about it, and decided to go ahead. One morning in 2001, Edwards woke up to see that Mayer had started using the Google.com home page to publish the progress of a Google employee's bike ride from California to Florida. Edwards flipped out. Mayer won out.

Years later, Edwards went for a long walk around Google's headquarters with Mayer to try and talk through all their differences.

He told her, "Look. You know, Marissa, I really appreciate how much you're getting done and all of the contributions you're making here, and I think you're doing great. I just want us to be more aligned in terms of communication."

Mayer seemed to agree. But then in the days ahead, she went back to acting unilaterally.

Many of Mayer's enemies were the people she worked with most closely: designers. Several of them hated her rules-driven, data-dependent approach.

Famously, a lead designer named Doug Bowman quit Google over it.

In a farewell blog post, Bowman wrote: "A team at Google couldn't decide between two blues, so they're testing 41 shades between each blue to see which one performs better. I had a recent debate over whether a border should be 3, 4, or 5 pixels wide, and was asked to prove my case. I can't operate in an environment like that. I've grown tired of debating such minuscule design decisions. There are more exciting design problems in this world to tackle."

Bowman went to Twitter.

Some people who worked for Mayer in design disliked her style for almost the opposite reason. They believed that she actually made her design decisions with her gut and would arbitrarily make up rules or tailor data retroactively to suit her choices.

Mayer's power over what lived and what died at Google also cost her friends.

For many years, the only way new products got any attention from users was if they were featured on Google's search results pages in a piece of on-screen real estate called the "One Box." Mayer made lots of enemies throughout Google because she would tell product teams: Sorry, you're not getting a link from Google's search results pages until you change your product the way I would like.

Once, there was a team of three or four engineers who got excited about a product idea called Google Music. A user could search for an artist, and at the top of the search results, they would see some song titles from that artist, linked to online stores where they could buy the tracks. The engineers built the product during their personal time. They got some positive signals from people in Google's product division.

When it was done, they took it to Mayer for review.

All they got from her was: "Why is this good? Why is this better than the search results below it?"

The product died.

One peer Mayer's style irked in particular was Salar Kamangar. Kamangar joined Google as its ninth employee. He drafted its original business plan and handled financing and legal early on. Younger than Mayer, he rose along with her at Google, though not as conspicuously.

Mayer and Kamangar clashed often.

The specific habit of Mayer's that drove Kamangar nuts was her ability to speak incredibly fast, not allowing him to reenter the debate.

The rivalry between Mayer and Kamangar was so intense

that when Kamangar was made a vice president before her, she threatened to quit the company. She got her promotion months later.

That kind of naked ambition was also hard for some people to take. Many early Google employees believed Mayer was too quick to take credit for successful products that were either first imagined by or built on the back end by others.

Starting in 2001, Mayer and a deeply respected Google search scientist named Krishna Bharat teamed up to build Google News. Bharat was one of the engineers who had followed Jeff Dean from DEC to Google. Bharat was renowned for his work in information processing and information retrieval—the real, gritty technical stuff that makes a search engine work.

Bharat had an interest in news—and in doing semantic analysis of documents. Those interests led him to develop the underpinnings of the technology that would eventually become central to Google News. With Mayer, he worked to turn that technology into a product for normal users. To the equation, she brought a sense of how users would actually interact with Google News.

It was a healthy relationship for a long time. Then Google News began to get very popular. It was one of Google's first noncore search products to achieve escape velocity. Rightly, both Bharat and Mayer felt pride of parenthood. The difference was that Bharat, like many engineers, was the quiet, cerebral type. Mayer was more of a self-promoter with outward-facing responsibilities. In the press, at conferences, even in lectures at Stanford, she would casually discuss Google News as a product she had led to launch. Over time, it began to sound to Bharat that Mayer was claiming the idea as her own and taking all the public credit for the success of Google News. Their relationship soured.

Another Mayer habit that annoyed colleagues was one she picked up straight from academia. For many years at Google, Mayer insisted that if her colleagues wanted to meet with her, they had to do so during her "office hours." Mayer would post a spreadsheet online and ask people to sign up for a five-minute window.

When Mayer's "office hours" rolled around in the afternoon, a line would start to form outside her office and spill over onto the nearby couches.

Office hours are socially acceptable in an academic environment because the power dynamic is clear. The students are subordinate to the professor, who is usually their elder and mentor.

But Mayer's office hours were not just for her subordinates; they were also for her peers.

So there, amid the associate product managers waiting to visit with Mayer to discuss their latest assignment or a class trip to Zurich, sat Google vice presidents—people who had been at the company as long as Mayer and in some cases held jobs as important as hers.

There was nothing especially abhorrent or uncommon about Mayer's behavior as an executive. She was headstrong, confident, dismissive, self-promoting, and clueless about how she sometimes hurt other people's feelings. So were many of the most successful executives in the technology industry. Steve Jobs was famous for his petulant tirades. Larry Page never bothered with pleasantries or human emotions. There's a whole movie based on the alleged betrayals of Mark Zuckerberg. Bill Gates is infamous for his heartless product reviews, where he would shout: "This sucks!"

It's also fair to say that some of the resentment toward Mayer had a sexist tinge to it. Though the people who did not like Mayer were as often female as male, women are, unfortunately, just as likely to dislike a powerful woman because she is a woman as a man is. Facebook COO Sheryl Sandberg wrote a book about it. The fact is: Google was a mostly male environment, and by standing out in her Oscar de la Renta, Mayer made herself a target.

Mayer had a style that some people didn't like and, unfairly or not, it made her enemies. As long as those enemies were disgruntled designers, product managers, or—and especially—people from marketing like Douglas Edwards, Mayer was always going to be fine. She had worked hard to belong at Google, and none of those people were going to knock her out of the "secret cabal" at the top.

The problems came when she made a different kind of enemy.

In May 2006, Marissa Mayer shared a view with many others at Google: Its flagship product remained deeply flawed.

That month, Mayer gave a guest lecture at Stanford. During a Q&A session at the end, someone asked her how search would look in the future. In her usual rapid-fire style, Mayer said, "I've been at Google for seven years. I've been responsible for the look and feel of the site for most of it. My friends and family are starting to give me a hard time.

"They say, 'So you're responsible for Google's look and feel?'

"I say yeah.

"They say, 'But it looks the same.'" A beat. "'What do you do all day?'"

Mayer laughed her "nnn" laugh. Then she said her friends were probably right.

Mayer told the Stanford class that Google needed to move beyond serving up ten links for every search query users put to it. If a user asked, "How do you cut up a chicken?" Google should show that user a video. If a user typed, "What does Britney Spears look like?" Google should show a photo.

What Mayer was saying was that Google needed to create a hybrid search engine—one that could display photos, video, and maps alongside text.

Inside Google, Mayer had been saying that since 2001.

Back then, Google CEO Eric Schmidt had asked Mayer and a few other Googlers for big new ideas for search.

Mayer made a few mock-ups. One was a design she called Universal Search.

It was a fake search results page for the query "Britney Spears." Instead of just ten blue links, it featured news, images, groups, and links.

Schmidt—and, more important, Larry Page—loved the mock-up.

For the next several years, Page pushed for Google to rebuild its search engine around Universal Search.

Finally, in 2006, Google hired a new leader for its search quality team. This was Udi Manber, the former Yahoo search leader. The Universal Search project started to gain real momentum. By 2006, Google engineers had developed an engine that could index the entire web, not just text but also video and images. The only remaining challenge was to figure out how to rank those results and show them.

This task would ultimately fall to two people and dozens of their proxies: an engineer named Amit Singhal and Google's vice president for search products and user experience—Mayer. Supervising the project would be Bill Coughran, Google's senior vice president for engineering.

Chubby-cheeked, with oval glasses, Amit Singhal was the best engineer on Manber's team—and one of the most talented search engineers in all of Google. Singhal grew up in India. In the late '70s, his family got a TV. It had two channels. One showed lots of programming for farmers. The other showed black-and-white reruns of *Star Trek* episodes. Singhal watched *Star Trek* over and over. He became obsessed with the computer on board the *Enterprise*—how it could provide Captain Kirk with whatever answers he needed as he flew around the galaxy. Singhal studied search when he was a graduate student at Cornell and then as a research fellow at AT&T Labs. In 2000, Krishna Bharat convinced Singhal to join Google.

His hire almost immediately paid off. Soon after joining, Singhal decided the code Google used for figuring out how to rank its search results needed a major overhaul. It had been written by Sergey Brin, and it was very sloppy. Singhal rewrote the whole thing in two months, adding huge improvements to relevancy and speed. In 2006, Singhal was named a Google Fellow, an award with a prize in the millions of dollars. He earned a nickname around campus: King of the Ranking.

All of Singhal's success boosted an already healthy self-esteem. By the time Singhal began working with Manber and Mayer on hybrid search results in 2006, he felt that Google search was his baby—and that everyone at Google knew it and respected him for it.

Coughran was aware that the collaboration between Singhal and Mayer would be a battle of egos. But that was typical for Google, and he was certain he could keep them from strangling each other.

He was right. For a time.

On May 14, 2007, Mayer published a post on Google's official blog announcing Universal Search. From then on, Google search results would blend results from Google Images, Google Maps, Google Books, Google Video, and Google News.

Mayer wrote: "While today's releases are big steps in making the world's information more easily accessible, these are just the beginning steps toward the universal search vision. Stay tuned!"

Google held to Mayer's promise.

For the next three years, Google rolled out massive changes to Google search, unlike any it had come up with over the preceding decade.

In December 2009, Mayer, Singhal, and another executive, named Vic Gundotra, hosted a press event to announce Realtime Search—an expansion of Universal Search to include social media updates from Twitter and other networks.

Then, less than a year after that, on September 8, 2010, Mayer and a search engineer named Ben Gomes held another event, this time to announce Instant search. It was a radical design change. Now, search results would actually begin to show up as the user typed their query.

It was the last thing Marissa Mayer ever had to do with Google search.

Almost from the start of the Universal Search project, Singhal and Mayer didn't get along.

The surface issue that the two disagreed over most was: Should Google allow only algorithms to determine the ranking of its search results, as Singhal argued? Or should Google sometimes use human editors to curate its results, as Mayer argued?

To make her case, Mayer's favorite example was a search query for "suicidal thoughts." Using purely algorithmic ranking, Google did not bring up the National Suicide Prevention Lifeline. Mayer felt the number should obviously be included, and near the top of the page. Why shouldn't Google just include it? Shouldn't Google serve up the best results, even if they had to be included manually?

The very idea of it infuriated Singhal. Surely Mayer realized her editorial results would never scale the way his algorithmic results could.

The debate played out vocally in product-review and launch-calendar meetings in gray conference rooms in building 43 on

Google's campus. For years, Mayer had dominated those meetings, but in Singhal, she encountered someone who had an ego to match hers. Like Mayer, Singhal felt supported by Google's higher-ups, and he would not back down.

Singhal and Mayer would sometimes argue through proxies. The product managers on Mayer's staff would spout her talking points, and then the engineers on Singhal's would respond with his. For many on both staffs, it felt like a war between sects of the Google faithful—the algorithmic orthodox versus the editorially reformed.

Even more than Mayer's arguments for including editorial results, Singhal loathed how, when his team was ready to roll out a change, Mayer would insist it pass through her UI review—a process that could take weeks.

Ultimately, the contest between Singhal and Mayer was not over any one issue. It was about authority.

Singhal—and Manber, too—believed that the engineers who created the hard-core technology powering Google search could more than handle user interface design. How hard could it be to draw mock-ups? Not as hard as developing an algorithm. Ultimately, Singhal and Manber wanted engineering to own the Google product. They felt the product would improve faster if they didn't have Mayer bottlenecking the whole process.

Mayer, meanwhile, felt that she was the one coming up with brilliant products—like the idea for Universal Search way back in 2001. Why shouldn't she have direct control over Google's engineering resources to implement what she wanted to do?

In his many years running large technology organizations, Coughran had seen this kind of battle for power over and over. There was a natural tension between product management and engineering. At Google, this tension was intentionally fostered. Larry Page had always preferred to run the company by setting up heated debates between his direct reports so he could hear both sides of an issue and then pick his way forward.

And for a few years, Coughran and Google's two cofounders managed the battle between Singhal and Mayer in the same way. Maybe they would pick a single leader for the product someday, but not yet.

Then, in 2010, Larry Page decided that Google was moving too slowly. He wanted the whole company to move as fast as its Android and Chrome divisions.

One impetus for this decision was a memo from a longtime Googler named Urs Hölzle. It reminded everyone that social networks, and Facebook in particular, had become a dominant force on the Internet. It said that Google was nearly blind to all the knowledge stored on Facebook. Hölzle pleaded with his colleagues to focus on social media, or else the company could be swept away in an oncoming wave.

Page took the memo to heart, and put Vic Gundotra in charge of developing a social network for Google. The project was code-named Emerald Sea, after a Japanese painting in which a boat is about to be wiped out by a huge wave. Gundotra's team built a prototype in a hundred days.

The speed impressed Page. He realized that one thing Android, Chrome, and the Emerald Sea project had in common was that each had a single person in charge. He wondered if it was time to put one person in charge of search.

Page consulted with Coughran. Coughran said he could no longer peacefully referee what was becoming an increasingly hostile relationship between Singhal and Mayer. Coughran said that a couple times a week, one or the other would be in his office, complaining and asking to lead the organization.

"We're going to have to pick somebody here," he told Page.

Gundotra, suddenly vested with influence thanks to the Emerald

Sea project, made it known that he did not like working with Mayer. With all her reviews and processes, she slowed things down too much.

Page thought about the future of Google and its past. To him, the strength of the company was that it developed machines that could learn what humans wanted and then provide it to them. He believed that Singhal better understood how to make the technology that powered those machines. Page believed that made Singhal more capable of pushing Google products to their technological limits.

Page didn't make Coughran break the news. He summoned Mayer into a one-on-one meeting and told her she was done working on Google search.

In October 2010, it was made official. Mayer was removed from the top of Google's search organization and put in charge of Google Maps and other "local" products.

Technically, this was a lateral move, if not a promotion, because Mayer retained her vice-president title and she was, at the same time, given a seat on Google's operating committee—then-CEO Eric Schmidt's round table of top executives from the company.

In reality, it was a demotion. Mayer was no longer in charge of what Google's most important product looked like or how it worked. At Google, there was search, which generates nearly all of the company's revenues and profits, and then there was everything else. Running Google search, Mayer was managing the most important product at the world's most important Internet company. Running Google Maps, she was not.

Still, there was the mitigating factor that Mayer was on the operating committee, and she therefore reported directly to CEO Eric Schmidt.

That went away, too.

In December 2010, Page announced that, a decade after giving the CEO job up to Eric Schmidt, he was going to take it back.

When Page formally took control of Google in April 2011, he dissolved the operating committee and created a new council of executives who would report directly to him. This group came to be known as the L-Team. Mayer was not named to it.

To make matters worse for Mayer, Page put another Google executive, Jeff Huber, in charge of Local and Geo, the group Mayer had been tasked to run only months before. Mayer now reported to Huber, who joined Google in 2003—four years after her.

For Mayer, losing her seat on the operating committee was the hardest blow of all. Harder even than losing search. She had been kicked out of the secret cabal that ran Google. Eleven years after that night in July 1999 when all Mayer wanted was to belong on a team full of such amazing talent, Mayer felt ousted. She went into a funk.

Over the next year, she tried to get out of it by focusing on her work. But Mayer was an ambitious person, and she knew that there was no path forward for her at Google. Not anymore.

Then, one day in September 2011, Mayer got an idea.

It came from Gabriel Stricker, the soft-spoken PR hand from the world of politics who had so successfully developed her national profile.

She was sitting with Stricker at Google's headquarters in Mountain View. They were wrapping up a meeting.

Stricker looked at Mayer. He asked her if she'd heard the news about Yahoo. Carol Bartz had been fired.

Mayer said she had.

Stricker said, quietly, "You should pursue that job."

He said: You're exactly the kind of technologist that company has always needed.

Mayer said, "I would do it. But the board situation is so messy. I wouldn't be set up for success."

Mayer had heard all about Roy Bostock, Yahoo's obstinate chairman, and there was no way she would ever go to Yahoo if it meant working for him.

Little did Mayer know that at that very moment, three thousand miles away, Dan Loeb, a force of nature in a suit, was preparing for an all-out brawl—one that, if he won, would remove Bostock from Yahoo and clear the way for the arrival of Marissa Mayer, CEO.

PART

III

7

Win Win Win

Eric Jackson got off a plane in Hong Kong. It was December 2010, three and a half years since his Internet campaign to get Terry Semel fired ended in success.

The years had been good to Jackson. In the aftermath of Semel's resignation, Jackson had become a minor business media celebrity. Bloomberg sent a satellite truck to his condo in Florida, upsetting a bunch of neighbors. That same year, Jackson tried to repeat his success with an activist campaign against Motorola management. The media paid attention. Motorola management did not. Jackson dropped the effort after three months.

A friend who used to work at a large New York hedge fund encouraged Jackson to start one. So Jackson did. He raised about $5 million and launched in February 2008. The fund, called Ironfire, held Yahoo stock through the spring of 2008. But then, when it was clear Jerry Yang and Roy Bostock were going to fumble away Microsoft's offer, Jackson sold the position. Jackson thought he might be done with Yahoo forever.

Now, as he lugged his bags through Hong Kong International

Airport, he wasn't so sure. The reason: While in Hong Kong, Jackson was planning to meet with Joe Tsai.

Joe Tsai was the chief financial officer and vice chairman of Alibaba, the Chinese Internet startup Yahoo invested $1 billion in back in 2005.

Tsai joined Alibaba in 1999. He was working at a Swedish investment bank when a friend of his said he should go to the Chinese city of Hangzhou and meet a crazy entrepreneur named Jack Ma.

In May 1999, Tsai got on a plane and visited Ma in his apartment. What he found wasn't much to look at. Ma didn't have a company incorporated or anything: just a website, in English, that was supposed to connect Western companies with Chinese factories. Ma was running the whole thing from a PC hooked to a 56K modem. He was using an old-fashioned bookkeeper's ledger to keep track of orders. This was manageable because the site had just 28,000 registered users.

Tsai wasn't very impressed with the operation. Ma, however, he liked. Tsai liked his long-term thinking, his passion for helping small Chinese businesses connect to the West, and his egoless leadership skills. The sixteen people working for Ma's company at that point were all former students who had taken Ma's English class. Ma called them all cofounders.

Ma told Tsai he was looking for someone who could help him turn the website into a business and get financing. But, Ma said, he didn't want to hire someone from Taiwan, Hong Kong, or Shanghai. He didn't like the big-shot attitude of people from those places. Tsai thought: I'm finished. He'd grown up in Taiwan, lived in Hong Kong, and his parents were originally from Shanghai. Ma got over all that, and by July, Tsai was cofounder number eighteen.

Tsai's first job was to set up a corporate entity. He needed a lawyer. A friend recommended Fenwick & West, the famous Silicon Valley firm. So Tsai called up one of its partners, Joel Kellman.

Tsai told him, "This is a B2B e-commerce company. The founder is based in Hangzhou."

Kellman said, "Where?"

At the end of the call, Kellman said, "Joe, thanks very much for telling me all this. I'm sure we can help you. I'm interested. But to be honest, I have no clue who you are. So why don't you send me a check for $20,000 as a retainer and we'll talk."

So that's what Tsai did. He took out his personal checkbook and wrote a $20,000 check out to Joel Kellman at Fenwick & West. He put it in the mail. After that, Kellman and Tsai became good friends. When Ma and Tsai came to the Valley that summer, Kellman had lots of meetings set up with venture capitalists—although none with big-name firms like Sequoia or Kleiner Perkins. They weren't interested in Ma or Alibaba.

Most of the meetings were held at a Palo Alto sandwich shop. Kellman said it was the place to meet VCs. Tsai thought it was a dive. There were lots of offers, but Tsai didn't like them because the venture capitalists wanted all sorts of special rights as investors. They wanted something called "participating preferred stock." Basically, it meant that if Alibaba were ever sold, the VCs would get a greater than proportionate return.

The VCs would tell Tsai this was how these deals are always done. They weren't lying. But Tsai would do the math and say: I don't care. From the start, Alibaba was aggressive about doing financing in a way that benefited management, even if that meant ignoring business tradition.

Tsai told Ma that they should look for funding from different kinds of investors. They cast a wider net. Nothing came together, and Ma and Tsai went back to Asia.

Then, in August 1999, Tsai was walking through the lobby of

an office just off Exchange Square in Hong Kong when he saw an old friend of his from the world of investment banking—Shirley Lin from Goldman Sachs. Tsai hadn't pitched Alibaba to Goldman because it usually did large private equity deals. But Lin said she had recently been in Silicon Valley looking for small startups to invest in.

Goldman led the first outside investment in Alibaba, putting in $5 million in October 1999. The valuation was smaller than what the VCs had been offering, but there was none of that "participating preferred" junk.

Tsai thought he was done fund-raising for a while. He was wrong.

Shortly after closing the Goldman deal in October, he got a call from Hangzhou. It was Ma. He said, "Joe, we've got to go to Tokyo."

Ma and Tsai had been summoned to the offices of Masayoshi "Masa" Son, the billionaire CEO of Japanese telecom conglomerate Softbank. Masa was a Goldman Sachs client. When Goldman told Masa about its latest investment in Asia, Masa said he wanted to meet Ma and Tsai and perhaps invest in Alibaba, too. Masayoshi Son prided himself on meeting two hundred entrepreneurs every three months.

Tsai, on the phone, told Ma, "We just raised this money. We don't need any more money."

Ma said, "No. When Masa asks you to go to Tokyo, you have to go."

"Okay," said Tsai. "Fine."

They met in Tokyo in November 1999.

When they got to Masa's office, one of the Goldman guys pulled Tsai aside to prep him for meeting Masa. To prep him and to warn him.

He said, "This guy is larger than life. When most people meet him, they crumble. Don't give up. Don't compromise on anything."

Tsai said okay, sure. He wasn't nervous. He didn't really know who Masayoshi Son was, or about his reputation.

Ma and Tsai went into Masa's office. It was huge. Very Japanese, Tsai thought. There was a long table. Masa sat on one side, with five executives in suits on his left and five more on his right. Ma and Tsai sat down facing them all.

Ma described his vision for Alibaba. When he was done, Masa pulled out a giant old accountant's calculator. He punched some numbers in and then said, "I want to invest $30 million for 40 percent of the company."

Meekly, Ma said, "Well, Masa, that's too much."

"Okay," said Masa. He made a slightly reduced offer. Still too high.

Tsai saw that Ma was squirming in his seat. He remembered what the Goldman guy had said: Don't cave!

Tsai jumped in. He said, "Masa, I don't even need to take this offer back to our board. We're just going to veto it right here, just me and Jack."

Masa froze for a few seconds. The suits on either side of him were stunned. People didn't usually talk to Masayoshi Son like that.

Masa said, "Oh. Okay."

He went back to his giant calculator.

"How about $20 million for one-third of the company?"

They had a deal. All the particulars were settled by December, and the money was in the bank by February 2000.

A few weeks later, the Nasdaq crashed and the Internet bubble burst. At one point, Tsai had been unsure if Alibaba really needed Masayoshi Son's money. Now he felt lucky to have it. There was no way a startup like Alibaba would be able to raise that kind of money after the markets crashed. Tsai thought: Good thing I bumped into Shirley.

Over the next three years, Ma used Masa's millions to pursue his vision for a business-to-business portal between the West and China.

Then, in 2002, eBay bought a Chinese Internet company called EachNet. Like eBay in the United States, EachNet was a site consumers could use to sell to other consumers. The acquisition made Ma paranoid. He decided Alibaba needed to get into eBay's consumer-to-consumer business. Tsai thought Ma was nuts. Alibaba didn't know anything about eBay's business model. The idea was put on hold.

Then, at the end of a business trip to Tokyo, Ma was on his way back to the airport to fly home when he got a call from Masayoshi Son.

"Jack, where are you?" said Masa.

"Well, I'm actually— I'm in Tokyo. Sorry I didn't come and see you. I was just in and out and I'm on my way to the airport now."

"Cancel your flight. I need to talk to you."

Ma told his driver to turn around.

Back in Masa's giant office, the Softbank CEO said he had an idea for Alibaba. It needed to launch a consumer-to-consumer e-commerce business—an eBay for China. Masa said his joint venture with Yahoo, Yahoo Japan, was in that business and it was suddenly generating 60 percent of the company's operating profits.

Ma said, "Guess what? That's exactly what I was thinking!"

They got all excited.

When Ma told Tsai about it later, Tsai was still worried that Alibaba didn't know enough about the consumer-to-consumer business and that if Alibaba failed in the new venture it would sink an otherwise very healthy business. He suggested that Alibaba and Softbank launch a joint venture. Softbank could put in all the capital and Alibaba would operate it. That way, if the new company flopped, it wouldn't affect Alibaba's financials. Ma and Masa agreed to Tsai's plan.

In 2003, the consumer-to-consumer site was launched. It was called Taobao. It did well enough that by late 2004, eBay flew three executives to Hangzhou to meet with Ma and Tsai, wave a white flag, hand over some cash, and sign a partnership.

eBay sent Bill Cobb, who was running eBay's auction business in North America, Rajiv Dutta, eBay's CFO, and Bill Barmeier, the dealmaker at the head of eBay's corporate development team.

In a conference room at Alibaba's headquarters, Cobb began the meeting by ticking off a list of metrics. He said, "Look, we're the largest player in China. Taobao is the little guy here. In terms of users, we're seven times your size. In terms of transaction volume, we're ten times your size."

On he went, listing four or five more stats. Then, done describing how tiny and irrelevant Taobao was, Cobb said eBay would like to buy it.

He turned to Barmeier to describe the offer. But Barmeier's computer had crashed on the flight over, and he didn't have any of his numbers. He threw out a figure that sounded right: $150 million.

Ma and Tsai retreated to a conference room next door to discuss. They considered $150 million a lowball offer. They supposed they were obligated to throw a number back.

Back in the room, Ma addressed some of the metrics Cobb had shared. He said that while it was true that eBay had 80 percent of the consumer-to-consumer market share, there were still only eighty million people using the Internet in China, and only 10 percent of those were shopping online. That meant there were seventy-two million people who hadn't started shopping on Taobao or EachNet yet. Behind them were another 1.3 billion who hadn't even started using the Internet. He said: Your market share today is totally irrelevant.

Then Tsai said Taobao's price: $900 million.

eBay's money man, Rajiv Dutta, immediately stood up. He said, "Thank you very much. We appreciate you spending time with us. You're very gracious. Let's go to dinner. We don't think we need to have this conversation anymore."

A few months later, eBay tried to restart the conversation. This time, it was willing to merely invest in Taobao. But by then, Tsai and Ma were quickly closing in on a deal with another American Internet company: Yahoo.

The first time Jack Ma met Jerry Yang, it was years before Alibaba existed, and Ma was a tour guide at the Great Wall of China. The next time they met, it was March 2005 at another wonder of the world: Pebble Beach, the golf course in Northern California.

Masayoshi Son, a mentor to both, put the meeting together. He felt the two could help each other.

Ma needed capital. Yang needed to invest capital.

Ma needed capital because Taobao was taking off, and it was quickly becoming clear that setting it up as a joint venture had been a bad idea. His management team was putting all this effort into building Taobao—and it was working—but half of all the value they were creating was accruing to someone else. He desperately wanted Softbank to sell its stake in Taobao to Alibaba. The problem was, Masa wasn't going to sell his stake cheap.

Meanwhile, Yang was looking to invest some of Yahoo's cash into a Chinese Internet startup. Yahoo had already tried breaking into the Chinese market twice and had failed both times. First, it bought some local startups and ran them as wholly owned subsidiaries. But the local management team proved not to be very loyal once their upside was capped. Then Yahoo launched Yahoo China. It wasn't getting much traction. By the time Ma and Yang were hitting golf balls together next to the Pacific Ocean, Yang and the rest

Jerry Yang and David Filo didn't start Yahoo to get rich or to run a company. *"Jerry & David, 1995," by Yahoo, available on Flickr.*

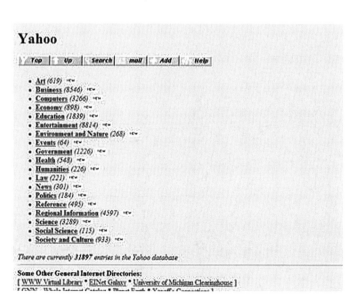

Back in 1995, the Yahoo home page linked only to 31,897 websites. That was pretty much the entire Internet. *"Our homepage in 1995," by Yahoo, available on Flickr.*

Terry Semel brought Yahoo back from the dot-com bust, but he whiffed on deals to buy Facebook and YouTube. *"Terry Semel @ Web 2.0," by Kris Krüg, available on Flickr.*

Sue Decker was Yahoo's CFO and then its president. Microsoft's offer, and the saga that followed, basically knocked her out of the company. *"El Presidente," by Yahoo, available on Flickr.*

Sue Decker, Carol Bartz, and Jerry Yang. After Bartz arrived, Decker quit. Bartz mistrusted cofounders like Yang. *"Sue Decker, Carol Bartz and Jerry Yang stand before Yahoos," by Yahoo, available on Flickr.*

Carol Bartz and Microsoft CEO Steve Ballmer. Bartz got a lot of credit for signing a search deal with Microsoft. Years later, it's viewed as a mistake. *"Steve Ballmer signs the Microsoft-Yahoo! agreement," by Yahoo, available on Flickr.*

Eric Jackson led an Internet campaign against Terry Semel and later brought the world's attention to the value of Yahoo's stake in Alibaba. *Eric Jackson*

When Marissa Mayer joined Yahoo in July 2012, employees hung posters on the wall that read "HOPE." They mimicked the style of Shephard Fairey's famous Barack Obama posters. *Hunter Walk.*

Scott Thompson's tenure at Yahoo didn't last long, thanks to a bruising battle with Dan Loeb. *"CEO Scott Thompson greets Yahoos at Sunnyvale HQ," by Yahoo, available on Flickr.*

Dan Loeb took on Yahoo CEO Scott Thompson and Yahoo chairman Roy Bostock—and won. *Third Point LLC*

Marissa Mayer and her husband, Zachary Bogue. Bogue and Mayer had a baby just months after Mayer became CEO of Yahoo in 2012. *"Marissa Mayer, VP at Google, and her husband," by Robert Scoble, available on Flickr.*

TechCrunch writer Greg Kumparak, Yahoo mobile boss Adam Cahan, and Marissa Mayer at the Crunchies in 2014. Mayer put Cahan in charge of building a team of mobile developers at Yahoo. *"The 7th Annual Crunchies Awards on February 10, 2014 in San Francisco," by Steve Jennings for TechCrunch, available on Flickr.*

For more than a decade, Yahoo has held its all-hands meetings in its cafeteria, called URLs. *"Yahoos welcome CEO Scott Thompson at his first All Hands event," by Yahoo, available on Flickr.*

Yahoo chairman Roy Bostock took a "combative" stance toward Microsoft when it offered to buy Yahoo at a huge premium in 2008. *"Chairman Roy Bostock welcomes Scott Thompson," by Yahoo, available on Flickr.*

Yahoo's Sunnyvale, California, headquarters. *"Y! Campus," by Yahoo, available on Flickr.*

Tumblr CEO David Karp and Yahoo CMO Kathy Savitt. Mayer hired Savitt to run Yahoo marketing, but she eventually took over Yahoo's media business, too. *"Yahoo/Tumblr White House Correspondents Dinner Brunch," by Yahoo, available on Flickr.*

Marissa Mayer and the Yahoo board hired Henrique De Castro without vetting him fully, and he left the company before his second year was over. *Photo by NRKbeta.no, available on NRKbeta.no.*

of Yahoo management believed the only way Yahoo was going to expose itself successfully to the growing Chinese Internet would be by taking a large minority stake in a fast-growing native company.

Per usual, Masa was right about the deal—it made perfect sense to both Yang and Ma for Yahoo to take a large minority position in Alibaba. Joe Tsai and Yahoo deals man Keith Nilsson hammered out the particulars over six weeks of negotiations between May and July 2005. The last couple nights of negotiations took place on the eleventh floor of an office building in Palo Alto. Every night, it was sushi from Tamarine for dinner.

In August, the companies announced the deal: Yahoo gave Alibaba $1 billion in cash, a license to use Yahoo technology, and Yahoo China in exchange for a 44 percent stake in Alibaba. Alibaba used some of the money to buy out early Alibaba investors. Then Alibaba used $360 million and some of that reacquired Alibaba stock to buy out Softbank's stake in Taobao.

No one was happier with the deal that Masayoshi Son, sitting at his huge desk with his giant accountant's calculator.

First off, there was the cash he was getting from Alibaba. His original investment in Taobao had been $80 million, so he was getting a 400 percent return after two years. Not bad. Next there was the fact that the deal made Alibaba a much stronger company, because it now fully owned Taobao. This pleased Masa because Softbank remained a one-third owner of Alibaba. Likewise, a strengthened Alibaba also benefited Yahoo—another major position in the Softbank portfolio. It was a win-win-win for Masayoshi Son.

For the next three and a half years, Joe Tsai marveled at the healthy relationship between Softbank, Alibaba, and Yahoo. It helped that Taobao was doing so well that keeping tabs on its progress was almost boring.

During one board meeting, Tsai was in the middle of going

over yet another excellent quarter when Ma got up from his chair and began to practice Tai Chi. A few minutes later, with Tsai still going on and on, Yang stood up, grabbed a golf club, and started practicing his swing. Finally, Masa got up and walked over to a collection of samurai swords in a rack and picked one out. He started swishing it around.

That boring, wonderful peace lasted a relatively long time—from 2005 to 2008.

Then came 2009, and with it, a new Yahoo CEO: Carol Bartz.

In March 2009, Ma, Tsai, and nine or so top Alibaba executives traveled to Sunnyvale. Jerry Yang greeted them at Yahoo headquarters. Yang was no longer Yahoo CEO, but he was still Yahoo's representative on Alibaba's board. He walked with the Alibaba executives through the halls of Yahoo, taking them to Phish Food in building D.

Then a weird thing happened: Yang introduced Bartz. Ma and Tsai expected Yang to sit down and join the meeting. He didn't. He awkwardly ducked out—as though he couldn't get out of there fast enough. Tsai soon realized why.

Everyone sat down and the Alibaba executives presented the state of the company to Bartz. Taobao was booming. It had destroyed eBay's efforts in China and was now the most dominant e-commerce site in China. Ma and his team were certain Bartz would praise their efforts and thank them for turning Yahoo's $1 billion into a huge multiple of that.

But that's not what Bartz did.

She shamed Ma and his team for their failure to do anything with Yahoo China.

She said, "I want you to take my name off of that site because it's embarrassing. It's terrible."

It was true that Yahoo China wasn't doing great. But when Alibaba took it over, it was already the sixth-ranked portal in China—a doomed loser. The Alibaba executives couldn't believe Bartz wasn't able to appreciate the bigger picture. They also couldn't believe Bartz knew so little about the customs of Chinese business that she so harshly criticized Ma in front of his team of executives—one of whom was his wife. Chinese business culture dictated that the appropriate way for Bartz to rebuke Ma would have been to ask him to remain in the room after the wider meeting. This would have allowed her to get her message across and him to save face.

Ma went into a sputter. He said, "Well, why don't you let us— If you want, we can take you through our strategic plans to try to improve the site." He went through the plans, and the meeting ended cordially.

But inside, Ma was seething.

His resentment contributed to another growing desire, one that Tsai shared: Just as they had wanted to buy out Softbank's stake in Taobao, so that the value Taobao was creating would accrue more directly to Alibaba, they now wanted to buy out a portion of Yahoo's stake in Alibaba.

In late 2009, Tsai approached Bartz about a friendly transaction—one where Alibaba management would be able to own a greater piece of the company and Yahoo would be able to bag a huge return on its $1 billion investment. He figured she would go for it, considering the weakened state of Yahoo's core business. Yahoo could use the money to buy companies or even just give it to shareholders. But Bartz wouldn't bite. She believed Tsai and Ma were trying to get Yahoo's Alibaba stake cheap.

Through 2010, Tsai and Yahoo CFO Tim Morse worked on a deal. The problem was, they could never come to an agreement on how much Alibaba was worth. Alibaba kept growing so fast. Every time a deal seemed at hand, new Alibaba sales figures would come in, or some similar company would have a great IPO, or Yahoo would hear about how well another Chinese Internet company was doing, and the price would go up and Tsai would balk.

By December 2010, Tsai was revving up for one more crack at negotiations with Morse. The people at Softbank had an idea for a deal that would help Yahoo avoid paying taxes on its big gains. Tsai wasn't very optimistic about the deal's prospects.

By then, Tsai was resigned to the fact that, with Alibaba only going up in value, Yahoo was under no pressure to sell.

If the deal was ever going to happen, someone was going to have to provide that pressure.

Tsai wondered who that could be.

Then he got an email from Eric Jackson, asking for a meeting.

Tsai, Jackson, and Jackson's Ironfire partner, Stephen Chang, talked for an hour or two at Alibaba's office in the Wan Chai district of Hong Kong.

Tsai told Jackson and Chang about the size and growth of Taobao and the behavior of Carol Bartz.

Tsai explained how, when Taobao launched, there were only 80 million Chinese people online, with just 8 million shopping. Now, he said, there were about 500 million Chinese Internet users, with 250 million of them shopping. He told Jackson how, more than any other Chinese e-commerce property, Taobao had successfully ridden that wave in two ways—by not charging its buyers or sellers fees and by creating a service called Alipay, which kept buyer payments in escrow until sellers shipped their goods.

He explained how Taobao made its money. Taobao was basically a giant search engine like Google, only all the searches were for things to buy. That made Taobao's search results pages very attractive real estate for advertising.

Tsai told Jackson how frustrated he and Ma were with Bartz. He said that Alibaba was almost ready to go public—creating a massive liquidity event for Yahoo and its shareholders—but that an IPO was going to be impossible so long as so much of Alibaba was foreign owned. He said that Alibaba wanted to buy back some of Yahoo's stake—giving Yahoo billions of dollars in cash, by the way—in order to fix the ownership mix and get on track for an IPO. He asked Jackson if Bartz was really acting in the best interest of shareholders, the way she was handling the situation.

Jackson agreed that Bartz was not looking out for common shareholders.

But that wasn't his main takeaway from the meeting.

His main takeaway was: Yahoo owns 44 percent of a huge Internet company, and nobody knows about it.

As he and Chang walked out of Tsai's office, Jackson turned to his partner and said: "Man. We've got to go buy some Yahoo stock right now."

Over the next month, Jackson dove into research. He found an especially good report on the Chinese e-commerce market from a firm called iResearch. He read local reporting on Taobao and dug into work by an analyst named Marianne Wolk.

He decided that Taobao alone was worth at least $50 billion, and maybe $100 billion.

A valuation of $75 billion meant Yahoo's 40 percent stake was worth $30 billion. Because Yahoo would have to pay a lot of taxes on any Alibaba shares it sold and because there was no way Yahoo would ever be able to sell such a huge stake in one transaction, Jackson discounted that $30 billion by another 40 percent to $18 billion.

Meanwhile, Yahoo also still owned a 35 percent stake in Yahoo Japan, its joint venture with Softbank. Yahoo Japan was a publicly traded company, so it was easy to calculate that Yahoo's stake was worth more than $8 billion.

Then there was Yahoo's stake in another public company, business-to-business portal Alibaba.com (not to be confused with Alibaba). That was worth $3 billion.

Then there was all the cash in Yahoo's bank account. Along with deferred revenue, that total came to $4.3 billion.

Jackson added up all the figures. When he was done, he was shocked.

He realized that Yahoo's assets, not including the core Yahoo .com business being run by Carol Bartz, were worth about $35 billion.

This number made Jackson giddy. Because in January 2011, Yahoo's market cap was only $24 billion. For whatever reason—probably ignorance—the market was overlooking the value of Taobao.

Jackson bought a bunch of Yahoo stock.

Then, on February 23, 2011, Jackson made his position public. He wrote an article on TheStreet.com doing a sum-of-the-parts valuation, concluding that Yahoo stock, which closed that day at $16.58 per share, should actually be worth $31.04 per share.

"Almost no one assumes it is possible for Yahoo to ever get its stock higher than the old Microsoft offer for the company in 2008," Jackson wrote. "But, on a sum-of-the-parts basis, I believe that is a very realistic goal between now and the end of 2012. And I like it that Bartz has a big incentive to make something happen. If she and Softbank decided to do a deal with Alibaba management, it could work out to be a beautiful win-win-win.

"In the meantime, I'm happy to patiently wait, owning an asset worth $1 that is trading for 55 cents."

For the next six months, Eric Jackson used every outlet he could to shout about how the market was undervaluing Yahoo.

But nobody would pay attention.

Jackson would write about Apple for his blog or TheStreet.com or *Forbes*, and CNBC producers would call him up and ask him to come on and talk about it. The same went for Facebook and Google. They never wanted him to talk about Yahoo.

Meanwhile, Yahoo stock went nowhere for most of the spring.

Then in May, disaster struck. Yahoo announced that Alibaba had spun out its payments service, Alipay. Yahoo said that Alipay was now owned by Alibaba management and not by Alibaba shareholders. Bizarrely, Yahoo said Alibaba had done this without Yahoo's knowledge way back in August 2010.

In its own statements, Alibaba said it was forced to spin Alipay out because the Chinese government forbade payment companies from being foreign owned.

The scandal raised all sorts of questions, like: Would Alibaba management steal Taobao, too? How bad had the relationship between Alibaba management and Yahoo gotten that this was surprise news for Yahoo?

Inside Yahoo, the belief was that Alibaba management had stolen Alipay in order to force Yahoo back to the negotiating table and allow Alibaba to buy some of its stake back.

Yahoo stock started tanking.

Jackson thought what Yahoo shareholders needed was an activist investor who could buy a bunch of stock and then demand that the Yahoo board do a deal with Alibaba.

In the summer of 2011, Jackson approached Pershing Square Capital Management, the hedge fund run by Bill Ackman. He met with an Ackman lieutenant named Paul Hilal.

Hilal said to Jackson, "Everyone comes in here every week pitching me on Yahoo. Come on. Tell me something I don't know."

Pershing Square passed.

The whole thing drove Jackson nuts. He kept looking at the numbers. They couldn't have been clearer. Even after the Alipay spinout, the sum of Yahoo's parts was worth far more than Yahoo's market cap.

And yet, Jackson felt like no one was paying attention to him and his hypothesis.

He couldn't have been more wrong.

8

Bully Pulpit

Dan Loeb sat in his Park Avenue office, ten blocks uptown from Grand Central Terminal. Loeb noticed Yahoo's stock was tanking. Again.

It was August 2011. Since April, Yahoo stock was down 37 percent—from $17.70 to $11.08 per share.

Loeb emailed one of his analysts, Tim Lash.

"What do we think of Yahoo?"

Lash did a quick sum-of-the-parts valuation, adding up the value of Yahoo's core business along with its Asian assets. He used Eric Jackson's valuation for Alibaba. And, like Jackson before him, Lash decided that the market was undervaluing Yahoo.

Lash emailed Loeb: It's $11. Seems like good risk to reward. I definitely see it getting to $14, $15.

Loeb agreed. He started buying Yahoo stock. Lots of it.

Loeb knew his next decision would be a lot more difficult.

Did he really want to get back into the business of sending letters of mass destruction?

His choice would have huge consequences for Yahoo and Marissa Mayer.

Dan Loeb was the suited, slick, and handsome Wall Street type. He wore his salt-and-pepper hair short and messy on purpose. He was actually from Southern California, and sometimes he put off a surfer vibe.

When Loeb was a kid, he would sometimes get himself in trouble with his smack talking. He would say things to, and about, the bullies at school.

The bullies didn't like it, and they decided to beat the little guy up.

Loeb saw the threat coming. He went to one of the biggest kids in his school and offered to pay him a quarter every day for protection. The big kid agreed.

Loeb told everyone about the arrangement. The bullies never came around again. Loeb learned a lesson he'd never forget: You could win a lot of fights with a little money and a big mouth.

Daniel Seth Loeb, born in 1961 and raised in Southern California, grew up in a household that talked about business. His father was a lawyer specializing in corporate governance. His aunt Ruth Handler created the Barbie doll and founded Mattel.

Loeb developed an early love for investing. As a teenager, he started trading options. He worked at Paine Webber during his junior year in high school. He bought and sold stocks in college and graduated Columbia with $120,000 in his bank account.

It was all so easy.

Then it wasn't.

After college, Loeb invested all of his money into one company: medical equipment maker Puritan Bennett. Then the AP reported that Puritan Bennett machines were linked to several deaths. Loeb lost all his money, going $7,000 in debt to his father.

Burned by trading, Loeb started down a traditional business

career path. He worked at investment bank Warburg Pincus, and then in corporate development for Island Records. In 1991, Loeb joined investment bank Jefferies & Co. as an analyst. In 1994, he started selling junk bonds for Citicorp.

It wasn't the career he wanted. He admired big corporate raiders like Nelson Peltz and Carl Icahn. He wanted a career like theirs.

In 1995, he went for it. With $340,000 of his own money and another $3 million from friends and family, he launched Third Point, a hedge fund. For the first two years, Third Point mostly traded distressed debt—the junk bond market Loeb knew from Citicorp. In 1997, Loeb deployed a new type of trade—risk arbitrage, where he would buy the stock of companies involved in M&A talks. Third Point remained relatively small.

Loeb tried a new tactic starting around 1999. He found public companies he believed were destined for failure and bet against them, selling their stock short. To speed the process along, Loeb would log on to investor forums on the Internet and trash the companies.

By 2000, Third Point's assets under management had grown to $136 million. That was a lot compared with where Loeb started, but still tiny relative to the billions Peltz and Icahn managed.

Then Loeb saw how much further you could take the having-a-loud-opinion approach.

In March 2000, a hedge fund manager named Robert Chapman bought 5 percent of a company called American Community Properties Trust. Because American Community Properties was a public company, the Securities and Exchange Commission required that Chapman publicly announce his 5 percent stake with a form called a Schedule 13D. Usually, 13Ds are treated as a formality. But instead of issuing a standard 13D, Chapman wrote a vicious letter to the CEO, ridiculing his management style and demanding change. It worked. Embarrassed, American Community Properties made changes and the company increased in value, delivering a win for Chapman.

Loeb tried the tactic for himself in 2000. He bought more than 5 percent of a company called Agribrands. Agribrands was in the process of selling to Ralcorp for $39 per share. Loeb wrote a 13D letter accusing Agribrands CEO Bill Stiritz of taking a cheap offer because it benefited him, not Agribrands shareholders. Rattled, Agribrands reopened its sale process and eventually found a new buyer willing to pay $54.50 per share. Loeb had been right in a very visible way and he made a lot of money for his fund: $20 million in a few months.

Loeb learned another lesson. The bullies he had known in school had grown up to become self-dealing, incompetent CEOs, chairmen, and board directors of public companies, refusing or unable to look out for the shareholders to whom they owed a fiduciary duty. Loeb learned that not only could you still beat those bullies with a big mouth and some money, you could make a lot of money in the process. You just had to become a big shareholder yourself and insult the bullies until they respected you. Also, you had to be right.

Thus Dan Loeb began his rampage through the world of small public companies, righting perceived wrongs and making big money in the process. He began to call his attachments to 13D forms "letters of mass destruction."

In one particularly harsh campaign, Loeb attacked Irik Sevin, the CEO of Star Gas Partners, for putting his seventy-eight-year-old mother on the board of directors, paying himself a huge salary, riding around in an expensive company car, and maintaining subsidiary businesses solely for the purpose of giving friends and family jobs.

Loeb called Sevin "one of the most dangerous and incompetent executives in America."

Loeb told Sevin, "It is time for you to step down from your role as CEO and director so that you can do what you do best: retreat to your waterfront mansion in the Hamptons where you can play tennis and hobnob with your fellow socialites."

Between the activist campaigns and a big bet on risky credit in 2002, Third Point quickly became the kind of fund Loeb had dreamed of managing. In 2003, the fund grew 50 percent. In 2004, it grew 30 percent—quickly approaching $1 billion. New investment came pouring in.

By 2005, Third Point's assets under management were above $5 billion. Loeb narrowed his tactics down to one type of trade: event-driven investments. Third Point would invest in companies that were undervalued for some specific reason that Loeb had identified, and there was a catalytic event on the horizon that would change the market's perception in the next six to twelve months. Sometimes, that catalyst would be Loeb himself, agitating for an "event" like the election of a new board of directors.

Due to the size of his fund and the vitriol of his letters, Loeb became infamous in the hedge fund industry. He and Chapman fell out. There were lawsuits. People whispered that he called himself Don Corloebone. Loeb began to hear all sorts of strange-sounding narratives about who he was and what his motivations were.

Loeb realized that by targeting others for ridicule so frequently, he was inviting ridicule in return.

Through 2005, 2006, and 2007, the ridicule was fine. Third Point was exploding in value. Loeb was traveling around the world in his jet and on his yacht, surfing and practicing yoga in exotic locations. Let them talk.

Then came 2008. Thirteen years into the life of Third Point, it nearly died. By then, it had two funds. One was down 32 percent, the other 37 percent. Many hedge funds allow their investors to withdraw their capital only in small chunks. Third Point did not, and the firm's assets under management shrank precipitously.

Loeb's response was to pull back from the spotlight, build out Third Point into a more institutional firm and, in 2009, invest in a market he knew very well: risky, distressed debt. There was a lot of debt to bet on during the Great Recession, as governments and whole industries sought bailouts backed by high-interest loans. Loeb loaded the boat on credit. He stayed away from activism. After being publicly wrong and losing billions of dollars in 2008, it was time to be quietly right.

The back-to-basics approach worked. Third Point grew 38.5 percent in 2009 and 34.5 percent in 2010.

Now, it was August 2011, and Loeb faced a difficult choice.

After lots of research into the history of Yahoo, Loeb believed he had finally come across the ultimate boardroom bully: Yahoo chairman Roy Bostock.

The way Loeb saw it, Bostock was guilty of mishandling Microsoft's offer and refusing to do a deal with Alibaba. Worst of all, Bostock had hired Carol Bartz, an executive who Loeb believed had no business running an Internet company.

The more Loeb studied Yahoo, the more he believed it was the perfect activist target. But Loeb had just spent years repairing his reputation after 2008. Did he really want to stick his neck out again?

Relative to investing in debt, activism was a very hard way to make money. When Loeb bet on debt and lost, no one knew, and he could make enough money on other trades so that no one would care.

In an activist campaign, you become a public target. If you end up wrong, everyone in the world knows it.

One of Loeb's heroes, Carl Icahn, warned him to stay away from Yahoo. Icahn had led an activist campaign against Yahoo after the Microsoft saga in 2008. He managed to get on the board, but his experience had been an awful one. He said Yahoo insiders would never listen to a Wall Street outsider like Loeb.

In the end, Loeb felt he had to go forward with the campaign.

Third Point's primary strategy was still event-driven trading: betting on or against companies ahead of events that would reveal their true value. Midway through 2011, it was proving to be a year of few events. The recovery from the Great Recession was far enough along that the distressed-debt opportunity was over. But it wasn't far enough along that companies were ready to spend their cash piles on M&A. Starting an activist campaign was one way to create your own catalyst.

As August wore on, Third Point built its Yahoo stake to $1 billion and prepared for a fight.

Though Loeb always held Bostock most responsible for Yahoo's plight in August 2011, his letter was also going to target Yahoo CEO Carol Bartz.

Loeb believed Bartz was unfit for the job due to her lack of Internet experience and her temperament. He thought her f-bombs weren't fun or funny. He thought they made her sound unhinged. He heard awful rumors about her.

He was going to excoriate her publicly.

He never got the chance.

———

Roy Bostock fired Carol Bartz over the phone on September 6, 2011.

Loeb rewrote his letter and published it on September 8.

In it, Loeb slammed Bostock for hiring Bartz in the first place and for making "a gross error" in turning down Microsoft's $31-per-share offer in 2008.

Then Loeb called for blood. He wrote, "We insist that Mr. Bostock, who championed Ms. Bartz's hiring and led the charge against the Microsoft deal, promptly resign from the Board."

He concluded with a threat: If the Yahoo board didn't cooperate, Third Point would propose a new slate of directors to be voted on by shareholders at Yahoo's annual meeting the next summer.

"It is time for new leadership at Yahoo," wrote Loeb. "Yahoo's investors, employees, clients and users deserve it."

A couple days later, Loeb got on the phone with Bostock and Jerry Yang, who had remained on Yahoo's board after stepping down from the CEO job in 2008.

The call was very casual. Yang sounded relaxed. He even said, at one point, "Well, I wasn't really a great CEO."

Bostock was less pleasant. He made it clear he didn't want to answer any questions from Loeb. But Loeb pressed. He asked Bostock, "How do you rationalize being chairman, given your performance in the job?"

Bostock hung up on him.

On September 14, Loeb took a different approach. He sent a second letter, this time addressing it to Yang.

The letter began with a lament that Loeb, Yang, and Bostock, "a destroyer of value," were unable to finish their phone call due to "Mr. Bostock's abrupt unilateral termination of the call."

Then Loeb appealed to Yang as a potential ally.

"As a Founder and major shareholder of the Company, the abysmal record of the current leadership must be heart-rending to you personally, as well as damaging to your net worth. We urge you to do the right thing for all Yahoo shareholders and push for desperately-needed leadership change. We are prepared to support you and present you with suggestions on candidates who could help bring Yahoo back to its rightful place among the world's top digital media and technology companies."

Yang had no intention of joining up with Loeb's cause. The truth was, he was working on his own deal.

Eric Jackson and Dan Loeb weren't the only people who

realized how valuable Alibaba was, and that its value was not properly recognized in Yahoo's stock price in 2011.

It was a classic event-driven arbitrage opportunity, where easy money was to be made buying low in an ignorant market and selling high in an educated one. That kind of ignorance in the market was like blood in the water for the sharks of private equity.

In the spring, summer, and fall of that year, no less than five private equity firms expressed interest in buying huge chunks of Yahoo stock. They were: TPG, Blackstone, Providence Equity Partners, Bain Capital, and Silver Lake.

Providence Equity Partners spotted the opportunity earliest, in part because it had a former insider on its team: one-time Yahoo dealmaker Mike Marquez. After watching Terry Semel botch the Facebook acquisition in 2006, Marquez left Yahoo for CBS Interactive. There, he met Quincy Smith, the CBS division's CEO. After a few years, Smith and Marquez quit CBS and formed an investment banking firm called CODE Advisors. One CODE client was Peter Chernin, the former COO of News Corp.

Marquez developed a presentation—known as a "book" in the M&A industry—showing how Yahoo could be a next-generation media company, and that if it embraced that identity by bringing in big media personalities and sought-after content, revenues would start growing again. In his vision, the purpose of products like Yahoo Mail was to bring users back every day until they eventually began seeking out Yahoo content on their own. Marquez argued that Yahoo's stakes in Alibaba and Yahoo Japan set a floor valuation for the company, and that Yahoo was trading below that floor on the public markets.

Chernin loved the plan and he brought it to Providence Equity Partners, where he was an advisor. Over the summer, the group approached Jerry Yang to see if he would join them on the deal.

The problem for the Chernin group was that by the summer,

Marquez's book had spread far and wide—including to private equity firm TPG, which had its own ex-Yahoo dealmaker in Keith Nilsson, the guy who had orchestrated Project Godfather. In addition to all the private equity groups, News Corporation also expressed interest in a transaction with Yahoo.

The fact is: One reason the Yahoo board fired Carol Bartz when it did was that there were so many people who wanted to buy the company and fire her. So Bostock preemptively canned her and hired Goldman Sachs and Allen & Co. as advisors to help Yahoo start an M&A process.

By late fall, Yang and the Yahoo board narrowed in on TPG and Silver Lake. Both firms spent hours visiting with Yahoo executives in Sunnyvale. Silver Lake brought in Marc Andreessen to help figure out what Yahoo was worth. Twenty years after inventing the Mosaic browser that inspired Jerry Yang and David Filo to create Yahoo, Andreessen was now a blue-chip venture capitalist in the Valley. His conclusion: Yahoo was a conglomerate and its only good business was search, which it had disastrously outsourced to Microsoft. Its only hope was fixing or ending that deal and firing ten thousand people.

TPG and Silver Lake wanted to do something called a private investment in public equity, or PIPE, deal. They would buy as much as 20 percent of the company in one transaction and, in return, put new structures and governance rules in place that would effectively give them majority control over the company.

Both TPG and Silver Lake wanted to make sure they shared that control with Jerry Yang—which is why Yang never rushed into Loeb's arms in the fall of 2011.

When Loeb read news reports about the PIPE deal in November, he wrote an open letter blasting Jerry Yang. In it, he said that Silver Lake and TPG were trying to steal the company from Yahoo's common shareholders at a price that was less than its breakup value. He said that Yang was complicit in the theft.

What made Loeb really sick was how every party interested in Yahoo during fall 2011—including Yang, he believed—had an incentive to make the company look weak and worthless so that they could buy it, and its stake in Alibaba, on the cheap.

While all of this was going on, Joe Tsai and Masayoshi Son continued to apply relentless pressure on the Yahoo board throughout the fall of 2011. They had come up with a deal structure where both Softbank and Alibaba could pay Yahoo a lower price for its stakes in Alibaba and Yahoo Japan, and Yahoo wouldn't have to pay the US government billions of dollars in taxes on its profits. The deal was called a cash-rich split. Basically, Softbank and Alibaba would join to buy companies—they thought maybe the Weather Channel or Hulu—and trade those companies for Yahoo's Asian assets.

It was all so complicated. Finally, in December, Roy Bostock and the Yahoo board said: Enough. Wary of Loeb's righteous fury over the PIPE deal, the board told TPG and Silver Lake there would be no deal. The cash-rich split deal was dead, too, but Bostock said that Yahoo was willing to sell some portion of its Asian assets. Bostock believed the priority for Yahoo had to be its core business, and that if selling some portion of its Asian assets could help fund and fix that business, then a transaction should happen, even if it meant selling an asset still growing in value and ringing up a huge tax bill. He hoped the transaction would quiet some of the noise around Yahoo—from the press and from Loeb.

As the end of 2011 approached, Loeb and his Third Point team were actually very pleased with how their first activist campaign in four years had gone. It was true that Bostock remained on Yahoo's board, and that was disappointing. But at least he had done the right thing when it came to the PIPE deals and Alibaba. Even better, thanks to all the public shouting about how valuable Yahoo's Asian assets were, Yahoo's stock price had climbed from $11.08 per share in August all the way up to $16.00 by the end of the year. It was a nice win for four months of work.

One December night, Third Point analyst Tim Lash was at his suburban home thinking about how happy he was with the Yahoo investment. It was the first activist campaign he had ever been involved with, and it had already made the firm close to $300 million.

Lash reflected on where everything stood. The PE firms had been vanquished. Bartz was gone. Yahoo might soon have a bunch of cash it could invest in its core business or return to shareholders.

Lash thought: You know, the only risk remaining is that Bostock goes out and hires another terrible CEO.

9

The CEO Has No Clothes

For all the turmoil and noise going on around Yahoo in fall 2011, inside the company it was actually a quiet, productive time.

Tim Morse, the chief financial officer, was a perfect interim CEO. He knew the company and its financials extremely well. He was also the kind of executive who knew what he didn't know, and he didn't have ambitions to hold the job permanently. He relied heavily on two executives to help him make his decisions.

One was Ross Levinsohn, Yahoo's president of the Americas. Levinsohn, who worked in Yahoo's Santa Monica office, was the kind of West Coast executive who would point at the camera when he had his picture taken. He had a wide smile. His hair was combed back. He wore suits. He looked good in the fleece zip-up sweater vests they give out at Allen & Co.'s Sun Valley conference for media moguls.

Levinsohn joined Yahoo in October 2010 as an executive vice president in charge of the "Americas" region. That meant he oversaw Yahoo's media and sales organization. Previously, he'd run a venture capital firm he'd created with the former CEO of AOL, Jonathan Miller. Before that, Levinsohn was president of News

Corp's Internet division, then called Fox Interactive Media. There, Levinsohn had reported to CEO Rupert Murdoch and COO Peter Chernin. Levinsohn's major success at News Corp was acquiring MySpace for $580 million and then, in 2006, selling its ad inventory to Google for $900 million.

Levinsohn was at Yahoo for only ten months before Bartz was fired. But he had impressed shareholders with his performance at Yahoo's annual shareholder meeting in 2011, when he presented a vision for Yahoo as "the world's premier digital media company."

The other executive Morse leaned on was Blake Irving, Yahoo's chief product officer. Irving was totally bald, with a small soul patch. He came from Microsoft, where he had run the online division. One of Irving's most important tasks since joining Yahoo in May 2010 was unifying the technologies powering Yahoo's many products. Ever since the days of Jeff Mallett's pods and virtual sevens, Yahoo products around the world were built and run using whatever technology was at hand. By fall 2011, Irving was making real progress on the issue.

One reason Morse, Levinsohn, and Irving all managed to get along during the tumultuous fall of 2011 was that none of them were candidates for the CEO job vacated by Bartz. Levinsohn and Irving imagined themselves capable of doing that job, but assumed Bostock and the Yahoo board would hire a big gun for the position. Levinsohn thought maybe someone like his old boss, former News Corp COO Peter Chernin, might get the job.

Then, on January 4, 2012, Roy Bostock announced on a conference call that Yahoo's new CEO would be Scott Thompson. Thompson was the president of PayPal, a subsidiary of eBay. Like Carol Bartz before him, he had zero experience in the Internet advertising business.

The collective reaction from Yahoo and the rest of Silicon Valley was: "Who?"

When Third Point's Tim Lash heard the news, he thought: Fuck.

Lash's boss, Dan Loeb, agreed with the assessment.

Loeb had been traveling around Silicon Valley since the fall, asking important industry people who they thought should be the next Yahoo CEO. They all told him Yahoo needed someone like Mark Zuckerberg or Jeff Bezos or Larry Page—a web native with the aura and instincts of a founder.

Twitter cofounder Jack Dorsey told Loeb that Yahoo needed someone like this one Google executive.

Had Loeb heard of Marissa Mayer?

She would be the perfect candidate, said Dorsey.

Too bad she would never take the job.

Loeb looked at Thompson and saw the opposite of what Yahoo needed. He began working on a plan to get rid of him.

Veteran Yahoo employees were used to new CEOs coming into the company.

Every time, there was a little rush of euphoria and hope that maybe this time the right person was here and the company would finally start heading in the right direction again.

Imbued with that sense of optimism once more, the executives and employees of Yahoo tried very hard to like Scott Thompson.

At first, they did. He looked friendly enough. With a bushy mustache that he sometimes grew into a goatee, an aw-shucks smile, and a Boston accent, Thompson reminded everyone of Cliff Clavin, the mail-carrier character from the 1980s sitcom *Cheers*.

The goodwill did not last long.

One problem was that Thompson didn't seem to know much about Yahoo's business.

During his first day on the job, Thompson introduced himself to the company at an all-hands meeting in the URLs cafeteria. After, Ross Levinsohn asked Thompson if he wanted to join him in a meeting with senior executives from Interpublic Group (IPG). Levinsohn told Thompson that IPG was one of the four largest ad agencies in the world and one of Yahoo's biggest clients. Thompson said of course and headed up to Phish Food with Levinsohn.

In the meeting, Thompson launched into the same stump speech he'd given moments before downstairs. But it was fine. At the end, Thompson took questions.

One of the IPG executives, Quentin George, asked, "What role do you see agencies playing in the future of this business?"

The right answer for Thompson to give was that agencies were Yahoo's partners and collaborators. After all, it was usually the agencies—and not agency clients—that determined where big brands spent their money.

Thompson did not give the right answer.

He said, "Well, at PayPal, we generally liked to take the middleman out of the equation."

Levinsohn felt himself slumping back in his chair. He thought: You've got to be fucking kidding me. How did he get this job?

The other thing Yahoo senior executives thought was odd about Thompson was a strange, overly macho affect he sometimes put on. It seemed like every time he came into a meeting where there was a taller man present, Thompson would walk up to him and say, "You're a big guy. Well, big guys don't scare me."

The macho thing also surfaced during Thompson's introductory tour of the company, which amounted to a series of hostile interactions.

In front of whomever he was meeting that particular day, Thompson would say, "What have you guys done in the last quarter? Because I don't see anything new. I don't see anything innovative. I don't see anything coming out in the next quarter, either. What are you doing here?"

That's the right message, an executive thought during one such meeting. He's just delivering it in the wrong way.

Never was Thompson's macho bluster more in effect than when the name Dan Loeb came up.

Shortly after Thompson took the job, Loeb proposed four candidates for the Yahoo board. The candidates were Loeb himself, the former MTV president Michael Wolf, former NBC boss Jeff Zucker, and turnaround specialist Harry Wilson.

Loeb and Thompson had a phone call to discuss the proposal. Thompson said there was no way Loeb was going to be on Yahoo's board. He said Loeb wasn't "qualified."

Then Thompson hung up on Loeb.

"He doesn't fucking scare me!" Thompson told one Yahoo executive, and then another.

"He's not going to intimidate me. I fucking hung up on him!"

The big-shot attitude showed up in other strange ways, too. Thompson had access control turnstiles installed in building D, preventing everyone but executives with proper swipe cards from entering. The gates seemed utterly out of place at a company where the CEO used to work in a cubicle and one billionaire cofounder still did.

In April, Thompson began to roll out a plan for Yahoo that he developed with help from the Boston Consulting Group. He called it Project Alpha.

Project Alpha called for a drastic reduction of Yahoo. It would reduce its data centers from thirty-one to six. The search business was to be sold. Google would take over selling many of Yahoo's ads.

Thompson shrank a division called Yahoo Labs by 70 percent. "Why do we have all these PhDs here?" he asked.

Thompson initiated a bizarre layoff plan in which some people lost their jobs right away and many others were told that they would lose their jobs in the next six to eighteen months. Morale plummeted.

Thompson announced that Yahoo was going to sue Facebook over patent infringement. The move deeply embarrassed both the engineers at Yahoo, who thought that kind of behavior was for trolls, and the media people at Yahoo who depended on traffic partnerships with Facebook to build audiences.

To many of Yahoo's senior executives, Project Alpha seemed arbitrary—and incredibly destructive.

Chief product officer Blake Irving especially hated Thompson's cuts and let him know in a series of straightforward, vocal disagreements. Irving resigned on April 5.

The rest of Yahoo's senior leadership trudged forward, either resigning themselves to years more of Thompson's leadership or making plans for how they might also leave. A sort of foggy stupor set in.

The malaise remained as Yahoo's top 30 executives gathered for a series of off-site meetings at the Hotel Los Gatos near San Jose on May 3. The point of the meetings was to review Yahoo's various products in light of Project Alpha. That morning, the executives all met in a conference room on the hotel's second floor. They sat around a U-shaped table with Thompson at the bottom of the U.

By 11:45 a.m., the meeting had gotten painfully boring. Yahoo's editor in chief, Jai Singh, and product executive David Bottoms were presenting plans for the Yahoo home page.

Singh and Bottoms were going on and on, when subtly the atmosphere in the room changed.

Something happened.

On one side of the U, Ross Levinsohn was looking at his phone, eyes bugging out. Yahoo's executive in charge of infrastructure,

David Dibble, took out his phone. Across the table, Mickie Rosen, the head of Yahoo's media group, picked up hers. Tim Morse looked at his phone, HR boss David Windley at his. Soon, everyone at the table was staring at their screens.

Silently, they were all sending each other a single news story, just published by All Things Digital reporter Kara Swisher. They couldn't believe what they were reading.

Thompson had no idea anything unusual was going on. He was still watching Singh and Bottoms's presentation.

Finally, Yahoo PR executive Sara Bettencourt Gorman handed him her phone.

As he read what was on the screen, Scott Thompson did not look well.

He got up and left the room.

Right after the door closed behind Thompson, everyone in the conference room reached for their laptops. The room was silent as they all read the same words over and over.

The words were Kara Swisher's lede: "In a letter to Yahoo's board, activist shareholder Dan Loeb of Third Point is alleging that the company's new CEO Scott Thompson has inaccurately added a computer science degree to his resume."

—

On May 3, Loeb filed the ultimate letter of mass destruction with the SEC.

The letter pointed out that, in the biographies of Scott Thompson that Yahoo posted on its website and filed with the SEC, Yahoo said that Thompson had a bachelor's degree in accounting and computer science.

This was odd, because Thompson's alma mater, Stonehill College, did not begin awarding computer science degrees until 1983, four years after Thompson graduated.

Loeb wrote that during Thompson's time at Stonehill, the college offered only one computer science course: Intro to Computer Science.

"Presumably, Mr. Thompson took that course," Loeb snarked.

Loeb wrote that if Thompson had indeed embellished his academic record, it undermined his credibility as a technologist and reflected poorly on his character.

Loeb said the fabrication also called into question "whether the Board failed to exercise appropriate diligence and oversight in one of its most fundamental tasks—identifying and hiring the Chief Executive Officer."

Loeb and Third Point had been sitting on the information for weeks. They found it through a simple Google search—nothing more complicated than the basic research Third Point did when it hired anyone. Half of Thompson's bios online said he had a degree in accounting and half of his bios said he had a degree in accounting and computer science. It was only a matter of calling Stonehill College and finding out the truth.

The truth turned out to be that, somewhere along the line, Thompson had, at the very least, begun allowing people to believe he had more of an education than he actually had. Thompson never corrected the mistake—not even when a reporter asked him about the degree in an interview.

Loeb held back from publishing this information for a time because in February, Roy Bostock, Jerry Yang, and two other directors unexpectedly announced their resignations from the Yahoo board. That meant there would be some vacancies on the board. It also meant Loeb had defeated the bully he'd originally targeted, Bostock. Loeb hoped he could fill those seats with some of the nominees from his slate—and that he could either influence Thompson's strategy for Yahoo or, failing that, push him out without having to nuke him publicly.

At first, it seemed like Loeb's hope would come true. Yahoo director Patti Hart called to say that Yahoo was willing to interview his candidates. Then ten days went by without any of the candidates hearing from Yahoo. When Loeb asked why, Hart told him she didn't have their phone numbers. Loeb provided them.

Over the next couple days, Yahoo directors reached out to Zucker, Wilson, and Wolf for perfunctory interviews.

Thompson and Loeb began a frustrating series of phone conversations. First, Thompson called Loeb to say that Third Point's candidates weren't going to be invited onto the board—but did Third Point want to review Yahoo's preferred choices? Loeb said that was unacceptable. Thompson called back later and said that Yahoo would be willing to accept Wilson, but that was it. Again, Loeb said that wasn't good enough—he wanted to be on the board himself. His firm had a $1 billion investment in Yahoo, and he wanted to look after it.

Loeb proposed that Yahoo take him and Wilson and that's it. Thompson said no way. And then he said the thing that really made Loeb mad.

Thompson said that Loeb wasn't qualified for the position. Technically, Thompson told Loeb that Yahoo's candidates were more qualified than him. But what Loeb heard was Thompson telling him that he did not have the proper qualifications.

Qualified? thought Loeb. What are your qualifications? Your computer science degree from Stonehill College? The one you made up?

Loeb decided to publish the letter. And when he did, he thought to himself: How do you like them apples?

After the letter came out on May 3, Thompson spent the rest of the afternoon in the hotel's courtyard talking to his wife, Yahoo board members, and his PR team, trying to figure out how to respond.

That evening, the rest of his executives went out for a previously scheduled team dinner.

A couple hours into the meal, Thompson surprised everyone by showing up.

"It's all okay," he said, sitting down, "Everything's fine."

Everything was not fine. Not for Thompson, anyway.

By the next morning, the scandal was national and international news. CNN, NBC, CNBC, and *Business Insider* picked it up. So did the British newspapers.

Thompson denied the allegations. He met with as many Yahoo vice presidents as he could and told them all that he did not misrepresent his credentials. He started to blame the scandal on the PR people at his old company, PayPal. He said they fabricated the degree and he never caught it.

He started acting paranoid. He called all of his executives into an empty office a couple doors down from his. He said he didn't do anything wrong, and that he expected support from everyone in the room.

He said, "Do I have your support?"

None of the executives said a word. Most of them thought Thompson should have resigned with dignity when the scandal first broke. Now they thought he should just resign.

Finally, news broke that Thompson had begun blaming the fabrication on the firm that had recruited him into PayPal. Loeb's consultant, board nominee, and ally, Michael Wolf, saw the reports and forwarded them to the headhunting firm Thompson had implicitly accused of error, Heidrick & Struggles.

"I think he's talking about you," Wolf wrote.

Heidrick & Struggles finished Thompson off. It sent the Yahoo board a cache of documents, including emails Thompson sent to the firm before he joined PayPal, citing his fabricated degree.

Over the weekend of May 12 and May 13, Yahoo board directors

Brad Smith and David Kenny reached out to Loeb and Third Point and apologized for the behavior of their colleagues. They said the board was ready to capitulate.

Five directors resigned immediately. Thompson also resigned, citing health issues. Ross Levinsohn was named interim CEO. Loeb, Wilson, and Wolf gained board seats. Yahoo agreed to pay for Third Point's activist campaign expenses. Third Point agreed not to buy any more Yahoo stock. Third Point also agreed that, if its stake in Yahoo ever fell below 2 percent, Loeb, Wilson, and Wolf would leave the board.

The new board launched an investigation into Thompson's hiring. Eventually, the new board learned some board members had known about inconsistencies in Thompson's biography before Thompson was officially hired.

The settlement put the Third Point directors in charge of key board committees. Loeb would chair the board's transaction committee, which meant he would have sign-off power on any sale of Yahoo's valuable Asian assets.

Wolf would lead the executive search committee. It was his job to find Yahoo's next CEO.

He already had someone in mind.

⸻

Before Wolf could start looking for a CEO, something remarkable happened, something that would definitely make that CEO's job easier.

Yahoo CFO Tim Morse reported to the new board that, over the past four months, he and Joe Tsai of Alibaba had finally reached a deal.

The terms were that Yahoo would immediately sell half its Alibaba stake for $7.1 billion. In addition, Alibaba would pay Yahoo a $550 million fee to terminate its license to use Yahoo technology.

Perhaps most important of all, the deal started an approximately two-year countdown clock till Alibaba's IPO.

It was great news for Yahoo shareholders and Third Point. Yahoo would be able to return most of that $7.1 billion to shareholders and use the rest to invest in its core business.

Even better, for the next two years, Yahoo would be just about the only way for investors around the world to invest in a humongous, fast-growing Chinese Internet company ahead of its imminent IPO.

That fact was sure to boost Yahoo's stock price. Thanks to Dan Loeb's campaign, Eric Jackson's sum-of-the-parts valuation for Yahoo was becoming the norm.

For whomever Wolf found to be CEO, the soaring stock price meant two solid years where Yahoo's core business could be fixed without the normal scrutiny of the public markets.

10

The Unicorn

On the morning of Thursday, July 12, 2012, Yahoo's interim CEO, Ross Levinsohn, still believed he was going to be named permanent CEO of the company.

He had just one meeting to go.

It was a board meeting, to be held that day in a room on the second floor of Yahoo's Sunnyvale, California, headquarters. The room was big, with a large horseshoe table and video screens on the walls.

The agenda for the meeting: Levinsohn was going to brief the directors once more on his plan for Yahoo, should he get the job.

Levinsohn walked into the room; all of his top executives followed.

There was Jim Heckman, Levinsohn's top dealmaker, who'd spent months negotiating with Microsoft. There was Shashi Seth, Yahoo's top product management executive, already planning a long-overdue update to Yahoo Mail and the Yahoo home page. There was chief financial officer Tim Morse, who'd just completed a critical, company-saving deal to sell a portion of Yahoo subsidiary

Alibaba. There was Mickie Rosen, a News Corp veteran whom Levinsohn had hired to run Yahoo's media business. And there was Mollie Spilman, whom he'd just made CMO.

Heckman, Seth, Morse, Rosen, Spilman, and a handful of others sat off to the side.

All of them believed that the meeting was a formality—that Levinsohn was going to get the job.

They had good reason to be confident. For the two months prior, the new chairman of Yahoo's board, Fred Amoroso, had made it clear that he was going to do everything he could to make sure Levinsohn and his team would be running the company for the foreseeable future.

Amoroso told Levinsohn this in private. He announced it to Yahoo employees during an all-hands meeting in May. He'd even joined a sales call to express support for Levinsohn to Yahoo advertisers—an oddly hands-on move for a chairman.

In June, Amoroso helped Levinsohn recruit a high-profile Google executive named Michael Barrett into Yahoo. During the recruiting process, Amoroso promised Barrett that Levinsohn's "interim" title was only temporary—that it was safe to leave Google.

Levinsohn had another reason to be hopeful: For the past few months, he'd been speaking with two of Yahoo's most important new directors, Dan Loeb and Michael Wolf, almost every day.

Levinsohn began his presentation. It was going to be a doozy, as he planned to seriously alter the direction of Yahoo.

He wanted it to stop competing with technology businesses like Google and Microsoft and instead take on media and content businesses like Disney, Time Warner, and News Corporation. As part of this transition, Levinsohn planned to spin off, sell, or shut down several Yahoo business units. He said doing so would reduce Yahoo's headcount by as many as ten thousand employees and increase its earnings before taxes and interest by as much as 50 percent.

In fact, Levinsohn announced during his presentation that he and his team had already started down this road.

Levinsohn told the board that, under his direction, Heckman had begun negotiating a deal with Microsoft to exchange Yahoo's search business for Microsoft's portal, MSN.com, and large payments in cash. Levinsohn and Heckman had also been talking with Google executive Henrique De Castro about turning over some of Yahoo's advertising inventory. Furthermore, there was talk of unloading some of Yahoo's enterprise-facing advertising technology businesses into a joint venture involving New York–based ad tech startup AppNexus.

It was during this part of his presentation that Levinsohn began to feel the CEO job slipping away.

Others in the room got the same sinking feeling.

Wolf, the man in charge of the committee tasked with hiring a permanent CEO, began to question the wisdom of the deal.

Wolf asked, in a loud voice with a sharp tone, "I understand why this is good for Microsoft, but why is it good for Yahoo?"

Harry Wilson, another director brought onto the board by Loeb, joined Wolf in his criticism of the deal as "shortsighted."

Their cross-examination of the deal eventually boiled down to one question: Had Levinsohn and Heckman made any irreversible commitments to either Microsoft or Google?

It was obvious to several people in the room that Wolf and Wilson wanted to make sure another candidate for the CEO job would not be forced to follow through on a deal they had not negotiated.

This was a bad sign for Levinsohn's candidacy.

But Wilson and Wolf's loud complaints about the Microsoft deal weren't the worst sign for Levinsohn's chances; Loeb's behavior during the meeting was.

During Levinsohn's presentation, Loeb looked bored. He wasn't paying full attention. As the interim CEO talked, Loeb stood at the back of the room and played with his BlackBerry.

One person in the room remembers watching Loeb texting for a while and then, "during the most important part of the presentation," getting up and going to the bathroom for ten minutes.

This person remembers thinking: "Oh, okay. Sorry, Ross, you're not CEO anymore."

After the meeting, Barrett, the Google executive Amoroso had helped Levinsohn poach, called Levinsohn to ask how it went. Levinsohn told him he no longer felt like he was getting the job.

But who was?

That night, Levinsohn flew to Sun Valley, Idaho, where investment bank Allen & Co. holds an annual retreat for big-name media and technology executives.

Over the weekend, Levinsohn played a guessing game with venture capitalist Marc Andreessen, Square CEO Jack Dorsey, and Twitter CEO Dick Costolo. With each of them, Levinsohn and the other Silicon Valley bigwigs ran through a long list of names, trying to figure out who might be getting the job Levinsohn had so hoped for. For each name they came up with, they thought up a persuasive reason why that person could not be it.

Whom had Wolf and Loeb so clearly already decided on?

Finally, late Sunday night, Levinsohn got a call from a friend of his at Google.

This person said: You won't believe who else interviewed for the Yahoo job.

Shortly after Roy Bostock announced on January 6, 2012, that Scott Thompson would be Yahoo's next CEO, Dan Loeb and Michael Wolf flew to San Francisco. The purpose: to find someone better than Thompson, just in case Third Point actually won control of the Yahoo board.

One morning during their trip, Loeb and Wolf drove south to meet with venture capitalist Marc Andreessen, Silicon Valley's go-to wise man, for breakfast at his house.

Loeb and Wolf asked Andreessen if he would join their slate for Yahoo's board. He refused to participate in a deal perceived to be hostile to Yahoo's founders and current management, but said he was happy to talk about Yahoo strategy. After all, he had spent much of the fall thinking about it.

The New Yorkers asked him: Whom should Yahoo hire—a media person or a product person?

By a "media person," they meant an executive who could run Yahoo almost like a television network or magazine publisher, but on the Internet. This person's specialties would be the ability to identify great content and close deals with the people who create it and those who could distribute it, and the skill set to sell ads against it. CBS chief executive Les Moonves and former News Corp chief operating officer Peter Chernin were this kind of executive. So was Michael Eisner when he spent twenty years transforming Disney from a sleepy studio into a corporate giant.

By a "product person," Loeb and Wolf meant someone who could get teams of engineers and designers to build software tools that consumers find useful, addictive, or fun. Facebook CEO Mark Zuckerberg was this kind of executive. So was Apple cofounder Steve Jobs.

Almost since its beginning, Yahoo had struggled with its identity.

Should it act like a media company—one that tries to attract consumers by producing and buying content and distributing it through Yahoo.com? Or should Yahoo act like a products company—where Internet software tools like search, webmail, stock charts, and photo storage attract users?

Andreessen said: If you get the chance to run Yahoo, the only way you'll be able to save it is if you hire someone who can make great Yahoo products.

Andreessen talked about the difference between technology companies and "normal" companies. He said the output of normal companies is their product: cars, shoes, life insurance. In his view, the output of technology companies is innovation. Whatever they are selling today, they will be selling something different in five years. If they stop innovating, they die.

Andreessen said the person at the top of Yahoo would need to know how to pioneer and produce a steady stream of innovative products if the company was going to survive in a competition with large companies like Google, Facebook, and Apple, or even some of the Valley's many startups.

The message stuck.

Shortly after the Yahoo board settled with Third Point on May 13, and Wolf was put in charge of finding Yahoo's next CEO, he hired executive recruiter Jim Citrin of Spencer Stuart and gave him a description of the Yahoo CEO job.

The document Wolf gave Citrin said Yahoo needed to hire someone who could "modernize" Yahoo's "user experiences" on mobile devices by building a culture that attracts the best "content, developer, product innovation, advertising, marketing, and managerial talent." The document said the board sought someone who could "reestablish Yahoo's credibility and reputation in the tech-innovator community" and build partnerships with companies such as "Microsoft, Apple, Facebook, and Amazon."

At Citrin's first meeting with the board, the week of May 21, 2012, he told the directors there were only a few people in the industry who could do the job described in Wolf's document. Citrin said those people were at companies like Amazon, Apple, and Google.

He warned that it was going to be very difficult for Yahoo to hire any of them.

The board came up with a list of candidates for Citrin to approach.

Though he was a "media," not a "products" executive, the top prospect for most of the directors was Ross Levinsohn.

Among the other names were Nikesh Arora, the chief business officer at Google; Eddy Cue, Apple's senior vice president of Internet software and services; and Jason Kilar, then the CEO of web TV site Hulu.

The board also asked Citrin to approach Google's Marissa Mayer.

Citrin cautioned that Mayer appeared to be a lifer at Google and was unlikely to be interested in the job.

Many of the directors wondered whether Mayer was actually capable of leading a large public corporation. They asked questions like: Had she ever managed a balance sheet? Hadn't she been demoted only a year before?

Citrin said he'd call Mayer anyway. For a while, he couldn't reach her and had to keep leaving messages.

The truth was, Mayer was ignoring Citrin's calls because she thought he was approaching her for a non-CEO job. Also, she was in China.

When Citrin finally got Mayer on the phone, he could tell Mayer was unenthusiastic about having a conversation with him.

He told her what the job was: Yahoo CEO.

Mayer thought back to her conversation with Gabriel Stricker nine months before.

Citrin said: You aren't interested in this, are you?

Mayer said: Actually, I am.

Citrin said: You are?

In the middle of June 2012, Marissa Mayer sat on a plane, thinking and preparing.

Mayer was flying to New York to have dinner at Michael Wolf's Manhattan apartment with Wolf, Citrin, and three other Yahoo directors: David Kenny, John Hayes, and Thomas McInerney.

After thirteen years at Google, she was ready to leave for the right job.

The past two years at Google—since she was, according to the rest of the world, "demoted"—had been quieter than the first eleven but in many ways more challenging and exciting.

In local and geo, she'd taken over a much more massive operation than the one she'd been running at Google.

Whenever people asked her about the "demotion," as Wolf and the other directors might over dinner, Mayer always pointed out how she had gone from managing 250 product managers in search to supervising a considerably larger, more diverse group of managers—1,100 people managing engineering, design, marketing, and sales. Mayer would tell people that she was supervising some 6,000 contractors.

She'd figured out that the geo and local piece of the company, which she was running, represented something like 20 to 25 percent of the company's overall headcount. She felt that, for the past two years, she had been learning a lot from a bigger job than she'd ever had before.

As she flew to New York that day in June 2012, Mayer also believed she was now ready for an even bigger one.

On the evening of June 24, Mayer arrived at Wolf's modern, Fifth Avenue apartment. An informal dinner was served.

Mayer read for the part of Yahoo CEO.

Throughout the conversation, Mayer touted a surprisingly

thought-out plan for overhauling Yahoo's culture, executive bench, and product lineup.

After Mayer left, one of the board directors said to Citrin: "That's the next CEO of Yahoo." The committee agreed that Wolf would stay in touch with her.

Michael Wolf and his pro-Mayer allies on the board had a problem. They were outnumbered.

On the day Wolf joined the Yahoo board in mid-May, he attended a town hall meeting in midtown Manhattan for Yahoo's New York–based employees. Fred Amoroso stood up and gave a speech about how he was going to do whatever he could to make Ross Levinsohn CEO.

After the town hall, Amoroso and Wolf went out for a cup of coffee. Amoroso told Wolf he didn't see any reason for there to be a CEO search. Levinsohn was obviously the guy for the job, and the longer the board waited to make it official, the more damaging it would be to Yahoo morale. Talented people would leave the company, Amoroso warned.

By mid-June, several other Yahoo directors had come around to Amoroso's view of things and had decided that interim CEO Ross Levinsohn should get the full-time job.

After Thompson resigned in the middle of May and Levinsohn was named interim CEO, Levinsohn sent a memo to all Yahoo's employees. He wrote, "I'm fired up and I hope you are too. I believe in the power of what we're doing. We have an incredibly talented team, unparalleled strengths in key areas and most importantly, I see the purple pride building everywhere. Let's move forward quickly with conviction and confidence."

Levinsohn ran with the opportunity, and by the end of June—really, just a few weeks—he'd accomplished a lot. He'd signed a deal with Facebook over patents. He was able to quickly recruit impressive talent into Yahoo, including Google advertising executive Michael Barrett. Levinsohn and Jim Heckman had nailed down several content partnerships, including one with on-demand music service Spotify. Levinsohn and Heckman were also busy finishing larger deals with Microsoft, Google, and AppNexus.

The reason Levinsohn was able to move so fast was that he was working off an elaborate plan he and Heckman had devised nine months before. During fall 2011, when News Corp and all those private equity firms came out of the woodwork with bids for Yahoo, Levinsohn and Heckman began to wonder why they, too, weren't trying to take control of the company. In their off-hours, using non-Yahoo computers, the two of them put together a plan for what they would do if they owned Yahoo. Then they took the plan and pitched it to private equity firms. Bain Capital showed the most interest, but talks went nowhere because PE firms did not want to launch a hostile bid.

As Levinsohn worked from his plan during the summer of 2012, Yahoo directors began to come under pressure from the rest of the industry to hand him the job. Levinsohn's allies across the media, advertising, and entertainment industries wrote Yahoo directors letters recommending him.

At the *Wall Street Journal*'s D: All Things Digital conference, former Yahoo executive Jeff Weiner, now the CEO of LinkedIn, enthusiastically endorsed Levinsohn and said Yahoo would finally be in good hands if it put him in charge.

After several weeks went by without Yahoo naming a full-time replacement for Thompson, even Marc Andreessen wrote a note to Loeb suggesting that Yahoo should just put Levinsohn in the job permanently and commit to a media strategy, since it seemed unlikely they could get a top-end product CEO, and continued delays would permanently damage the company.

Meanwhile, All Things Digital reporter Kara Swisher seemed to be actively pushing for Yahoo to hire Levinsohn. She said the only reason the board hadn't hired him yet was that it was looking for a "'unicorn CEO'—one who actually does not exist but who sounds just dreamy."

By the beginning of July, several board members were almost completely sold. They wanted Levinsohn to keep the job.

On the morning of Wednesday, July 11, 2012, a small bus pulled in front of the Four Seasons Hotel in East Palo Alto, California. As the bus idled, about a dozen middle-aged executives quietly boarded.

These executives were the Yahoo board of directors, and as they boarded that bus, they had no idea where they were going. Their destination was a secret, because these people—people who would soon have to come together and decide the fate of Yahoo—did not trust each other.

That day, the board was going to interview, for the last time, four finalist candidates for the Yahoo CEO job.

The search committee had decided that if the entire board knew where the final interviews were taking place, one of the directors would inevitably leak the location to All Things Digital's Kara Swisher.

David Kenny was particularly insistent on secrecy. The fall prior, before Scott Thompson was hired, Kenny had interviewed for the CEO job at Yahoo. Word of his meetings in Sunnyvale had gotten out, and Kenny had to resign from Akamai, where he was president. Kenny recovered nicely—he'd become CEO of the Weather Company, parent of the Weather Channel—but he didn't want the same thing happening to any of the executives interviewing that day.

The directors rode in the bus for exactly five miles—south on

University, south on 101, off the highway at Oregon Expressway, and continuing onto Page Mill Road.

After ten to fifteen minutes, the bus pulled into an office park and everyone got out.

They'd arrived at the offices of Third Point's law firm, Gibson Dunn. The location was ostensibly picked by headhunter Jim Citrin, who'd also provided the bus. But some of the directors took it as a signal from the Third Point board members about whose show this really was.

Citrin had also arranged for a car to pick up Levinsohn, who had no idea where he was going, either. Nor did he know who the other finalists were.

Levinsohn went first. He presented his plan, which the board was already familiar with. He wanted to get Yahoo out of the "platform" business—where it was competing with Google, Microsoft, and Facebook—and move it into the content business. Levinsohn knew some of the directors were worried that he'd ignore Yahoo's engineers and product development people, so he talked about how he'd been spending a lot of time with product boss Shashi Seth and his team.

The interview felt strange to Levinsohn. He'd been talking to Loeb a handful of times every day. He said, "You guys know where I'm at. You know what I'm doing."

After, Jim Citrin told Levinsohn he'd done well. If the board decided to go in the "media" direction, the job was his.

Levinsohn left.

After enough time had passed to ensure that they wouldn't spot each other, Mayer arrived by limo.

Anyone remotely familiar with her childhood, studies, and career could have predicted what happened next.

Mayer walked into that room at Gibson Dunn and blew them away.

She described her long familiarity with Yahoo and its products. She described how Yahoo products would evolve over time under her watch. Her presentation included an extraordinary amount of detail on Yahoo's search business, audience analytics, and data. She talked about fixing Yahoo's culture with more transparency, perks, and accountability. She named her perceived weaknesses, and explained how she planned to address them. She said she would hire people who had the skills she didn't have.

It helped that Third Point's Tim Lash had prepared a report on Yahoo for Mayer to study, and Michael Wolf had gone over it with her, helping her understand the key points Yahoo's other directors would want her to address.

When Mayer was done, Jim Citrin told her he'd call with the board's decision by eight p.m.

She left. The board still had a tough final decision to make.

A number of the Yahoo directors continued to oppose hiring Mayer. They argued that she didn't have enough corporate experience. Some of the directors favored Levinsohn because they felt that the Third Point directors were just trying to install someone they could control.

The directors who opposed Mayer—most vocally Amoroso, but also Brad Smith and David Kenny—argued that Levinsohn, with his "media" strategy, had a better plan for Yahoo than Mayer and her "products" strategy.

They argued that Mayer may present a greater upside—she was more likely to come up with the next Facebook or Google Maps or Twitter—but that Levinsohn was the safer bet, a more guaranteed return.

Loeb, who had fought a bloody fight to get onto the board, and whose vote undoubtedly mattered the most, didn't mind that Mayer was a high-risk, high-reward play. In his view, the sale of Yahoo's Asian assets and the returning of those proceeds through share buybacks or dividends would provide enough of a floor in Yahoo's value that it was worth betting on the greater upside Mayer brought to the table.

Loeb was also somewhat aware that Mayer had a reputation for being unable to relate to and connect with other people. That she would sometimes struggle to hold eye contact, for example. He wrote this off as a trait typical of Silicon Valley geniuses like Larry Page, Mark Zuckerberg, and Max Levchin. For Loeb, Mayer's awkwardness was almost a selling point. It helped her look the part.

As for Levinsohn's plan—Loeb was unenthusiastic. Heckman had forwarded Third Point analyst Tim Lash a bunch of spreadsheets that laid the plan out. At first, Lash had been impressed, because projections were huge. Then he right-clicked on some of the spreadsheet cells to see how Heckman had come up with the figures. Lash was stunned to see that the numbers had been hardcode plugged-in. They were guesses. Lash told Loeb there was nothing there. Loeb believed the whole plan was a Potemkin village.

Loeb also favored Mayer because of a conversation he had with Yahoo cofounder David Filo, who was still solving problems for the company from his cubicle. Filo told Loeb: "These properties have been underinvested in for years. They just need proper care and feeding." What Loeb heard was that Yahoo needed someone who could do what it already did, but better. Not someone who could take the company off on an adventure.

The 8:00 p.m. deadline came and went. Mayer, at a dinner party on the other side of town, tried to stop checking her phone.

At 9:45 p.m., the board still hadn't called her. She signaled to her husband, Zachary Bogue, that she wanted to leave the party.

Back in the boardroom, Wolf lobbied his fellow directors in favor of Mayer to the point of annoyance.

Finally, the pro-Mayer directors proposed a solution. What if they made Mayer the CEO and offered Levinsohn a huge amount of money to stay on as her chief operating officer? That way, she'd be able to pursue her "products" strategy, and he could keep running the sales force and making deals with major media companies.

An informal vote was cast. The pro-Mayer directors were in the majority, with Amoroso and others voting against.

It was over. A formal vote was cast.

This time, the board unanimously voted to name Marissa Mayer the new CEO of Yahoo.

On the other side of town, Mayer and Bogue were finally leaving their dinner party. As they began to say their good-byes, Mayer's phone rang. It was Jim Citrin. She let it go to voice mail.

Citrin told her: "Marissa. You should be smiling. We're smiling. Call me ASAP."

When the board reached Mayer to offer her the job, she did not accept it right away.

First, she had some news to share. She was five months pregnant.

Mayer's pregnancy wasn't supposed to be some huge secret. Lots of people around Google knew. But the only person on the board who knew until that last phone call was Michael Wolf. He hadn't told anyone because he didn't think it was their business.

The offer stood. She accepted.

The next day—Friday, July 13—Mayer called a meeting in her apartment at the top of the Four Seasons.

The people in the room were Michael Wolf, Third Point lawyer Josh Targoff, and Gabriel Stricker, the Google communications executive who first gave Mayer the idea to go for the job. Stricker was now the head of communications for Twitter, and he was helping Mayer with her transition purely as a favor. On the phone was Elissa Doyle, Third Point's head of investor relations and marketing.

The purpose of the meeting was to decide how to break the news of Mayer's hire. Everyone agreed to two goals. One was that the coverage needed to correctly characterize what Mayer had been doing at Google since her job changed in late 2010. Too many reporters were calling it a demotion.

The other goal was: Make sure All Things Digital reporter Kara Swisher didn't get to break the news. Though he wasn't in the room, Loeb thought it was incredibly important to show that a new era of Yahoo had arrived, and that Swisher, the chronicler of the old era, was no longer in the know.

The group decided to give the news to Andrew Ross Sorkin, the CNBC host and *New York Times* columnist. Both the Loeb and the Mayer people knew and trusted him. They also thought it would help that Sorkin had two outlets.

After the meeting, the next thing Mayer did was fly out to Wisconsin to spend the weekend with her parents.

Back in California, Wolf, Targoff, and Doyle—who had flown in to help—met with David Filo on Sunday, hoping to convince him to throw his support behind Mayer when the news became official.

Sunday night, Doyle and Wolf briefed Sorkin. He was floored by the news: "This is a great story!" Doyle and Wolf told him they would give him the green light to run the story after the market closed on Monday.

The only thing left was for Mayer actually to sign the contract.

At six a.m. Monday morning, Mayer drove up to the Palo Alto offices of Gibson Dunn in her ten-year-old, hunter-green BMW 325. She was wearing one of her flowery dresses and a little cardigan. Her hair was still wet. You could kind of tell she was pregnant.

She sat down inside. The only people in the whole office were Mayer, Wolf, Doyle, Targoff, and a receptionist who seemed annoyed to be at work so early on a Monday.

Mayer flipped through the pages of her contract, the details of which she had spent the weekend negotiating with Wolf. It would pay her an annual cash salary of $1 million, with a cash bonus up to $2 million. The big money was in equity. There was an annual award of $12 million worth of stock and options, a one-time award of $30 million in stock and options, and a $14 million "make whole" stock grant intended to compensate her for the Google stock she was abandoning. Including further bonuses and awards, the deal was worth up to $100 million over five years. If Yahoo's stock took off during Mayer's tenure, she would make even more.

Mayer initialed every page, and then she signed her contract. She looked up at the three people in the room.

Doyle said to her: "Good!"

Mayer looked emotional.

Mayer said, "Okay. I'm going to go talk to Larry and Sergey and Eric"—the two cofounders and chairman of Google.

Mayer stood up to leave.

Doyle said, "Do you want one of us to drive you? Or do you want to take a car? Do you want someone to go with you?"

It seemed strange for someone to show up in an old BMW, sign a $100 million contract, and then drive away like a normal person.

Also, Mayer was pregnant. Didn't she need help moving boxes?

"No, I'll be fine," Mayer said. "My mom is going to come help me clean out my office."

Andrew Ross Sorkin broke the news at exactly 1:00 p.m. Pacific time, 4:00 p.m. Eastern. His story included a rare quote from David Filo—an endorsement.

By then, Mayer was back at the Gibson Dunn offices in Palo Alto. She had to deliver her resignation to one of the Google cofounders over the phone, but otherwise everything had gone well. Google sent her along with blessings.

There was a conference call with reporters. Then, around five thirty, Kara Swisher buzzed Elissa Doyle's cell phone. Swisher told Doyle that she knew Mayer was pregnant and that she was going to go with a story. Doyle told Swisher she would call her back with a comment.

Mayer did not want Swisher to have the story. Mayer had a personal grudge against Swisher, going back several years. Swisher believed it had to do with an incident when Owen Thomas, the editor of tech gossip site Valleywag, crashed Mayer's *Sex and the City* birthday party in 2008. Mayer believed Thomas knew about the party only because of Swisher, who was married to a Google executive.

Mayer wanted to give the pregnancy story to Patricia Sellers from *Fortune*. Doyle was fine with that. It was in keeping with Loeb's plan to lock Swisher out, showing that this was a new Yahoo era.

Mayer called Sellers. Swisher was left to seethe over the double cross when, that night, Sellers reported on *Fortune*: "Marissa Mayer, the Google executive who today was named Yahoo's new chief executive, is pregnant.

"Mayer told *Fortune* exclusively that her first child is due October 7. It's a boy!"

On the Monday morning before Mayer's hire was made public, Ross Levinsohn went into work fairly certain he was not going to become Yahoo's permanent CEO. The night before, someone told him they heard Marissa Mayer had also interviewed for the job. When he heard her name, he knew it was over.

Yahoo had to report its second-quarter earnings that week, and that Monday at the office, Levinsohn worked with CFO Tim Morse's team to prepare some remarks for the company's conference call with analysts.

Levinsohn kept telling the team, "Don't write this for me, write it for a CEO. It should be generic."

When that was done, Levinsohn went back to his office to wait for the news. He'd wanted this job. He'd fought for it. He'd done well.

Finally, Fred Amoroso walked into Levinsohn's office and delivered the blow.

Saving Yahoo was up to someone else now.

She's a big name, thought Levinsohn. Wonder how she'll do.

Before Andrew Ross Sorkin finally broke the news of Mayer's hire into Yahoo, Third Point's Elissa Doyle and Michael Wolf had worried a lot about what the coverage would look like.

Yahoo's directors had made a lot of good points about some of her potential failings. She had never run a public company before, or even a division with its own profits and losses. She had only ever worked at one company since college. It wasn't really that clear if she had been demoted at Google or not.

But after Sorkin published his story, it quickly became clear that Doyle and Wolf had worried for nothing.

Between Mayer's pregnancy, Google pedigree, photogenic looks, and young age, her hire became a humongous, positive news story over the following days, weeks, and months.

There was one nasty bit of press, though.

Sharon Waxman, the CEO and editor in chief of TheWrap, was at a tech conference in Colorado when word spread about Mayer and Yahoo.

The next morning, Waxman published a story about how conference attendees reacted to the news.

One quote, attributed to "one Google executive at the Fortune conference who declined to be named," was particularly critical of Mayer.

The Google executive said, "It will be a struggle. She's never managed more than ten to twenty people. She's a product person who hasn't managed sales, business development, human resources and all that. Her problem is not product innovation—she's a great innovator. The question is about the rest of the company."

11

HOPE

Where do I park?"

It was eight fifteen in the morning on July 17, 2012—Marissa Mayer's first day of work at Yahoo. She didn't know where to put her hunter-green BMW.

Being so early—for sleepy Yahoo, at least—there were only a few employees milling around the headquarters entrance. One of them directed her to a spot.

Mayer got out of her car and walked up to Third Point's Elissa Doyle and board director Michael Wolf, who were waiting for her. The pair planned to stick around for a couple weeks to help Mayer's onboarding. They called it Project Cardinal.

Mayer asked Doyle, a fashionable blonde from New York, "Is it kind of weird that I came here with my hair wet?"

Doyle told her she looked great.

The three of them waited for a minute. Then out from inside came David Filo, Yahoo's cubicle-bound cofounder. For the big occasion, Filo was wearing a T-shirt and jeans.

Before allowing Mayer into Yahoo, Filo produced a flourish.

He ceremoniously unrolled a large purple carpet through the open doors of Yahoo. The group walked in.

Inside, there were big screens on the walls and on them, in big letters, the words "Welcome Marissa!" On the walls, someone had taped posters of Mayer's face illustrated in the style of Shepard Fairey's Obama poster. Under her face, in all caps, was the word "HOPE."

Yahoo security took Mayer's picture, gave her a badge, and escorted her to the elevators.

A large crowd got into the elevator with Mayer and, as it made its way up three floors, everyone introduced themselves to her.

Filo showed Mayer and her contingent to her office. It was already jammed with gifts. A couple years before, *San Francisco* magazine had profiled Mayer and written that she loved to make cupcakes. There were maybe a few hundred of them in her new office. Google sent over many bunches of balloons in different colors.

The Yahoo board had put Doyle's phone number on the press release announcing Mayer's hire, and by Tuesday morning, Doyle's voice mail box was full of messages from dignitaries calling to congratulate Yahoo's new CEO.

"It's Valerie Jarrett from the White House."

"It's Jamie Dimon from JP Morgan."

"It's Nancy Pelosi calling."

On that first day, Matt Lauer from the *Today* show called and asked for an interview. He begged Yahoo every day for the next several weeks. Mayer told Doyle to say no to all interview requests.

An IT guy came into Mayer's office and helped set up her computer, email, and phone.

When someone told her that the Marissa@yahoo-inc.com address was already taken by another employee and asked if she wanted to go with MarissaM@yahoo-inc.com, she said "No." Mayer, who is obsessed with divisible numbers and despises prime numbers, was very picky about her phone numbers.

One of Mayer's biggest concerns that first day was to have her computer set up properly. Specifically, she wanted to be able to use it to log in to the Yahoo code base and make changes, whether she was at home or in the office.

The IT guy was unable to help her with that. The reason: He wasn't an IT guy. He was Yahoo's interim general counsel, Ron Bell, and he had only meant to come by to say hello to the new boss.

Mayer's mom dropped by during the onboarding. So did Mayer's executive coach, who came in, said, "I'm so happy for you!" and rushed over to give Mayer a big hug.

Mayer worked through midnight her whole first week, fueled on a diet of Carnation breakfast drinks, regular Coca-Colas, yogurt pretzels, and salads with Catalina French dressing.

On Wednesday, Mayer's second day, she ventured down to URLs, Yahoo's cafeteria, for lunch. She was swarmed by employees the second she stepped on the floor. The mob was so deep she could hardly move. The food at URLs was all of Mayer's favorite things. The Yahoo chef had called the Google chef and asked what she liked.

On Thursday, Mayer sent out an email to the whole company saying hello and inviting people to come by her office in building D on the third floor. She said she wanted to hear their ideas for Yahoo's future.

Yahoo's employees took Mayer at her word, and they started showing up in droves.

During Mayer's first meeting with Yahoo media boss Mickie Rosen, there were about nine people outside her office door wanting to come in to say hello. Mayer would go into the hall and people would stop her to take pictures with her. Then they would post them to Yahoo's photo-sharing site, Flickr.

Yahoo's celebrity, superhero, savior CEO had arrived.

⸻

Mayer's first big lesson on what it meant to be CEO of a huge public company came in early August.

It had to do with the deal CFO Tim Morse made with Alibaba in May. The deal stipulated that Yahoo would, that summer, sell 20 percent of its stake in Alibaba to Alibaba for $7.1 billion.

After the Yahoo board's transaction committee, headed by Dan Loeb, approved the deal, Yahoo announced that it would return all of the $7.1 billion to shareholders, possibly in the form of buybacks.

A buyback is when a company uses its cash to buy its own stock. Buybacks tend to increase the share price of a company because, when a company buys back shares, it removes those shares from its total outstanding shares. And, just as reducing the number of slices in a pie makes each piece bigger, reducing the number of outstanding shares in a company makes each worth more.

Investors were pleased with the promise of buybacks, and Yahoo's share price began to rise during the summer from $15.01 on June 4 to $16.09 on August 8.

Then, on August 9, Yahoo filed a notice with the SEC saying it might not actually use the money for buybacks. Mayer was not sure buybacks were the best use of Yahoo's money.

She thought: What about acquisitions? What about investing in the core?

Yahoo's stock immediately began to drop, and was down 9 percent by the middle of the following week. Like that, billions of dollars were erased.

This was the moment Mayer learned that, though she was

trained as a software engineer, she was going to have to be as much a financial engineer in order to do her new job well.

It was also a moment that reemphasized for Mayer the pivotal role Yahoo's Alibaba stake would play in her turnaround.

The fact was, because of that stake, for the next two years, Yahoo's stock price was likely to go up no matter how well or poorly Yahoo's core business performed.

The reason for this was simple: Alibaba was the hottest Internet company in all of China. Thanks to Eric Jackson, lots of fund managers knew it. Those fund managers wanted to put money into Alibaba in order to benefit from its growth. But they were not able to because Alibaba was not a public company.

The next best thing for the fund managers to do, then, was to invest in a public company that itself owned Alibaba stock—for example, Yahoo.

The point was: As Alibaba grew in value over the next two years, so would the value of Yahoo's stake in the company—and that would drive up Yahoo's stock price.

Mayer's situation was one most public-company CEOs in turn-around situations could only dream of: She was going to be able to do the messy, hard work of fixing Yahoo without Yahoo investors paying any attention at all. They would be watching Alibaba boom.

If turning around a company is like building a bridge in the middle of a war zone, with bombs dropping out of the sky every minute, then Marissa Mayer was the lucky army engineer who got to build a bridge from Yahoo's past to Yahoo's future under perfect air cover—air cover provided by Alibaba.

The only downside to Mayer's situation was that, after almost exactly two years, Alibaba's air cover would go away.

The deal Alibaba signed with Morse gave Alibaba major incentives to go public around the end of 2014. It stipulated that during the IPO, Yahoo would sell half of its remaining shares.

From then on, the only reason for an investor to buy Yahoo stock would once again be because that investor believed in the strength of Yahoo's core business.

At the end of two or so years, Mayer was going to have to have Yahoo ready for scrutiny.

Specifically, Mayer was going to have to show that under her, Yahoo had a plan to reverse the trends that had doomed Carol Bartz.

In 2011, Yahoo had shrinking search market share, shrinking display advertising revenues, and shrinking traffic. It was almost nowhere in mobile. Yahoo Mail usage was declining. Talented employees were fleeing. Yahoo's brand had lost all its cachet.

In 2012, after a year of turmoil, things were worse. Quarterly revenues were below 2005 levels.

It would be impossible for Mayer to fix all those problems before Alibaba's air cover lifted sometime in the second half of 2014. But she was going to have to show that, thanks to her two years of effort, the company was finally on the right trajectory again.

The clock was ticking.

After setting up her office over her first couple days at Yahoo, Mayer began hosting Yahoo's top executives for one-on-one meetings.

She needed to know whom she could count on and whom she was going to have to replace.

She was going to have to replace Ross Levinsohn.

Despite personal pleas from Yahoo chairman Fred Amoroso and whispers of a generous compensation package, Levinsohn had decided not to stay as Mayer's chief operating officer. Since he took the interim job in May, he'd warned the board that if he didn't get the permanent gig, he was going to try to become a CEO somewhere else.

If Levinsohn ever had any notion of reconsidering, that was squashed by his first scheduled one-on-one meeting with Mayer.

After he learned that Mayer was getting the job, Levinsohn flew back home to Los Angeles. Mayer said she wanted to meet, and he agreed to fly back up to Sunnyvale. But when he showed up at the appointed time, Mayer's assistant told Levinsohn that Mayer was running late.

Levinsohn said to the assistant, "My office is three doors down. I'll be in there."

Suddenly anxious, the assistant said, "You have to wait here."

She wanted him to wait so that when Mayer was done with whatever she was doing, Levinsohn would be immediately available.

Levinsohn said, "Not so much." He walked away.

Soon he walked out of the building for good.

Jim Heckman would quickly follow. Heckman met with Mayer during her first few days at Yahoo. It was a clash of personalities. Heckman wasn't afraid to break rules. He was squinty-eyed and caffeinated. He made deals. He used your first name—too much. He quoted the comedian Daniel Tosh of *Tosh.0*. He didn't care about the headcount; he cared about the bottom line. Once, at a Yahoo party held on a yacht during the Cannes Lions festival in France, Heckman brought a date who decided to go topless.

In his meeting with Mayer, Heckman laid out the plan he and Levinsohn had been working on for the past year, ever since they began compiling a pitch deck for outside private equity investors. If the plan had been implemented, it would have completely changed the way Yahoo did business.

Heckman told Mayer he believed partner ad technology would immediately raise Yahoo's ad rates.

Moreover, with the money Yahoo would save by getting rid of the people it had working on ad tech, it could go out and buy high-quality video content from Hollywood studios. He argued that advertisers would be willing to pay much higher ad rates if Yahoo's content quality were higher. He said rates could go from under $2 per 1,000 impressions to $20.

He told Mayer that he'd negotiated a deal with Microsoft CEO Steve Ballmer, wherein Yahoo would turn over its entire search business—patents and all—in exchange for Microsoft's large online media property, MSN.com, and long-term, guaranteed cash payments.

Heckman said his plan would allow Yahoo to run with just 4,000 full-time employees, far fewer than the 15,000 full-timers and thousands more contractors Yahoo employed. He told Mayer that Yahoo's EBITDA (earnings before interest, taxes, depreciation, and amortization) would increase by 50 percent if she closed his deals.

Mayer heard him out, taking notes the whole time.

Within twenty-four hours, Mayer let Heckman know that she'd canceled all his deals and that his services were no longer needed by Yahoo.

Heckman flew to Ibiza, Spain, for a thirty-day vacation.

One by one, the rest of the senior executives from the prior regime came through Mayer's office. Many of these people were meeting Mayer for the first time, and they expected to sit across from the woman they'd read about in so many fluffy profiles and had seen on TV or onstage at conferences, someone who was charismatic and warm—personal.

Other than the $10,000 maternity outfit straight from the pages of *Vogue*, that was not what they got.

Each walked in and sat down at a table across from Mayer. Mayer would say, "Hi, I'm Marissa" and then launch into questions. She asked: "Where did you get your education?" "Where are you from?" "What do you do here?" And so on.

A typical follow-up question: "I'm sorry, I didn't catch where you said you went to undergrad."

As Yahoo executives answered, Mayer took notes on their answers with pen on paper, hardly looking up. When she did, she would flutter her eyes, avoiding direct contact. She wouldn't smile.

Mayer didn't bother with pleasantries. She didn't try to relate to the people who had just watched the man who hired them, Ross Levinsohn, walk out the door, leaving their lives in flux.

One Yahoo executive attended such an introductory meeting between his boss and Mayer. His boss asked Mayer, "Would you like to meet the people I brought?"

Mayer looked at them.

"No."

The truth is, the person Yahoo's top executives sat across from in those first meetings was not the Marissa Mayer they thought they knew from the media coverage of her. It was the Marissa Mayer from the Philosophy 160A study sessions.

Just as during those all-nighters almost twenty years before, Mayer wasn't at Yahoo to socialize. In one early meeting, Mayer said that Yahoo was going to fail—shut down—in the next few years if it did not get things going soon. She told a top product executive that Yahoo lagged in innovation and talent, and that its culture was broken.

She was there to save the company, and that was going to take a lot of work. It was past time to get started.

Over the next couple months, most of the old regime exited Yahoo, including Tim Morse, the CFO. He had exhausted himself on the Alibaba deal and was ready to join a startup.

Mayer asked Mickie Rosen, the News Corp veteran Ross Levinsohn had brought in to run Yahoo's media business, to stay. Mayer told Rosen she didn't know much about media, and she needed help. Rosen agreed to stick around.

A couple days into the job, Mayer was at lunch in URLs when

an employee walked up to her and said he was Tony. "I'm a mobile engineer. I'm on the mobile team."

Mayer said to Tony, "Great, how big is our mobile team?"

"Thirty people!"

Mayer's face betrayed that she was shocked by the tiny number.

"Oh, but there's more," said Tony. "They're in the teams."

"How many more?" asked Mayer.

"Maybe sixty."

Mayer knew that Yahoo was behind on mobile, but she couldn't believe prior CEOs had actually put so few people on the job. She thought Tony must be mistaken.

She went to engineering management and said, "How many people do we have working on mobile at the company?"

"Like, a hundred."

Mayer said, "Like an actual hundred or like sixty rounded up to a hundred to make me feel better?"

"Well, maybe more like sixty."

Mayer was desperate to grow that number. Mayer believed that the best way for Yahoo to reinvent itself was to ride the shift from PC to mobile—to become a really great apps company.

The more she studied Yahoo, the more convinced she was that the key to its success would be going "back to the future" and doing what Yahoo had always done best.

Just as Yahoo's original success had come from making the early Internet user-friendly for normal people, Mayer believed Yahoo's renewed success would come from making the mobile Internet user-friendly. The big difference would be that Mayer wanted Yahoo to narrow its product portfolio down from more than a hundred products to approximately a dozen. She did some market research and found a list of common user activities on mobile devices. She called this list the "Daily Habits." The habits included news reading, checking weather, checking email, and photo-sharing. Mayer was determined to make sure Yahoo had the best mobile app available for each.

To lead this effort, Mayer began looking for someone who could direct a mobile task force at Yahoo. She knew it would be one of her most important hires.

Michael Wolf, the board director who had pushed so hard to hire Mayer, told her he knew exactly whom she should give the job to.

Years before, when Wolf was a director at consulting firm McKinsey, he worked with a young executive named Adam Cahan. When Wolf took over MTV for Viacom, he brought Cahan with him.

Now Cahan was working for Yahoo. Cahan had come into Yahoo when it bought his startup, a social networking app called IntoNow, in 2011.

The weekend before Mayer officially signed her contract, Wolf saw Cahan in the Valley. Wolf was looking to put someone he trusted close to Mayer, and he suggested to her that Cahan should have a big job in her administration. Mayer trusted Wolf, so she looked for something Cahan could do. IntoNow had been a smartphone app, so running mobile was considered.

Cahan developed some mock-ups of what Yahoo's mobile product suite could look like. In November, Mayer introduced Cahan to the rest of Yahoo as its new senior vice president of emerging products and technology, overseeing mobile, connected video, and Flickr.

With the promotion, Cahan leapfrogged Shashi Seth—a former Googler who, as SVP for Yahoo's "Connections Business Unit," had been Cahan's boss. Seth would leave Yahoo at the beginning of 2013. Everyone in Yahoo's product organization noticed the aggressive power grab.

One way Mayer planned to grow the number of mobile

developers working for Cahan was to go out and buy startups that had made slick-looking, innovative smartphone apps that had, for some reason or another, not really taken off with consumers. These kinds of cheap deals were known as "acqui-hires." Mayer needed someone who could execute them one after another. Since this person would solve a staffing problem, Mayer thought of the job as an HR position that required dealmaking and corporate development skills—a rare mix.

To find such a head of HR, Mayer turned to Martha Josephson, an executive recruiter Mayer worked with a lot at Google. Josephson suggested several HR veterans—and someone with zero HR experience named Jackie Reses. Reses was blond, bespectacled, and from New York. There was something Tina Fey-esque about her. She was very direct in her manner of speaking.

At first blush, Reses appeared to be an odd fit. Reses was a partner at a giant private equity firm called Apax Partners. Before that, she ran a dot-com-era startup for a year and spent seven years at Goldman Sachs. She had come to meet with Josephson weeks before to beg her to please help her find a job in Silicon Valley. Reses was desperate to get out of the boring side of corporate America, where she felt she had been since her very first internship, at PNC Bank in Philadelphia years before.

Mayer picked Reses out of Josephson's packet of suggestions, and the two hit it off in a meeting. Mayer announced Reses as Yahoo's new executive vice president of people and development on September 7.

Mayer asked her industry connections to help her find a CFO to replace Tim Morse. Frank Quattrone, the legendary investment banker, suggested Mayer ask a friend of his, Ken Goldman, to lead a search. After about a week, Goldman came back to Mayer and said he'd done an exhaustive survey, and the best available candidate for the job was . . . him. He started in late October and quickly developed a reputation for penny-pinching. When, in May 2013, he announced that he would allow Yahoo to buy some picnic tables for employees to sit on outside, the entire company broke into laughter and applause. Mayer called it a "shock."

During his time as interim CEO, Ross Levinsohn appointed Mollie Spilman as the company's CMO. Spilman made it through a couple weeks with Mayer, then went on a vacation in August. While she was away, Mayer hired another CMO.

Her name was Kathy Savitt. Mayer knew her from *Fortune*'s Most Powerful Women conference series. Shortly after Mayer got the Yahoo job, Savitt sent her an email saying: Hey, I'm in San Francisco, are you around? Mayer told her to come by. When Savitt got to Mayer's office, she locked the door, walked to Mayer's desk, and said, "Make me your CMO." Savitt was a friendly, vivacious woman, obsessed with something she called Generation Z and other people called children and teenagers. Her first moves as CMO were to bring marketing spending back in-house and build out Yahoo's customer service call centers in the United States.

Mayer made Ron Bell—not an IT guy—Yahoo's permanent general counsel on July 27. She eventually gave big jobs to Yahoo veterans Scott Burke and Laurie Mann. Burke would become the senior vice president for ad technology and display advertising. Mann would head search and search monetization.

Finally, Mayer turned to the most important hire she had to make: chief operating officer.

Though Marissa Mayer was a longtime veteran of the Internet industry, she had close to zero experience in Google's advertising business. She had focused almost entirely on product development, leaving the monetization of those products to others. Even when Google's sales executives sometimes invited Mayer to meet with their clients, Mayer would often decline.

Mayer knew that among the most important things she had to do in her early days at Yahoo was hire a COO who could run the business side of the company for her. It was a hire she could not screw up.

Mayer would have been perfectly happy to work with Levinsohn. But because he wanted to be a CEO and because she had been rudely late to her first meeting with him, that option was out.

Next, Mayer considered another Yahoo veteran: Rich Riley, the executive who, years before, had successfully signed a multibillion-dollar deal to outsource Yahoo search to Google, only to see the pact fall apart under the withering gaze of the DOJ.

Mayer told Riley she was looking for someone who could fix Yahoo's advertising business while she worked on its products. She said Filo told her she needed to find a place for Riley on her team. Maybe COO was the spot?

The problem was, Riley lived in New York, and he wasn't willing to move for the job. She offered Riley the Americas region. He passed, and soon exited Yahoo.

On his way out, he told Mayer she should consider Levinsohn's big hire, Michael Barrett, for the COO job. But Barrett and Mayer did not jibe personally. He found her habitual lateness unbearably rude (Riley just thought it was odd). Besides, he saw a path where Yahoo would pay him a huge severance to leave the company and not work for a while. He became scarce around Yahoo headquarters and eventually got the package he was looking for.

Mayer never actually found a COO.

He found her.

Part of Scott Thompson's big overhaul plan for Yahoo, code-named Project Alpha, was to outsource much of Yahoo's ad sales efforts to Google. Thompson put Jim Heckman and Ross Levinsohn in charge of negotiations. At Google, their counterparts were chief revenue officer Nikesh Arora and his lieutenant, Henrique De Castro.

After meetings with Google, Heckman and Levinsohn would laugh about how horribly Arora treated De Castro in front of them. Arora would sharply critique De Castro's ideas and even call him an idiot.

So it was no surprise to Levinsohn when De Castro eventually started nosing around about a job at Yahoo. Thompson interviewed De Castro for Head of Sales. Thompson ended up going with Rich Riley. Then Thompson had his scandal. Levinsohn demoted Riley and hired Michael Barrett. Then came Mayer, and the whole thing was back in flux.

After Mayer's hire, De Castro sent her an email asking if she was available for a dinner. She said she was. He suggested a place Mayer thought would be far too conspicuous. She countered with a quieter place and even arranged to get a table in the back.

At dinner, De Castro deeply impressed Mayer. Because of the long negotiations with Heckman and Levinsohn, he actually knew Yahoo's business incredibly well and had specific ideas for how to get it growing again. De Castro was able to talk credibly about what he had learned at Google, where he reported directly to Arora. De Castro was handsome, stylish, and extremely confident in his bearing. He indicated the obvious, that he wanted to be Mayer's COO. He could take care of revenue while she did what she did best.

At the end of the meal, Mayer said to De Castro: Is this a serious thing? If you're saying this to me, it had better be serious, because if you are, I'm going to move forward with it.

De Castro soon let Mayer know he was very serious. Then, for several mornings in a row, they would exchange emails going back and forth over his terms. Every night, Mayer would finish her day thinking she had made an offer that De Castro would have to accept. Then she would wake up and find a long email with a list of more conditions.

At last, she reached her limit and said: Henrique, this is going to have to be good enough. He said, Okay, let's move forward.

Mayer went to the Yahoo board and asked for final approval of her offer.

The directors were floored by the amount of money De Castro would get. It was somewhere around $100 million, depending on the value of Yahoo stock. De Castro had been very good at negotiating over email. He had done especially well convincing Mayer that Yahoo needed to make up for any stock compensation he would lose out on because he was leaving Google.

Mayer presented an energetic case for the hire. She said that without De Castro, Yahoo would lose out on revenue equating to many multiples of his compensation. With him, Yahoo would make back many multiples. Basically, he paid for himself, she argued.

The board's compensation committee, staffed by Sue James, Peter Liguori, Maynard Webb, and Harry Wilson, approved the offer. De Castro accepted it.

One thing bothered some of the board directors: Yahoo hadn't asked De Castro for any references. He hadn't really been vetted at all.

Directors David Kenny and Michael Wolf said they knew De Castro, and that he had a good reputation.

Still, others pressed: Wouldn't it be a good idea to call some people who actually worked with him at Google?

Mayer said Yahoo should not. De Castro was a very important person at Google, and vetting him would tip off people there that he was looking for another job.

It was too risky.

Marissa Mayer spent a lot of time in URLs, Yahoo's big-windowed cafeteria, during her first week on the job. Over and over, employees would come up to her and tell her what Yahoo needed to do to turn around.

At the end of almost every conversation, each employee would say: You know, no one from management ever talks to us.

Mayer would answer: Well, it's hard for there ever to feel like there's enough communication in a big company. I'll try to do better, but it's hard.

Then, during Mayer's second week, she went to her corporate communications team and said she was ready to meet with the company now.

She asked, "When's the weekly meeting?"

The answer was: "What weekly meeting?"

Mayer said, "When the executives talk to the employees and take their questions."

For its entire history, Google had a meeting like that every week, called TGIF.

The communications executive asked Mayer if she meant Yahoo's quarterly all-hands. Mayer said no, that's not what she meant. The quarterly review was for the CFO to go over financials. "I'm talking about the thing where we talk about how the company's going, our strategy, feedback, questions."

The comms exec said: Right, that's the quarterly all-hands.

Mayer said: "You mean the executives only talk to the company once a quarter?"

"Yeah."

Mayer thought: Oh, so the employees say that nobody ever talks to them because nobody ever talks to them.

Mayer fixed that on July 27, 2012—ten days after she joined the company. That Friday at four p.m., she stood in the middle of a temporary stage at the far end of URLs. In front of her sat rows and rows of nearly two thousand Yahoo employees in folding chairs. Along the rows there were columns, and on those columns, TV monitors showing Mayer onstage.

She began to speak.

"Hey, good afternoon. I'm Marissa Mayer and I'm very, very happy and excited and honored to be here. I want to thank all of you for coming out to our inaugural FYI meeting."

Then Mayer explained what an FYI meeting was and how it would work.

FYI meetings were weekly meetings that all full-time employees were expected to attend. They began with a confidentiality reminder. Then Mayer would read the names of new employees. She would go over Yahoo anniversaries of five, ten, and fifteen years. She would list "wins of the week." Mayer or other executives would go into "deep dives" on new products, technologies, and business lines. Finally, Mayer and the rest of her direct reports would come onstage together and take questions from the employees in the audience and from a forum on Yahoo's internal network.

The idea, Mayer explained, was to make Yahoo a more open and transparent company, where employees would be able to communicate with executives and hold them accountable. The idea was also to take away an excuse from Yahoo employees: They would now have access to all the information they needed to succeed.

Mayer hoped, too, that the FYIs would slow down leaks to the press, especially to Kara Swisher. To encourage employees to turn in leakers, Mayer told the story of how once, when she was at Google, she turned in a colleague of hers.

"Back at my former gig, we had one meeting and it was a meeting [where] we were deciding whether or not to buy DoubleClick or build it in-house, and it was a really schizophrenic meeting and, as often happened, Larry and Sergey, our two founders, kind of started going back and forth debating and had a lot of different, very insightful but very abstract perspectives, to say the least.

"And when we walked out the meeting, my friend who I walked out with, as we walked down to lunch, said 'Gosh, that meeting was so awkward. It was like watching your parents fight.'

"Then, eighteen months later, I was reading the *Wall Street Journal* about Google having bought DoubleClick, and as I was reading it, it said an anonymous source said the meeting was so awkward it was like watching your parents fight, and I knew something. I knew that my friend was the source. And at that time I got up from my desk and I walked down to the security office and I told them what I knew.

"Did I know something? Maybe I did, maybe I didn't, right? Maybe what it came down to is maybe somebody else heard that phrase and thought it was so funny that they should repeat it.

"But the fact that it was the exact same wording meant something. So if you know something...please come forward. It's in all of our best interest."

By early 2013, FYIs were global, with offices in places like Munich, Milan, and Madrid hosting "weekly viewing parties" to catch up.

Instituting FYIs was only Mayer's first step toward increasing transparency at Yahoo. She set up town hall meetings with the company's vice presidents, of which there were a few hundred. In October, Mayer began showing the rest of the company the same slides she showed during her quarterly meetings with the board. In early 2013, she began allowing employees to vote on "highlights" and "lowlights" she should review with the directors at those meetings. In November, she added a page called Product Central to Yahoo's internal network. There, Yahoo employees could look up the launch calendars and road maps for all Yahoo products. Mayer would also post the notes from her product reviews to the network. Mayer published her phone number on the network and told everyone in the company to call her anytime they needed her right away.

In February 2013, Mayer directed corporate development/HR boss Jackie Reses to explain how and why she was acquiring start-ups for Yahoo and to ask the employees for suggestions.

Mayer became an active participant in a forum called "dev random" for Yahoo developers on the company's internal network, Backyard. She set up an email address, awful@yahoo-inc.com, that employees could use to send anything they believed was "yawful," which she defined as things Yahoo had done "that don't feel right. Things that you just look at and you say, 'If I was a user of Yahoo, I wouldn't want that experience.'"

When, at an FYI in January 2013, an employee asked why Yahoo was allowing Microsoft to test new search algorithms during the middle of a weekday, thereby considerably slowing down Yahoo search for users, Mayer said she appreciated the drama of bringing up the issue at FYI, but "When this kind of thing happens, please email me, please email any [level two executive] you know, please keep ringing the bell until someone answers, because these are the types of things where every day and every minute and every search that takes longer than a second counts."

The push for transparency and accountability was part of Mayer's plan to change Yahoo's company culture.

At Google, Mayer had been obsessed not so much with how Google's products looked as with the pathway users took through them—the user experience. When she arrived at Yahoo, she decided to take a similar designer's perspective to the job of managing approximately fifteen thousand people. She wanted to redesign the user experience of being a Yahoo employee.

Eventually, Mayer wanted Yahoo to feel like Google had for her that late night in July 1999 when Georges Harik jumped up off his exercise ball and said life would never get better. She wanted Yahoo to be a place where people could manage themselves well because they had access to a broad array of information and because they felt empowered and independent and driven to succeed.

But first, she just wanted to make it suck less to be a Yahoo employee—to make it the "absolute best place to work."

During that first FYI, Mayer announced that, starting July 30, Yahoos would get free breakfast, lunch, and dinner at the office.

She ripped out the access control turnstiles Scott Thompson installed in building D. "The turnstiles which were apparently there to protect me," she told employees. "I don't need them. I'm pretty tough."

At an FYI on September 14, 2012, Mayer extended the meeting to announce, in the mode of Steve Jobs, "one more thing."

"When I got here, I got all kinds of emails from people all over the company saying 'Why are we all still issued BlackBerrys?' And I said, 'That's a good question,' because I think that a lot of Yahoo's future does lie in the world of mobile, and we've already seen that.

"So we want to make sure that everyone here can experience smartphones. So we are saying goodbye to the BlackBerry. We're not issuing any more BlackBerrys," Mayer said.

She clicked forward to the next slide on the big screen behind her. Then, over growing cheers and applause from the two thousand Yahoos before her, she said, "We are announcing smartphones/smart fun, which means everyone here gets their choice of an Apple iPhone 5, the Samsung Galaxy S3, the HTC One X, or HTC Evo 4G LTE, depending on which carrier you use, as well as a Windows 8 phone, the Nokia Lumia 920."

The new smartphones came in November, and in December came 4,500 new MacBook Airs.

Mayer set up an organization called PB&J, which stood for "Process, Bureaucracy, and Jams." PB&J's sole purpose was to take complaints from Yahoo employees and address them. Mayer put a fellow ex-Googler named Patricia Moll Kriese in charge of PB&J and gave her a staff of twenty people to get things done.

Things got done. Ever since the Terry Semel years, when Yahoo moved into its big new headquarters in Sunnyvale, there had been a problem with some of the bathroom stalls. The partitions between stalls didn't go all the way to the wall. Sitting on the toilet, you could see your neighbor doing the same. For years, people hung toilet paper to try to fill the gaps. It was demoralizing. But then Mayer came to Yahoo and set up PB&J, and one day, the old partitions were gone and new ones were in. Over the first few months, there were literally thousands of little fixes like that around the company that improved the daily lives of Yahoos. Morale lifted. The culture improved.

At the end of February 2013, Jackie Reses sent a memo to everyone in the company, asking employees to cease working from home.

It read:

Yahoos,

Over the past few months, we have introduced a number of great benefits and tools to make us more productive, efficient and fun. With the introduction of initiatives like FYI, Goals and PB&J, we want everyone to participate in our culture and contribute to the positive momentum. From Sunnyvale to Santa Monica, Bangalore to Beijing—I think we can all feel the energy and buzz in our offices.

To become the absolute best place to work, communication and collaboration will be important, so we need to be working side-by-side. That is why it is critical that we are all present in our offices. Some of the best decisions and insights come from hallway and cafeteria discussions, meeting new people, and impromptu team meetings. Speed and quality are often sacrificed when we work from home. We need to be one Yahoo, and that starts with physically being together.

Beginning in June, we're asking all employees with work-from-home arrangements to work in Yahoo offices. If this impacts you, your management has already been in touch with next steps. And, for the rest of us who occasionally have to stay home for the cable guy, please use your best judgment in the spirit of collaboration. Being a Yahoo isn't just about your day-to-day job, it is about the interactions and experiences that are only possible in our offices.

Thanks to all of you, we've already made remarkable progress as a company—and the best is yet to come.

Jackie

The work-from-home ban was polarizing at Yahoo, but much more so in the media outside the company. Professional women seemed particularly upset. Working from home was a convenient way for many of them to continue their careers after giving birth. Why was Mayer taking such a stance against it?

Inside Yahoo, the ban affected 164 people in a 15,000-person company. Many of them worked nowhere near a Yahoo office. Yahoo told them they either had to move to be near enough to an office so they could come in every day, or they would have to find a new job. Yahoo said it would pay for their moving expenses and even give them raises to cover increases in cost of living from rural to urban and suburban areas.

Aside from those 164, the ban was most annoying for Yahoo's managers, who, in the months leading up to its enforcement, had to go over every remote employee's circumstances and review whether an exception could be made. It was particularly tough for Yahoo's media organization, which had writers all over the country.

Most employees thought the ban was smart, if tough and poorly messaged.

Still, Mayer felt she had to address the controversy at an FYI on March 1, 2013. She said exceptions would be made. She argued that Yahoo was in the middle of an "all-hands-on-deck moment." At that meeting, she allowed that if an employee's kid was sick, or they needed to wait for the cable guy or a package, working from home for a day or so was fine. The point was to get rid of long-term, awkward arrangements—like instances where whole teams worked in the office for managers who were remote.

Then she launched into a story about how much hard work it took for Steve Jobs to turn Apple around. She said it was going to be just as hard—or harder—to save Yahoo. It was an anti-whining, toughen-up message.

"I'm really excited about what we're all here to do," she said. "But we all do need to be really honest that it's going to be hard work."

At the end of the quarter, Yahoo employees voted to make Mayer's messaging of the ban one of the "lowlights" she had to present to the board.

That frustrated Mayer a bit. She wasn't sure what else she could have done other than saying that she thought it was the right thing for Yahoo right now and that it had nothing to do with the world outside the company. Also, she believed the ban was desperately needed. One of those 164 employees was busted for not working for a couple weeks in a row. He lived in Tahoe. When he was called out on it, he said: Haven't you seen the snow report? The snow has been awesome!

But Mayer had worked hard to make Yahoo a more open and transparent place, where she was made accountable for her decisions. She put the lowlight in her board slides and explained herself to the directors.

That was how Yahoo's culture worked now.

All of the Yahoo CEOs prior to 2012 believed their job was to conceive of a strategy, or perhaps just approve one thought up by their lieutenants, and then make sure the right people in the company were empowered to execute the plan.

That was not how Marissa Mayer did things. Not since the days of Jeff Mallett had Yahoo seen such an energetic, command-and-control leader as Marissa Mayer. She was the CEO who, on her first day on the job, set up her computer for coding.

Before Mayer went to a single high-level financial, business, or strategic review, she started going to product reviews and running them like she did at Google for thirteen years.

The first Daily Habit to get her full attention was Yahoo Mail. It was arguably Yahoo's most important product. For one, it was massive. In August 2012, thirty billion emails a day passed through Yahoo Mail—350,000 every second. Six hundred million images traveled through the system every day, 250 times more than the number of photos uploaded to Yahoo's Flickr. For another, Yahoo Mail was a product that fed traffic to other products in the Yahoo network of sites. Some people inside Yahoo believed the only reason anyone ever came to the Yahoo home page was because they thought that was the only way to get to Yahoo Mail. There were stats to back the theory up: Four out of every ten people who visited the Yahoo home page next clicked on a link to Yahoo Mail.

When Mayer arrived at Yahoo in July, the GM for Yahoo Mail, Vivek Sharma, told her that Ross Levinsohn had approved a plan to relaunch Mail on four platforms: the web, iOS, Android, and Windows 8. The project was code-named Quattro Launch. The target release date was the first quarter of 2013, or the last quarter of 2012 if possible. Mayer told him to have the relaunch done by December.

This was an ambitious deadline. The last time Yahoo rebuilt webmail, in 2010, the project took eighteen months. Now Mayer was asking Sharma to accomplish as much in a third the time.

Actually, she was asking him to do more. In 2010, Yahoo didn't truly build mail apps for Android and iOS. It just made it so that the Yahoo Mail website was usable on smaller, mobile screens. This time, Yahoo was going to make apps, and Mayer was going to be picky about their quality.

When Sharma showed Mayer the first, early version of the iPhone app, she stopped him and said, "Vivek, why is it so jerky?"

The answer was that it was a "hybrid app." It wasn't fully built out on iOS. The app was basically a web browser that loaded the mobile version of the Yahoo Mail website. Hybrid apps weren't as slick or usable as apps built specifically for Android or iOS, but they were much easier and faster to make. Mayer scuttled those plans and commanded Sharma to start working on "native" apps for both Android and iOS.

Whereas Yahoo CEOs in prior years would have given Sharma his orders and then backed off, Mayer dove in.

By September, she was meeting with his team three times a week in a conference room that started to look more like a design studio. Windows ran down one side of the room. On the other side, projectors hung from the ceiling, rendering screens on the wall. Between the projections stood twenty or thirty huge pieces of foam core pinned up with a collection of ideas about what a new Yahoo Mail could look like.

Whereas CEOs in the past would have, on their rare visits with product teams, restricted their questioning to only the most senior leaders in the room, Mayer would grill everyone present on the finest details of the product's look and user experience.

It was a level of energized scrutiny none of the people on the Mail team were used to. It was bracing and intimidating.

Some of the people in the room were growing frustrated with the pace, but eventually, as the weeks wore on, others began contributing. Mayer learned whom to trust. Those trusted people began to grow in confidence, and they started to contribute even more.

One day during the fall of 2012, a member of the team named Dave McDowell found himself sitting next to Mayer in one of the thrice-weekly reviews. After minimal pleasantries, Mayer asked a question about the topic that was most important to her: the path users would take as they used the product, their "clickstream."

McDowell had an answer for her. Then she had another question. He had an answer. Another question.

For forty-five minutes, Mayer and McDowell were eyeball to eyeball as she grilled him on clickstream data. From across the room, where Vivek Sharma sat, it felt like McDowell was getting hit by a fire hose.

But in the weeks after that long test, Mayer's relationship with McDowell visibly changed. He had passed a test.

Once the Yahoos learned to operate on Mayer's level of intensity, the meetings became more interactive and warmer. The atmosphere lightened. Jokes started to fly around.

This was Mayer in her ultimate element, the tough professor leading a seminar on advanced product design.

She was pushing the pace as she had those late nights working on problems for Philosophy 160A. She was teaching, as she had three thousand Stanford undergraduates. She was creating, as she had those pompom routines twenty-five years before. She was using data to empathize with hundreds of millions of people all at once, as she had learned to do at Google.

By November, the Yahoo Mail team was working nights and weekends, racing to finish by the insane early-December deadline.

Finally, the Mail team finished its work at the end of November.

But then Yahoo learned another lesson about what making products would be like with Marissa Mayer as CEO.

One day before the new Yahoo Mail was set to launch, Mayer called a meeting with CMO Kathy Savitt, Sharma, and the entire product and engineering leadership team—about ten people in total. They met in Phish Food.

Everyone settled in; Mayer dropped a bombshell. For months, it had been decided that the new Yahoo Mail's colors would be blue and gray. The thought was that users were going to be looking at Yahoo Mail on their phones all day long, so it was best to choose the most subtly contrasting colors possible.

Mayer wanted to change the colors entirely—from blue and gray to purple and yellow.

Sharma's body language shifted immediately. He looked deflated. He was going to have to tell his people the news.

Changing the color of a product like Yahoo Mail was not easy. Some unlucky group of people were going to have to go and manually change the color in literally thousands of places—all while working under a deadline.

Sharma's team got the changes done, but there was fallout from Mayer's decision. The lead Yahoo Mail designer quit and went to Google. The lead engineer left and founded a startup. Sharma himself quit for a job at Disney.

Others had a different perspective. Their view was that Mayer refused to launch a product that she didn't think was finished. A product's color may seem superficial, but Mayer was obsessed with data, and the data shows it is not. At Yahoo's scale, if you can change a color a little bit and affect the performance by a factor of 0.01 percent, that translates into millions of dollars.

In this view, when Mayer forced already burned-out people to work even harder at the very last minute to make sure a product went out as good as it could be, she set a marker for the new era of Yahoo.

Shortly after a new version of Yahoo Mail came out in early December, so did a new version of Flickr, Yahoo's photo-sharing social network. Then came a new Yahoo home page. Then Mayer's Yahoo overhauled all three products again—all within a year, even as it launched new apps like Yahoo Weather and Yahoo News Digest.

Mayer spent as much time with each product as she had with Mail, pushing the teams at breakneck speed. In the three quarters prior to Mayer's arrival, the team working on a new home page created and tested five different new looks. In Mayer's first two months, Yahoo prototyped thirty-seven variations.

The speed was a direct result of Marissa Mayer having several attributes that her predecessors lacked.

Unlike Terry Semel or Carol Bartz, Mayer knew how the products worked and knew enough about the technology that powered them that she didn't need to be brought up to speed over and over just to make one decision in a series of hundreds. She was a native user and builder of web apps.

One time, a product manager came into a review ready to go over all the bugs that his team had fixed since their last meeting with Mayer. As he began to speak, Mayer cut him off.

She said, "Yeah, I use this product all the time. I know the bug. I saw that you fixed it. It's good that you're getting these results. Let's move on."

The next time the product manager met with Mayer, he prepared only one slide, because he knew he could start with the hard stuff. The meeting was forty-five minutes shorter than it would have been under Bartz.

Yahoo under Mayer was fast also because she brought a certain clear-eyed toughness to the place that anti-corporate Yahoo had often lacked. In September 2012, Mayer told four SVPs and two VPs that she wanted them to get a new version of search out by December. When they protested, she said, "Tell me if you can do it. Otherwise, I'll find people who can."

Finally, Yahoo got faster under Mayer because Mayer was willing to fail.

At her second FYI, Mayer said, "I have all kinds of different theories around failure.

"The first and foremost is: It's totally okay to fail; you just need to fail fast, right? So the idea is: Go ahead, take a chance, fail. Maybe you succeed, maybe you fail, but if you don't end up overinvesting a ton of time in it, you can move on and do the next thing.

"Hopefully that will be successful."

In the middle of all this, Marissa Mayer had a kid.

One minute she was in a Saturday-afternoon meeting with executives from Microsoft, insisting that they update Yahoo's search features as often as Bing's—the next, she was in labor.

On September 30, 2012, Mayer gave birth to a baby boy. For weeks, Mayer and her husband, investor Zachary Bogue, called their child only "BBBB," for "Big Baby Boy Bogue." They would eventually name him Macallister.

Mayer's pregnancy had been a fascination of the media, women around the world, and plenty of her Yahoo coworkers.

When news of the pregnancy broke, TechCrunch pointed out that Mayer was the first-ever pregnant CEO of a Fortune 500 company.

The *Los Angeles Times* wondered, "Will Marissa Mayer's high-profile pregnancy help end pregnancy discrimination?"

In *Forbes*, Amy Keyishian wrote a story headlined, "The Pregnant CEO: Should You Hate Marissa Mayer?"

She wrote, "I'm not going to pretend I could do what Marissa Mayer is doing."

How would Mayer handle having a newborn while trying to turn around a multibillion-dollar public company?

Some of her closest advisors found out on October 21, 2012. It was the Sunday before Yahoo's third-quarter earnings call—the first on which Mayer would actually speak to analysts. Mayer was determined not to take any missteps on the call. So she got on the phone with a bunch of advisors and rehearsed over and over. The call lasted ten hours. Most everyone on the call contributed with helpful suggestions and relevant data. One fairly vocal participant did not. All that came out of his mouth was nonsense.

This was Macallister Bogue, audible to everyone on the conference call for much of the ten hours.

Mayer made the baby-raising part look easy. She took just a two-week maternity leave. Then, two months after giving birth, Mayer told the audience at a conference on women in business: "The baby's been way easier than everyone made it out to be."

What Mayer didn't say was that, thanks to her incredible wealth and power at Yahoo, she had a lot of help with Macallister. At home, she had a full-time staff. At Yahoo, she knocked down a wall in her office and set up a nursery so that Macallister—and his nanny—could come to the office with her every day.

The comments upset a lot of women. Lisa Belkin of *The Huffington Post* wrote an open letter to Mayer, in which she said, "Dear Marissa Mayer...Putting 'baby' and 'easy' in the same sentence turns you into one of those mothers we don't like very much."

Other women were upset about the brevity of Mayer's maternity leave. They thought it set a bad example. In *Slate*, Allison Benedikt wrote, "Mayer didn't just have foot surgery. She birthed a tiny human being. A baby who needs stuff."

Rachel Wilner of the *San Jose Mercury News* wrote that she was "aching" for Mayer.

"I know plenty of accomplished moms," she wrote. "Not one thought her months-long maternity leave was too lengthy. All were still discombobulated, sleep-deprived and confused—if not clinically depressed—when they went back to work."

The whole topic gained a lot of extra heat because, in the past, Mayer said she was not a feminist and that she was "blind to gender."

Mayer addressed the issue at an FYI on April 19, 2013, when Macallister was about six months old.

She stood onstage and, on the giant screen behind her, there was a picture of her boy.

"So this is a picture of my son," she said. "Many of you ask me about him from time to time. He's very, very cute. He just got his first two teeth and he's starting to crawl this week."

She clicked to the next picture.

"And this is what he looks like when he's surprised."

Behind, a giant picture of a very surprised-looking baby.

Mayer said she had a surprise for Yahoo.

"I think that because I had only been here for twelve weeks, it wasn't really possible for me to take a maternity leave, which I was okay with. But one of the things that has bothered me is that I think internal-to-Yahoo and external-to-Yahoo people have gotten the impression that I don't think that maternity leave or paternity leave is important.

"Today, we're happy to announce new and improved maternity and paternity benefits here at Yahoo."

Mayer said that all new parents—surrogates, adopted, or whatever—would now get eight weeks of paid leave, and that new moms would get sixteen.

URLs broke into applause.

———

Marissa Mayer talked to her mother on the phone every single day.

It was during one of these phone calls, sometime around the end of 2012, that Mayer's mom said, "You know, Marissa, you just seem really, really confident. It seems like you have a really hard job. Should you really be this confident?"

Mayer said, "Well, thanks, Mom."

Mayer went to bed thinking about what her mom said. It was true, she did feel confident about the job she was doing at Yahoo. It was also true that it was a really hard job and that Mayer had huge goals. Should she feel so good about how she was doing? The next morning, Mayer woke up and decided the answer was yes. The fact was, things were going really well at Yahoo.

At a board meeting on December 10, 2012, Mayer had walked into Phish Food and had the pleasure of telling the directors the stock was up 24 percent since the last time she saw them.

Then she bragged to them about how, when she came to Yahoo in July and said she wanted to do FYIs on Friday, everyone said that was foolish, because people at Yahoo were gone from the office for the weekend by Thursday afternoon.

And it was true; for Mayer's first couple weeks, it had been easy to get a parking spot on Friday. It had been easy to find a chair in URLs at lunch.

But now, Mayer told the directors, things were different.

That very Friday, she had an off-campus meeting at ten thirty and was unable to get to the office till later. Guess what. When she got to the Yahoo parking garage, she couldn't find a space on the first or second floors. Not one. Then, when she came down for lunch at one fifteen, URLs was still jammed. She and her chief of staff, Andrew Schulte, had nowhere to sit.

She told the board: When I got here, you couldn't have an effective meeting on Friday afternoon at this place. But now, morale is riding high. Everyone is working really hard. We're achieving great things and great launches.

In January 2013, Mayer traveled to Switzerland for the World Economic Forum. She was in huge demand and had meetings from seven a.m. to midnight every day. Finally, she sat down for a televised keynote interview. Outside, the line of people trying to get into the audience for the interview went around the block.

In March, Yahoo stock was up to $22 per share and rising. Mayer added a tool to Yahoo's internal network that allowed employees to see how much their stock compensation would be worth in the future.

Around that time, Mayer started announcing "boomerangs" at FYIs—people who had left Yahoo during the dark ages before her arrival and were now coming back. Résumés from the wider world were also flooding Yahoo. In May 2013, ten thousand came in a single week.

At a board meeting in April, Mayer admitted that Yahoo under her watch had not yet identified a "breakthrough product." But she said she wasn't worried about it. She still had lots of ideas. She reminded the board that Steve Jobs didn't come up with the iPod until five years into his return at Apple. And even then, the iPod didn't catch on for a while.

Brimming with all this confidence about the state of Yahoo in the spring and summer of 2013, Mayer took two huge steps to make the place more fully hers.

She outbid Facebook by a couple hundred million dollars to buy a company called Tumblr for $1.1 billion. Tumblr was two things:

a suite of tools that made blogging really easy, and a social network built around a Facebook News Feed–like stream called the Dashboard. Tumblr had a lot of younger, mobile users. It fit perfectly into Mayer's vision for Yahoo. She had money lying around thanks to Tim Morse's deal with Alibaba. It was, in the end, an easy call.

A harder call: Mayer decided that spring that she didn't want the board directors most responsible for hiring her—Dan Loeb, Harry Wilson, and Michael Wolf—on the Yahoo board anymore.

Loeb in particular took his board director's duty to hold the CEO accountable very seriously. When he got on the board in May 2012, he couldn't believe how little detail about the business was included in the board books. Loeb wanted to be fully briefed. He wanted to give advice. He wanted to feel that he was being heard.

It didn't seem like Mayer appreciated the effort. She didn't seem to listen.

In board meetings and outside of them, Loeb and his analyst, Tim Lash, would pressure Mayer to do things with Yahoo that she was not comfortable doing.

Right from the start, Loeb and Lash clashed with Mayer over when Yahoo should start using cash from its Alibaba sale to buy Yahoo stock. Loeb and Lash begged her to start buying back stock right away, before the rest of the market caught on to Eric Jackson's sum-of-the-parts valuation and Yahoo's stock price started to rise, making the transition more expensive for the company. But Mayer waited and the Third Point people grew frustrated.

At one point, Loeb suggested that Mayer use some of Yahoo's cash to hedge its exposure to the Japanese yen. It was something he would do with Third Point's cash. Mayer didn't particularly understand. She told Loeb she wasn't comfortable with green-lighting those sorts of transactions. She said such decisions were up to her CFO, Ken Goldman. Loeb went around Mayer and talked to Goldman himself. The billionaire hedge fund manager managed to convince the CFO his trade would help protect Yahoo capital. Yahoo went ahead with the trade and made hundreds of millions of dollars.

Most of all, Loeb and Mayer disagreed over cost cuts. Loeb believed that Yahoo needed to fire as many as ten thousand people. Mayer thought she could cut some costs and manage out Yahoo's poor performers through QPRs, the quarterly performance review employee ratings system. They never agreed on the issue.

Finally, on July 19, 2013—almost exactly a year after Marissa Mayer took the job at Yahoo—Mayer went to Loeb and told him that Yahoo would buy forty million of his Yahoo shares at $29 per share. That was more than twice what he paid for them in the summer of 2011.

The deal would reduce Third Point's stake in Yahoo below 2 percent, forcing Wolf, Wilson, and Loeb to step down from the board, per Third Point's settlement from the year prior.

Loeb was surprised. He thought he and his two guys were Mayer's best board members—the only ones really pushing her.

But a deal like that? Loeb wasn't going to say no. He knew when to say "I win."

Third Point walked away from the Yahoo trade with $1 billion in profits.

Marissa Mayer was on her own.

12

Time to Shine?

On Friday, July 12, 2013, a Yahoo employee stood up at FYI and said, "Hi, Marissa. My name is Margaret Mish and I work in Advertising Data for Scott Burke.

"I understand you have a one-year anniversary coming up this week, and so we at Yahoo were trying to figure out how could we possibly get some sort of messaging to you—"

Mish saw that Mayer was going to say something.

"I hate to be superprecise but I think I'm five days short, but okay," said Mayer, with a smile.

"We knew that—" said Mish.

"Plus or minus 2 percent," said Mayer, interrupting again, still smiling.

Some people in URLs laughed.

"So we had a brainstorming a couple of months ago," said Mish. "We put out a secret portal that said 'Thank you, Marissa.' It went global, all around Yahoo, for everyone to thank you for your one-year anniversary."

Mish handed Mayer a coffee-table book. Its title was *Thank You, Marissa!* Onstage, Mayer flipped through it. On the first few pages it listed her executive staff and "First Year Facts"—including that Yahoo stock was up 60.6 percent since Mayer joined and that Yahoo had launched twenty products in the interim. Then, over another few hundred pages, the book had short messages from Yahoo employees.

From a Sunnyvale employee: "Thank you for raising the bar!"

From a Taipei employee: "Happy Birthday Marissa and all the best for the future."

The first note in the book was from David Filo.

It read: "Having experienced all the highs and lows of the past eighteen years, this past year easily ranks as one of the most impressive in our history. Looking back to just a year ago, few would have imagined that the energy, passion and excitement that exists today could be possible.

"Your focus on the people, building a great culture and creating products that we're all proud of have inspired Yahoos everywhere to transform Yahoo into a completely different company. Can't wait to see what the next year brings. Yahoo!"

As Mayer read that note, Filo, ordinarily so shy, stood onstage and gave a message just like his note in the book. Then he said that he had a gift for Mayer—a new email address, reclaimed from a Yahoo user who had abandoned it: Marissa@yahoo.com.

It was a moment that felt like many others during the spring and summer of 2013 at Yahoo. In May, Apple gave Yahoo a design award for its Yahoo Weather app. That same month, ten thousand job applications came in one week. *Vogue* editor Anna Wintour asked to send a reporter and a photographer to Yahoo for a story. In late July, Yahoo had a company picnic with a zip line, a man-made pond with paddle boats, go-karts, and a Build-A-Bear workshop. On top of it all, Mayer bought out most of Third Point's stake in Yahoo, thereby essentially taking control of the board. At times, the whole summer felt like one long victory parade.

After Filo finished his speech, the FYI returned to its normal proceedings, concluding with the usual question-and-answer session.

Mayer was disappointed to see that someone had a question about QPRs, the employee-rating system she had implemented to lower costs and boost talent.

The person said that the way Mayer's stack-ranking system was set up, employees were getting punished for having "achieves" ratings.

"It's very demotivating," the employee said.

Mayer couldn't help feeling a little exasperated. She'd been through this before. Why weren't the employees getting it?

The truth is, even as Mayer accepted the giant *Thank You, Marissa!* book and the praise of David Filo, Yahoo faced a growing number of difficulties.

Some were the result of Yahoo's immense inherent challenges. Search market share was still shrinking. So were display advertising revenues. Yahoo's revamped products were barely maintaining or adding to the previous year's traffic levels, and everyone was calling it a huge victory because the desktop Internet was shrinking so fast.

But beyond the secular trends, some of Yahoo's issues in the summer of 2013 were Marissa Mayer's fault. It was becoming clear she had made a number of bad hires and possibly promoted the wrong people. She was also being asked to do a nontechnical job she had no talent for.

Yahoo stock was still up—way up—from when Mayer joined. But that had nothing to do with her. Revenues still weren't growing. In fact, they were shrinking—down 5.5 percent year-over-year in the second quarter.

Everyone knew: The stock price was the result of air cover from Alibaba.

Everyone also knew: There was only one year of it left.

⸻

Marissa Mayer and the Yahoo board should have vetted Henrique De Castro.

Even a casual pass would have revealed he had a very poor reputation among the people who worked on the advertising side of Google's business.

There was widespread talk among the company's current and former advertising executives that De Castro had one of the lowest ratings of anyone on Google's senior leadership team.

One gossipy story going around Google was that De Castro so refused to ever be held accountable for his own mistakes that when he once spilled milk on a kitchen floor at Google, he decided not to clean it. In one Google executive's telling, De Castro just walked out and left it for someone else.

De Castro wears skinny ties and suits. At Google, many of De Castro's colleagues openly referred to him as "the Most Interesting Man in the World," after the older, bearded, accented man in the Dos Equis beer commercials. They gave him this nickname not just for his thick Portuguese accent, but also because De Castro carried himself with an exaggerated swagger. In broken English, De Castro would make grand, awkwardly worded pronouncements about business and life.

There was a Twitter account, called @HdCYouKnowMe, that Googlers believed featured real-life quotes from De Castro.

One: "To incentivize the sales force, you need to hit them with the carrot."

Another: "Product is like snakes...slippery—we need someone with a big hammer."

Ultimately, De Castro's reputation at Google was as someone who was very brainy and had big ideas—but who was a little lost operationally and had very weak relationship-building skills. Certainly, no one who worked closely with him would have done what Mayer did: make him responsible for Yahoo's revenues, sales force, and media business.

The Yahoo sales team found out how ill equipped De Castro was for sales in January 2013. Over three days at the end of the month, Yahoo held its annual sales conference in Las Vegas. The point of the conference was for Yahoo's thousand or so salespeople to meet the people who build the Yahoo products they were selling to Madison Avenue. It was also De Castro's big speaking debut in front of a sales group he was supposed to be leading.

But instead of rousing the crowd, De Castro sapped its energy with a long, pedantic talk.

After, Yahoo's various sales VPs were stunned. This was the guy Mayer had chosen over Michael Barrett? Why hadn't she been able to hang on to Ross Levinsohn?

One sales VP walked up to Vivek Sharma, who had given a presentation on Mail, and begged him to come on the road to meet clients so De Castro wouldn't have to come.

The VP needn't have worried. De Castro was allergic to meeting with ad agency buyers. He found them fratty and unsophisticated. He avoided them.

Greg Coleman, the former Yahoo sales boss who had been good at working with clients, was now one himself. He was president of a firm called Criteo, which spent upwards of $30 million per year on Yahoo ads.

Over the winter and spring of 2012–13, Coleman was extremely irritated with how hard it was for him to get a meeting with De Castro.

Finally, he sent him a hot email. The subject: "WTF." The

contents: "Dude, I'm spending $30 million a year with you. You're my friend. I can't meet with you?"

De Castro finally responded to Coleman.

Jon Suarez-Davis, the senior vice president of media at Kellogg's, another huge ad buyer, likewise felt ignored by De Castro. Unlike Coleman, he never got through. So Suarez-Davis spent Kellogg's money elsewhere.

De Castro's plan for growing Yahoo revenues was through user-generated content, like what's available on YouTube, Instagram, or Twitter.

De Castro believed that Yahoo could quickly grow revenues again if it owned a product like YouTube, where the users contributed all the video content. The content would be low quality, but De Castro believed Yahoo could easily make up for that with technology that was able to target the right ads to the right consumers based on their demographics, their Internet browsing history, and the time of day.

In December 2012, De Castro reshuffled the Yahoo sales force so that it would sell more ads against user-generated content instead of against the "premium" content made by Yahoo's writers and video producers. The problem was: Yahoo didn't have enough user-generated content for the reorganization to be useful. Meanwhile, traditional sales suffered.

The closest De Castro came to seeing his vision come together was when, in the spring of 2013, Yahoo almost bought Dailymotion, a YouTube clone. Dailymotion had tons of videos that De Castro believed he could monetize right away, to begin growing Yahoo revenues. But Dailymotion was a French company, and the French government didn't want it sold to an American company. The deal died.

At first, De Castro's new Yahoo colleagues were impressed with his big, needle-moving, creative ideas—much as Mayer had been over that first dinner. But as the months went by, sales struggled, and De Castro began to alienate himself from others with an aggressive and arrogant attitude his former Google colleagues would have recognized all too well.

Once, after one of his direct reports gave a presentation in front of De Castro and forty other executives, De Castro said, "I think your strategy's more of a fantasy. You make it up. You just make it up."

The direct report could tell that De Castro was trying to be funny and warm. It wasn't working.

The more junior executive left the room outraged, thinking: No, I didn't make it up. I actually worked my ass off on it with my head of business operations and finance for two and a half weeks. There's a time and a place to tease, and it's not when you're in front of a room full of forty executives.

De Castro's direct reports also hated how working for him felt like working for a consultant, not an operator. All he wanted to do was review strategy presentations, suggest revisions, and then review them again. Over and over.

To some of the veterans of Yahoo's advertising business, it often seemed like De Castro didn't know what he was talking about. The rate Yahoo is able to charge for its ads is almost always set by the wider online advertising market, which is priced through very liquid auctions held by third parties. So it was strange—and somewhat embarrassing for De Castro—when, in an early big review, he suggested the way to fix Yahoo's revenues was simply to charge more.

Worse than his style of management and salesmanship were De Castro's results. Revenues continued shrinking in the first quarter and again in the second and third quarters of 2013.

Mayer, who had no reason to notice De Castro's relationship with his direct reports or Yahoo's clients, did notice the poor performance. Yahoo's first-quarter revenues in 2013 were $1.14 billion, down from $1.22 billion the year before—and from $1.8 billion in 2008. In the late spring, she started getting more involved in the advertising side of Yahoo's business through emails, conference calls, and meetings. Often, she would publicly contradict positions held by De Castro.

Then, in June, all of Yahoo's top advertising and media executives traveled to France for the Cannes Lions festival. Cannes is a hugely important event in the world of advertising sales, because all the biggest brands and their agencies attend, hang out on yachts, and party. Mayer didn't go, leaving De Castro to be her delegate.

But then, while the festival was still going on, Mayer learned Yahoo's second-quarter numbers. They were bad: $1.13 billion versus $1.21 billion the year before, smaller even than the prior quarter. Second-quarter earnings rarely underperformed the first quarter at Yahoo. It had happened only twice in the prior ten years.

Mayer began holding daily revenue calls with all the executives still in France. She pulled them out of meetings with clients. It was a top priority. The calls would last an hour or two. The weird thing was, throughout these calls, Mayer did not address De Castro at all. She would speak directly to his lieutenants and act as though he did not exist.

Finally, De Castro stopped joining the calls. Mayer didn't seem to care or even notice.

De Castro's failures with display ad sales would have been easier to take if Yahoo's search business was doing better.

When Mayer came into Yahoo, she believed one easy way she could get its revenues growing again would be to improve the company's search market share. It had shrunk considerably since Carol

Bartz signed a deal with Microsoft in July 2009—from 19.3 percent to 13 percent when Mayer joined in July 2012.

The deal with Microsoft meant that Yahoo had no control over the algorithms that crawled the web and ordered search results. The deal allowed Yahoo to innovate only on the user interface of its search results pages. Mayer was fine with that.

For a number of reasons, including that Microsoft wasn't doing a good job selling Yahoo search ads at high prices, Mayer would have preferred Yahoo to control its search business entirely. But if Yahoo was going to control only the front end or the back end, Mayer was glad it was the front end.

She still believed that Larry Page had made a mistake giving control over Google search to Amit Singhal instead of to her. She believed that the back-end technology powering search engines was no longer a market differentiator in 2012. What mattered was her specialty: the user interface.

She told Yahoo employees that during an FYI in August 2012.

"I would say—as someone who's spent a lot of time thinking about crawling, indexing, ranking, speed, [and] user experience— the crawling, indexing, ranking, serving it fast? That part of it is becoming much more of a commodity across the industry. All of the innovations and all of the exciting things that you're going to see in search are going to happen in the feature and the user-experience layer."

In September 2012, Mayer made a bold prediction. "I don't see a reason why our search share should fall below 15 percent, which is where it roughly is today," she told employees at an FYI. "I also don't see a reason why it can't climb back up to the 20 percent that we had, by making some of the simple and obvious improvements to the user interface and the features that are being offered."

Some of the "simple and obvious improvements" Mayer believed Yahoo could make were: improving its multimedia search results, like Google had with Universal Search; displaying results as users typed in their queries, like Google did with Google Instant; and displaying information alongside links, like Google did with its Knowledge Graph.

Over the next year, Yahoo implemented most of those UI changes.

But Yahoo's search market share did not improve, and by the summer of 2013—just a year before Alibaba's air cover lifted—it was actually down to less than 12 percent.

———

Another nasty surprise for Mayer came in late April 2013. For weeks, Yahoo media boss Mickie Rosen and head of video Erin McPherson tried to convince Mayer that she absolutely had to come to their big event in New York at the end of that month.

It was Yahoo's "NewFront"—an event where, like TV networks did during their "upfronts," Yahoo would show off its video programming for the year ahead to a large audience of ad agency buyers.

Mayer took a little persuading. She was busy working on fixing Yahoo products like Mail and Flickr. It wasn't clear she knew what an upfront was. Finally, though, she agreed to come.

But on April 29, when Mayer showed up to the Best Buy Theater near Times Square, Rosen and McPherson wondered if they had made a mistake asking her to come.

This was a glitzy event. Rosen was in a cocktail dress. McPherson wore a tight black dress and high heels. Mayer, who would usually don a designer dress for any occasion that might call for it, looked totally out of place. She was dressed modestly in black slacks, a black top, and a purple-and-white cardigan. Her look was office casual.

Then the show kicked off and things got worse. Upfronts and

NewFronts are supposed to be funny and fast-paced. But Mayer went out onstage and read corporate speak from a prompter—putting the audience halfway to sleep.

Fortunately for the attendant ad buyers, Rosen and McPherson had booked enough talent to wake everyone up again.

Ed Helms, from *The Office* and *The Hangover*, and actor John Stamos, from *Full House*, went onstage and got laughs. Professional wrestler Big Show from the WWE showed up. The folk rock band the Lumineers played.

It was the rarest of events: Marissa Mayer had been caught unprepared.

When Mayer joined Yahoo, Rosen explained to her that Yahoo's media business was humongous, that it had three thousand employees and revenues of $1.5 billion. That was a big chunk of Yahoo's total annual revenues of roughly $5 billion. If Mayer was going to get Yahoo's revenues going before her twenty-four-month countdown clock was up, Yahoo's media business would have to play a big part. But it wasn't until that night that it seemed to sink in for Mayer how massive Yahoo's media business actually was—and how glamorous, too.

After the embarrassment of the NewFront, Mayer dug into Yahoo's media business during the summer and fall of 2013. She insisted that, going forward, any programming choices made by McPherson had to be approved by her first. She began sitting in on meetings, delaying their start because of her busy schedule.

In general, Mayer wanted Yahoo's media brands to move upmarket.

One morning while visiting New York, Mayer had breakfast with Anna Wintour, the bob-haired wearer of huge sunglasses who edits *Vogue*.

Mayer told Wintour she could use her help. Mayer asked her if there were any people Wintour could send to Yahoo. Maybe Yahoo could run some *Vogue* content?

"Marissa," said Wintour, "where would it go?"

Mayer told Wintour that Yahoo had a site for women, called Yahoo Shine.

Wintour leaned over the breakfast table and grabbed Mayer's arm. She said, "I know. I've seen it. It's dreadful."

Mayer could have brought up that Shine was actually very popular. Web metrics firm SimilarWeb reported that Shine saw nearly 75 million visits per month—about twenty times more than Vogue.com. She could have mentioned that Shine, as lowbrow as it might have appeared to someone like Wintour, brought in $45 million per year for Yahoo—less than *Vogue*'s print business for sure, but likely higher than its digital revenues.

But Mayer said neither of those things.

Instead, she felt like crawling under the table. Here was the queen of taste, telling her Yahoo's fashion site was awful.

Mayer was determined to reshape Yahoo's media brands into ones the Anna Wintours of the world would appreciate.

She began pushing for McPherson to follow Netflix's lead and commission full-length shows like *House of Cards* and *Orange Is the New Black*. McPherson explained to Mayer that those shows were extremely expensive to make, and that networks like Netflix and HBO could make them only because they generated their revenues through subscriptions—a much more predictable and less hit-dependent source of cash than Yahoo's advertising business. McPherson argued that Yahoo should do what Google was doing with YouTube and commission short-form video from startup production companies in Hollywood.

Over the summer, Mayer green-lighted a plan for Yahoo to hire one of her mother's favorite TV stars, someone who was surely

Wintour-approved: Katie Couric, the former anchor of CBS News and former cohost of the *Today* show.

In April 2013, Couric was hosting a failing daytime talk show. Yahoo invited her to interview Mayer onstage at an event for Yahoo clients in the Turks and Caicos. After, Couric told Mayer she wanted to do something big with Yahoo.

Couric had been working on and off with Yahoo since 2010, when Ross Levinsohn took her and her former producer Jeff Zucker out for lunch. Levinsohn thought Couric could do a daily show for Yahoo in which she would go over trending search queries. He wanted to pay her a couple million dollars and stick the video on Yahoo's front page.

That deal never came together, but in 2012, Couric did launch a video series on Yahoo called *Katie's Take*. She interviewed experts on topics such as health and parenting. Despite Couric's supposed star power, Yahoo users didn't click on the videos—no matter how Yahoo's editors positioned them on the page. Yahoo users preferred stories about celebrities.

Mayer ignored those metrics and, in mid-2013, made Couric Yahoo's "Global Anchor," giving her a deal worth $5 million per year.

Mayer's decision-making around media was very different than what many of her executives expected from her. They had heard stories about UI reviews where Mayer would test different shades of blue and pick one based on data. But when it came to media, Mayer seemed to make her decisions based on instincts—a deeply personal sense of what made for good content. She grew up sneaking into the living room to watch *Saturday Night Live* and could recite sketches during meetings—so Yahoo overpaid for the *SNL* archives. Mayer liked *Town & Country* better than Shine, so she started to starve Shine of budget, even though Shine was a commercial success and *Town & Country* content performed poorly on

Yahoo's home page. Even though actress Gwyneth Paltrow had a best-selling cookbook, Mayer thought it was a horrible idea to hire her to be a contributing editor for Yahoo Food. Why?

"She didn't even go to college!"

A few of Mayer's media executives believed that she did not understand Yahoo's middle-America, Walmart-esque brand—that it was always going to be something Anna Wintour did not like, but that was okay, because *Vogue*'s revenues were under $500 million and Yahoo's were more than $5 billion.

As summer 2013 turned into fall, Mayer phased De Castro out of Yahoo's media business. Mayer's push toward making Yahoo a more upmarket media brand was a departure from the user-generated content strategy Henrique De Castro had been pursuing since his arrival. De Castro was still Yahoo's COO, but a year after he was hired to run media and sales for Mayer, he was practically running neither.

Also during the fall, Ross Levinsohn protégée Mickie Rosen left the company. Despite Mayer's pleadings, so did Erin McPherson. McPherson left Yahoo to become chief content officer at Maker Studios, the kind of YouTube studio she thought Yahoo ought to have been courting.

With Rosen and McPherson gone and De Castro shoved aside, Mayer now had a chance to put someone in charge of media who shared her vision for Yahoo's brand. Mayer approached media industry veterans, including former NBCUniversal programming executives Lauren Zalaznick and Scott Sassa. None bit.

Soon, an executive already on Mayer's staff stepped forward for the job: CMO Kathy Savitt. Mayer made Savitt the de facto head of Yahoo's media business in fall 2013.

Kathy Savitt graduated from Cornell in 1985 and got a job making $12,500 per year at an ad agency. At thirty, she started her own marketing firm. Her clients were startups and companies in the middle of turnarounds. In 2000, she sold her company to IPG, the giant ad agency. She went to work for Amazon, where she ran marketing and communications. Next, she did the same for retailer American Eagle.

In 2009, Savitt started her second company, Lockerz. Savitt called Lockerz "the home page for Generation Z"—people aged thirteen to twenty. It was a website that gave away free stuff to visitors who watched videos or did other ad-supported activities on the site. The free stuff was nice. There were Apple gadgets and computers.

Giving away expensive toys proved to be an effective way to attract traffic, and Lockerz soon had huge numbers to brag about. In 2011, the company said it was getting 37 million unique visitors every month.

Savitt turned the big numbers into big investment from some very fancy venture capitalists, including Kleiner Perkins, the firm that backed Amazon.com and AOL. All told, $65 million went into Lockerz.

Lockerz quickly burned through all that cash and eventually sold for pennies on the dollar to a Chinese e-commerce company.

The reason: The 37 million people visiting Lockerz were not only members of Generation Z. They were also—perhaps mostly—Polish and Russian hackers gaming the system. That was not an audience marketers were willing to pay to reach, so Lockerz had little revenue coming in to help pay for an Amazon Web Services bill that totaled several hundred thousand dollars per month.

Compounding the problem, Savitt was not exactly a thrifty CEO. The gossip inside the company was that in 2010, Lockerz spent approximately $3 million to build an e-commerce platform that it could have licensed from an outside agency for somewhere between $25,000 and $50,000 per year.

Counting pennies was not Savitt's style. She liked to dream big.

Shortly before joining Yahoo, Savitt came up with a plan to get real web users finally to notice Lockerz. She told her executive staff: We should do a big runway show during New York Fashion Week and broadcast it live, and allow users to buy what the models are wearing right off Lockerz.

Someone pointed out it was a nice idea, but that it would probably cost at least $100,000 to make it work. The idea died.

Earlier in the history of Lockerz, when Savitt's startup still had money to burn, the idea might have come to life. Throughout her career, Savitt had loathed working with cynics. She valued optimists. When she became CEO of Lockerz, she was able to surround herself with them. They told her yes a lot.

Despite the failure of Lockerz, many of Savitt's former colleagues were thrilled for her when she got the big chief marketing officer job at Yahoo in 2012. People liked Savitt. They thought she was fun and personable. They also thought the job was perfect for her. The job of a CMO is to think big and spend big until the CFO says to stop. Her former colleagues were happy to hear she would have no real operational concerns to worry about.

The potential problem for Yahoo in the fall of 2013 was: While the CMO position was not an operational role, running Yahoo's media business was. And that's the job Mayer put Savitt into.

Now Yahoo's $1.5 billion media business was being run by two people with no experience in the field. There was Mayer, who had been hired specifically because she was a product-oriented CEO and not a media-oriented CEO like Ross Levinsohn. And there was Savitt, charming and effusive but prone to spending big and not getting results.

Mayer and Savitt came up with a plan.

For each vertical Yahoo was in—Food, Beauty, Travel, and Tech—it would launch new sites, built around Tumblr technology. They would be called "digital magazines."

To staff the magazines, Yahoo would hire big-name, expensive journalists—paying some of them hundreds of thousands of dollars, if that's what it took.

Savitt and Mayer hired *New York Times* gadget reviewer David Pogue to be the editor of Yahoo Tech, Page Six columnist Paula Froelich to edit Yahoo Travel, and makeup star Bobbi Brown to edit Yahoo Beauty.

And together, they plotted the shutdown of Yahoo Shine.

On May 1, 2013, Marissa Mayer ran into Jony Ive, the famous Apple designer, at an industry event.

Ive sidled up to Mayer and, in a confiding tone, told her, "I'm tormented by the Weather app, Marissa."

Yahoo had just released an app called Yahoo Weather. It drew from Yahoo's photo-sharing site, Flickr, to show users photos of their approximate location in weather conditions similar to the day ahead. So a snowy day in New York would feature a picture of Central Park covered in white.

"I'm so jealous," said Ive, in his British accent. "I don't get jealous."

Mayer replied, "Jony, if the Weather app made you jealous, we've got something up our sleeve on Flickr that's going to make you want to die."

"Oh, go to hell."

A month and a week later, Ive showed just how much he admired Yahoo Weather when, at Apple's annual developers conference, WWDC, the app won an Apple Design Award. It was a big deal. WWDC is well attended by executives from the entire consumer technology industry. Yahoo employees were universally thrilled by the news. But then, word started to spread about who had gone onstage at WWDC to accept the award for Yahoo: Adam Cahan.

Cahan was Yahoo's head of mobile, promoted into the job by Mayer at the suggestion of Yahoo director Michael Wolf in 2012.

When word got around Yahoo that Cahan had taken a bow over the Apple award, eyes rolled. People familiar with the story of how Yahoo Weather was made knew that Cahan actually had very little to do with its development. The idea for the app was born during a "Hack Day" in 2011. Hack Days, common at most Silicon Valley tech firms, were events where employees would break into small groups, brainstorm new product ideas, and, in one day, build rough prototypes to bring those ideas to life.

At Yahoo's Hack Day in 2011, three guys went onstage and showed off a prototype app that matched Flickr photos with weather data. One of the Hack Day judges saw the presentation and was floored by its possibilities. This was Kevin Doerr, a Yahoo executive then reporting to chief product officer Blake Irving. The prototype Weather app didn't end up winning the Hack Day competition, but Doerr told two of its creators, Marco Wirasinghe and Brian Chu, to quit their day jobs inside of Yahoo; they were working for him now. The pair resisted, but Doerr convinced them over lunch the next day.

Doerr and his team built a consumer-ready app for Android in eight months. The team didn't have very much access to weather data, so it focused on design flourishes. They figured out how to make the text and graphics showing weather data appear to slide over a Flickr photo, a design technique called parallax. When Irving saw the final product, he told Doerr to show it off at a big meeting with Yahoo ad buyers. Doerr and his team started working on an iOS version.

Then Mayer came into Yahoo in July 2012 and told Doerr and his team to keep going. The iOS app launched in mid-April 2013.

Everyone who knew anything about the behind-the-scenes story of the app believed that Doerr was the one who shepherded the product into existence, pulling people from their day jobs and convincing them their idea was a big one. Cahan was Doerr's boss, sure, but Cahan only oversaw the last bit of the product's development.

And yet, there was Cahan, onstage at WWDC, acting like it was all his idea. Meanwhile, Doerr didn't even find out Yahoo won the award until Mayer wrote a blog post about it.

This made people mad.

Mayer's plan to get Yahoo ready for when Alibaba's air cover expired in fall 2014 depended on the company building mobile apps users loved. That made Cahan one of the most important people in the company. But the fact was, by the summer of 2013, Cahan was regularly making talented people who worked for him angry—and some of them were leaving the company because of it.

Some of Cahan's behavior was straight from a Dilbert cartoon. Before product reviews with Mayer, he would come to the product team a half hour early and ask what everyone was going to say to her. Then, during the meeting with Mayer, he'd bring up their points as if they were his own.

Cahan was a screamer, too.

One day, Cahan was in a review with Mayer and three people from his team—a product manager and two of his staffers. After the meeting was over and Mayer left, Cahan and the remaining three began talking about scheduling. Cahan started getting upset. He asked the two junior people to leave him alone with the product manager. After they did, Cahan started shouting.

The product manager said, "I don't understand why you are screaming at me."

"You don't get it!" said Cahan. "These people are not working fast enough! They are not working hard enough!"

No one likes getting screamed at, so the product manager accelerated the project. Then, after the product launched, his team had to go back and fix a bunch of foundational tech issues caused by rushing.

In general, Cahan lacked interpersonal negotiation skills—the art of sandwiching a piece of criticism between two encouraging compliments.

People recognized that Cahan had every right to be rude and that Yahoo wasn't supposed to feel like kindergarten all the time. They even recognized that Yahoo needed someone compulsive and hard-driving to grow its mobile organization from less than a hundred people to more than five hundred in under twelve months.

But as much as people could admit that Cahan was effective in the big picture, it didn't mean they liked working for him. They started gossiping about him, telling stories about his brownnosing and sharing a salacious *New York* magazine story about how his first marriage fell apart.

Talented people from his organization started leaving Yahoo— including the real executive behind the app that made Jony Ive so jealous of Marissa Mayer, Kevin Doerr.

During the first year of her two-year grace period leading up to Alibaba's IPO, Mayer worked hard to improve the working life of the average Yahoo employee. She did this because she believed happy employees would be more productive and accountable. It was therefore odd that, as Mayer's first year expired, so many of the people who worked directly for her felt so miserable.

In communications with the vast majority of Yahoo employees, Mayer encouraged a healthy work-life balance. In an FYI on July 13, 2013, she talked about how important it was to find a personal working rhythm that avoided the buildup of resentment.

With her direct reports, Mayer was far more demanding.

Theoretically, Mayer understood that her lieutenants were

not able to operate on only four hours of sleep like she was, and that meant their working cadence would be a bit slower. In practice, when Mayer wanted something done, she wanted it done right away.

It would have been more tolerable if Mayer were an empathetic boss, armed with positive reinforcement.

She was not. While enthusiastic and emotive with big crowds, Mayer was still her shy self when it came to small group interactions. To her direct reports, it made her seem cold and closed off—unfeeling.

Most people, when presented with a product or idea they didn't like, would say, "I think we should reconsider that idea."

Mayer wouldn't even engage. She would let the person presenting the idea go on, but she would have a look of disgust on her face. Then she would say, "I think this is totally wrong. I think this is totally off," in the most cutting, unaware way.

People tried to come up with explanations for why Mayer was the way she was.

One of her direct reports was a great believer in the Myers-Briggs personality test. This person was convinced that, unlike most CEOs, Mayer was not an ENFP—an Extraverted iNtuitive Feeling Perceiving person—but an ISTJ: Introverted Sensing Thinking Judging. ENFPs are considered enthusiastic, friendly people who are able to inspire and motivate those closest to them. Sometimes, they gush over other people and flatter them insincerely. ISTJs, of which Mayer was believed to be one, are focused more on themselves. They are very literal. They believe in duty and never break rules. They work very long hours. They are not very aware of the feelings of others. They tend to thrive as accountants, optometrists, school principals, and judges.

Mayer's top lieutenants grew frustrated that she never seemed to listen to others. She appeared to believe she was always right.

Mayer would respect people who stood up to her and told her she was wrong, but she wouldn't change her mind. Because of that willfulness, because Mayer had so much trouble looking people in the eye, because of her genius with factual recall, and because she displayed certain types of tics—an eye flutter and that "nnn" laugh—her direct reports often whispered among themselves that perhaps she had Asperger's syndrome. One industry executive who is close to Mayer, and has a child with Asperger's, recognized in the CEO traits that child also possessed: her social difficulty, her shyness, her love of lecturing, and of course, her extreme talents.

Whatever its cause, Mayer's coldness was compounded by another two factors.

One was that she was a micromanager in the extreme. Throughout her first year, managers across the company would complain during FYIs that they had lost out on key hires because Yahoo's hiring process was too slow. The reason: For a time, Mayer insisted on personally approving every hire Yahoo made. At one executive meeting, Mayer spent as much time on Yahoo's parking policies as she did strategizing over the billions of dollars Yahoo would net from its final sale of Alibaba stock.

The other factor compounding Mayer's coldness was that she had the awful habit of being late, all the time.

Every Monday afternoon at 3:00 p.m. California time, Mayer's staff would gather for a three-hour meeting with the boss.

Mayer demanded all of her staff across the world join the call, so executives from New York, where it was 6:00 p.m., and Europe, where it was 11:00 p.m. or later, would dial in, too.

Inevitably, Mayer would show up at least forty-five minutes late. Some calls started so late that Yahoo's executives in Europe didn't hang up till after 3:00 a.m. their time.

Mayer had approximately two dozen people reporting to her during her first year at Yahoo. In theory, she was keeping up with each of them in a regularly scheduled weekly meeting. In practice, she would go weeks without talking to people because she was so busy.

For a while, each of those two dozen people thought that Mayer was just picking on them, individually. The people who had been at Yahoo before Mayer joined assumed that this meant she was going to fire them soon. The people Mayer had hired into the company, including HR boss Jackie Reses and CMO Kathy Savitt, were even more puzzled. Why had they been hired only to be ignored?

But then, during one of those long waiting periods after 3:00 p.m. on a Monday, a conversation unfurled that revealed all.

Making small talk, one executive said to another: "Did she cancel one of your one-on-ones again?"

A third jumped in: "Oh my God, she does that to you, too?"

It turned out that everyone in the room and on the call had been canceled on by Mayer, frequently.

Mayer was also constantly late to product reviews. The meeting would be scheduled for 2:00 p.m., and around 2:15 p.m., Mayer's assistant, Trish Crawley, would come out and say, "Really sorry. She's going to be late. We're not sure when she'll get here."

Then it would 3:00 p.m. and then 4:00 p.m., and then Crawley would come out and say the meeting was canceled.

The standard joke was that if you had a review with Mayer, you should expect not to know when it was going to be and that it would change at the last minute. It was annoying for people who worked in Sunnyvale. It was brutal for remote teams in India and Europe.

Sometimes the blowoffs angered people to their core.

When, in the fall of 2012, Mayer told the Yahoo Mail team that she wanted it to redo its colors at the very last minute, she told the executive in charge, Vivek Sharma, that she wanted to see early mock-ups the next morning. Sharma's team worked overnight. Mayer missed the meeting in the morning.

The coldness and the lateness were a brutal combination. It left the people who reported to Mayer feeling diminished.

Would the demoralization of Mayer's direct reports slow Yahoo down in its race to get into shape before Alibaba's IPO in September 2014? It seemed so when, in mid-2013, several Yahoo veterans, including global technical infrastructure boss David Dibble and Mickie Rosen, left the company. But most of the people taking their exit were pre-Mayer hires, and their departures were somewhat expected. The real danger was that word of Marissa Mayer's managerial style would get out and make it harder for her to hire talented executives. Joining a company in the middle of a turnaround was already daunting enough.

———

The honeymoon between Marissa Mayer and Yahoo's roughly fifteen thousand employees lasted about a year.

It began the day the HOPE posters went up all over Yahoo's walls. Then came the free food, phones, and computers. The euphoria peaked from December till May as new and revamped products launched to critical acclaim. It lasted through the Friday afternoon in July when Margaret Mish stood up and gave Mayer a *Thank You, Marissa!* coffee-table book. But, by fall 2013, less than a year till Alibaba's air cover would lift, the love affair between Mayer and Yahoo's rank and file was fading.

In part this was because the crown jewel of Mayer's revamped Daily Habits, the new Yahoo Mail, was suddenly going through a very public technical breakdown. After the Quattro launch in December 2012, Mayer and the Mail team decided to redo the product again in July 2013, this time more radically, and with design cues taken from the Yahoo Weather app. The project was code-named Postcard. Mayer pushed the team to move incredibly fast, and Postcard launched in October. It was an extreme acceleration from Yahoo's pre-Mayer pace. The Mail relaunch prior to Quattro, called Minty, had taken eighteen months. Quattro took six months. Postcard took three. The biggest catalyst for the speedup was Mayer's willingness to fail fast.

And, indeed, Postcard failed very fast. In the revamp, Yahoo removed lots of features from the product and changed it so that Mail's default background was a Flickr photo. Users hated it. So Mayer had the Mail team add the features back and make a flat purple the default background. It was disappointing for Mayer that the team had been wrong about what users wanted, but not a big deal. Mayer's whole product philosophy was to ship, see how people reacted, and adjust.

What *was* a big deal was that, starting in mid-October, the Postcard version of Yahoo Mail began to break down. In the rush, the underlying technology had not been properly tested. Then it was put under increased stress when features were added back in on the fly. Yahoo Mail started going down for days at a time for some users, many of whom were small business owners who depended on the service.

The worst part was, the outages kept happening. Throughout the fall, every time Yahoo thought it had a fix, Kara Swisher would report on another sweeping outage.

It was deeply embarrassing for Yahoo employees. They began demanding answers from Mayer at FYI.

Rank-and-file employees were becoming disenchanted with Mayer over other issues as well. There were reports that Yahoo was going to pay Katie Couric $6 million per year to be its Global Anchor. That seemed strange and out of touch—like a Terry Semel move, almost. Yahoo revenues weren't growing, either. Yahoo reported quarterly revenues of $1.14 billion on September 30, down from $1.20 billion during the third quarter the year before. Everyone inside the company was keenly aware how much Henrique De Castro was being paid to solve that problem—$60 million or more.

Meanwhile, inside Yahoo's product organization, there were murmurs that mobile boss Adam Cahan was such an unpleasant person to work for that the people behind Yahoo Weather had quit the company. With her Google pedigree, Marissa Mayer was supposed to have been some kind of search engine genius, and yet, Yahoo kept losing share in that market.

All of that was a sideshow, however, compared to the main source of angst and resentment for rank-and-file Yahoo employees that fall.

What they had begun to hate about the Marissa Mayer regime was her awful employee rating system—the QPRs.

In an effort to flush out some of Yahoo's poor performers and cut some costs in the process, Mayer had rolled a system where managers had to grade their employees on a fixed curve. Even on top-performing teams, someone always had to get a poor score. Poor and sometimes even average scores made it nearly impossible to transfer jobs, earn full bonuses, or get promotions. The system made employees feel like they were working against each other, not with each other.

The whole thing made Yahoo feel like a cutthroat, uncaring place.

In an FYI, someone asked Mayer if there could be an anonymous Q&A session, where people could ask honest questions about the system.

Mayer said yes. When the questions came in, they were extremely tough. They were not the kind Mayer hoped to read less than a year before she needed to have the company ready to show off after the Alibaba IPO.

We USED to work in an amazingly collaborative environment and feed off of and inspire one another. To ensure we retain our jobs QPR has left us with no other option but to shift how we work into an ultra competitive mindset instead of a collaborative one. Why would I help out my fellow designers, or other teams, or share an opportunity when I can just gather them up myself to ensure my job?

Originally Q3's QPR rating distribution asked for 5% OM [occasionally missed] and 5% Missed. At the last minute it was changed to 10% OM and 5% Missed because of "Marissa's decision." It created tremendous rework for the managers and frustration to the Talent Team who had to explain and apologize to various teams. Can we have more prudent thought on decisions from the very beginning?

How can you justify terminating employees with tangible and expert-level contributions to team and company goals simply because a year ago, when new to their teams, they received a low QPR rating without explanation or guidance to improve? These employees have since upped their ratings while increasing responsibilities and standing within their teams, becoming trusted, integral contributors, as well as examples of success, or so one would have thought. Direct management wasn't even consulted.

There have been quite a few times where we hear that it was changed by the SVP to meet the distribution or he felt based on past performances this is the right rating. First how would a SVP know whom to change and what a person did? Why is it that the manager is not even consulted on this one? Why waste 3–4 hours calibrating if somebody can change it without any reasoning, at least not communicating it.

I have seen good people getting pushed to occasionally misses to fit the curve. We need to either let all employees know that we are indeed doing bell curve fitting or don't force managers to fit the curve.

Why don't we simply lay off people rather than giving low QPR and terminating them? Some employees are destined to get a 'Sometime Misses' even though they don't deserve it. When these people will get negatively impacted, they won't just lose their jobs, they will lose their confidence, self esteem and reputation along with it.

It feels like we're headed in a precarious direction culturally. Fear, uncertainty, and doubt is tipping the scale in the wrong direction. What's the desired end-state, and how on/off course does e-staff think we are?

Finally, on Thursday, November 7, 2013, Mayer hosted a special company-wide meeting in URLs to go over the anonymous questions. She brought with her onstage a copy of her favorite children's book: *Bobbie Had a Nickel*. The point of reading it was to say how much she valued experiences and that she had loved her experience at Yahoo so far.

But when Mayer read the book onstage, none of the two thousand employees in the room got the point. Even if the employees had understood Mayer's message, they might have thought her meaning strange. Their questions were about *their* experiences, not hers.

The meeting only got worse after Mayer finished reading. She seemed hostile and defensive in her explanations for the QPR system. At one point, Mayer seemed to lie. She said that managers had never been told they had to grade their teams along a forced curve. Managers in the room boiled on the inside when they heard that. They had emails from their own bosses directly contradicting what Mayer had said.

As Mayer flopped onstage, it occurred to many of the people in URLs that perhaps she was not a CEO who could save Yahoo. There were merits to the QPR system: It held employees accountable; it flushed poor performers out of the company; it would help Yahoo cut costs. But the way Mayer was handling the problem was atrocious. Ten months till Alibaba would go public and investors would once again begin evaluating Yahoo stock based on the merits of Yahoo itself, morale inside the company was shriveling. Yahoo's performance wasn't much better. The company had no apps in Apple's top 100. Fourth-quarter revenues were coming in light, too. They would hit $1.27 billion, down from $1.34 billion during the same period the year prior.

The night after the anonymous Q&A, Marissa Mayer knew she hadn't done a very good job explaining herself that day. It had been painful. Rough. She doubted whether the point she was trying to make had come across when she read read *Bobbie Had a Nickel*. She realized how much she loved working at Yahoo, and she worried she was losing touch with all the employees who had so warmly embraced her when she joined.

How was she going to fix this?

13

Failing Fast

Along with her penthouse in the Four Seasons, Marissa Mayer and her family also kept a house in a leafy neighborhood in north Palo Alto. The neighborhood was not a long walk from Stanford, where Mayer used to rollerblade on the weekends when she worked at Google. Some people called the area Professorville. It looked like a classic American suburb, only there were more Teslas in the driveways than minivans.

Unlike the wealthy financiers around New York, who build bulky mansions in Greenwich, or the entertainment moguls near Los Angeles, who live in sliding-glass homes up in the hills, the tech elite of Silicon Valley spend their money trying to buy their way into Norman Rockwell paintings. They buy $5 million ranch homes with white picket fences, sidewalks out front, and small separate garages.

The really successful people from the industry, like Mayer, Google's Larry Page, and Facebook's Mark Zuckerberg, buy the homes around theirs, just to make sure the area stays nice.

Mayer loved the midwestern feel of Professorville, and she did as much as she could to contribute to it. She threw a big summer cookout every June for her birthday, and every October, Mayer would host a pumpkin-carving contest for her neighbors. Once, she turned a neighboring home she owned into a haunted house for kids. On Halloween, she and her husband always opened the door to all trick-or-treaters, giving out huge candy bars. Kids knew about it, and they would form a big line that lasted for hours. Mayer herself saw to every little ghoul.

None of Mayer's frolics compared to her Christmas party. It was always her most elaborate bash of the year.

In 2013, the theme was Christmas flannel—pj's recommended. Two hundred or so neighbors, friends, and colleagues came.

The first thing guests saw when they arrived at Mayer's house was real snow, all over her front lawn. This was unusual for Palo Alto, where the temperature hardly ever dips below forty degrees. Mayer had the snow shipped in.

Inside, there hung a big chandelier with Christmas ornament baubles dangling between the lights. Downstairs, Christmas movies played on a loop in a basement movie theater. In the theater's ceiling, little pinhole lights looked like stars. Occasionally, one would shoot across the room.

Out in the backyard, Mayer set up a series of fire pits, and around them, couches. There were s'mores kits for snacks.

And then, there in the yard was the best festive touch of all: an ice skating rink, nearly big enough for a regulation hockey game.

For when the ice in the rink needed smoothing over, Mayer had rented a mini Zamboni. After the party had been going for a while, it was time: The ice was chopped up from all the skating in circles. Another host might have asked one of the hired help to get on the Zamboni and do the job. Not Mayer.

Out from the house she came in flannel pajamas. She climbed on top of the mini Zamboni. She drove it onto the ice and started going back and forth.

It was a comical, cheerful scene, and another host might have laughed and waved at her guests as she rode the funny-looking Zamboni in her pj's. Not Mayer.

She was very serious. Sitting on top of the big machine, she concentrated on the ice beneath her. She wanted to smooth over every inch. She was going to get the job done herself and be excellent about it.

As 2013 turned into 2014, Marissa Mayer reflected on her first year and a half at Yahoo.

She had started with such great momentum. She fixed the culture. FYIs had added transparency. The free food and free phones improved morale. The work-from-home ban boosted productivity. Yahoo revamped its whole product lineup and even won an award from Apple. Mayer hired a team she was proud of. She bought Tumblr. She avoided layoffs. She booted Dan Loeb from her board. It felt like she would easily have the company in shape for renewed scrutiny after the Alibaba IPO in September 2014.

But then came difficulties. Morale started to hurt again thanks to the QPR mess. Henrique De Castro was failing to sell ads or do much of anything useful. There was no revenue growth. Despite her early bravado, search market share was shrinking quickly. Yahoo didn't have any new hit products. Mayer had been blindsided by the size and scale of Yahoo's media business. Yahoo Mail was breaking down.

After all her early success at Yahoo, Mayer had to admit that she was now dealing with failure.

But that was okay, Mayer thought.

Failure was good, she reminded herself.

Failure was good so long as you quickly recognized you were failing, corrected the problem, learned from it, and moved on to the next thing.

One thing Mayer didn't think needed correcting was her style of running Yahoo—micromanaging, bottlenecking, and dictatorial as some thought it was.

In the same way that Mayer was never going to be the person who let someone else jump on that Zamboni and smooth the ice at her Christmas party, she was never going to be a CEO who ran her company at a remove.

If anything, Mayer thought she needed to get even closer to the action. Time was running out. Alibaba's IPO was only nine months away.

Back at the office that winter, Mayer went to the conference room on the third floor of building A, where about twenty Mail engineers had been working on the outages for days straight. It was time to end the outages. When Mayer got there, the engineers were taken aback. Senior executives never came to meetings like this one.

There was such a contrast between the physical appearances of Mayer and the engineers. She was in a colorful, expensive cardigan with her hair and makeup done up. The engineers wore flip-flops and stunk from forty-eight straight hours of work. But Mayer didn't seem to notice. She told the team she knew from experience that what they were doing was extremely important and not easy. Then she said she was there to listen.

The engineers were upset and they let her know it. They said that the whole problem could have been avoided, but that Yahoo had pushed out a new version of Mail too fast. Yahoo had neglected core architectural issues. Mayer told the team that they were right, and that Yahoo was going to invest more in Mail.

A couple weeks later, Mayer promoted the product manager who had been in charge of the room that day. Her message to him was: I don't blame you for Mail's failures. We were moving fast. Let's keep moving fast.

Mayer moved out of her office and into a cubicle, a move from a high position to one down in the trenches, where Mayer could be a hands-on battlefield commander.

Next, Mayer corrected what she now recognized as her biggest mistake at Yahoo.

In early January, Henrique De Castro suddenly stopped going to all his regular meetings. He ceased hosting his regular conference calls with his staff. People were told that he was sick.

Then, on January 15, Yahoo announced that De Castro would be leaving the company effective the next day. In a filing with the SEC, Yahoo said De Castro would receive the severance compensation guaranteed to him in his employment offer letter.

After examining the offer letter, executive compensation firm Equilar estimated that De Castro's total compensation for fifteen months of work was $109 million.

Mayer explained why she fired De Castro at an FYI on January 31, 2014.

"At the end of the day, we discovered that Henrique was not a fit. That's not a decision we arrived at lightly.

"When you have someone who's not a fit, there's two things you can do: You can change their job to try and make them more successful or you can have them leave.

"In the case of Henrique, we tried both. We made many changes in the months leading up to the decision and ultimately those changes also failed to get us to a successful place, so we had to ultimately part ways. It wasn't something that I think was foreseeable. It also was not something that we arrived at easily."

Mayer tried to explain that De Castro's compensation was only so high because, in order to poach him from Google, Yahoo had to "make whole" the money he was leaving on the table by quitting Google. But that did not make the astounding figure any less real to Yahoo employees. It also revealed how desperate Mayer had been to get De Castro into the company—how desperately wrong, in the end.

Mayer took a lot of heat over the firing—inside Yahoo, with her board, and from the press.

But she knew she'd done the brave, right thing by firing him and taking the criticism. Hiring De Castro without properly vetting him had been a mistake—a big one. But Mayer spotted it quickly and moved on. She failed fast.

———

Firing De Castro left Mayer without a chief revenue officer and an official head of Yahoo's media's business. She solved one problem by formally moving Kathy Savitt to become head of Yahoo's media and editorial functions. Mayer fully trusted Savitt's sense of what made for a good, high-end media brand, and the two went forward with their Digital Magazines strategy.

Mayer solved the chief revenue officer problem in two ways. She hired a new head of Americas, Ned Brody, and she took on more work for herself. If growing Yahoo's revenues meant Mayer had to meet with a thousand Yahoo ad buyers in 2014, so be it. She already had a jam-packed schedule. What harm could a few more meetings do?

Mayer remained pleased with one of her earliest decisions as Yahoo CEO: putting Adam Cahan in charge of Yahoo's growing army of mobile developers. Yahoo now had 400 million people visiting its properties from mobile devices each month, up from 150 million in November 2012. Mayer gave Cahan a lot of credit for the growth. She believed he had stepped into a crisis and delivered. When Mayer gave a keynote at the Consumer Electronics Show in January, Cahan was one of only a few executives she brought onstage.

In March 2014, Marissa Mayer announced that she would, in a few weeks, do another anonymous Q&A session with Yahoo employees.

Once again, employees wanted answers about Yahoo's quarterly performance review system.

Mayer decided to handle the questions and the meeting a little differently this time.

In mid-April, she went onstage in front of the purple curtain in URLs and told the many thousands of Yahoo employees watching her that they were lucky she was willing to take anonymous questions from employees and answer them in public. She said that all of her CEO peers thought it was nuts.

Then Mayer told the employees that the problem was not with her system but with the one-in-five Yahoo managers who did not understand how the system worked. They were damaging it for everyone else.

Mayer said that instead of going over questions one by one, she had a few slides to show on how her QPR system worked.

She began to lecture.

Marissa Mayer arrived at Yahoo like a superhero. There was no cape, but there was a purple carpet, rolled out beneath her.

If this was a superhero story, it would be clear by now that, despite a few setbacks, Mayer was going to save the day.

But this isn't a superhero story, and as Alibaba's September 2014 IPO approached, it was not clear Mayer would be able to save Yahoo.

The spring and summer of 2014 were rough for Mayer.

It all started well in late April, when Mayer hosted Yahoo's 2014 NewFront. This time, she was prepared. She wore a designer dress and gave a dynamic presentation. Every program shown off that day had been personally approved by Mayer.

But the Digital Magazine strategy was not working yet. In May, Yahoo Tech, edited by the expensive *Times* veteran David Pogue, had just nine million visitors—putting it in seventh place among competitors, far behind rivals like CNET and Gizmodo. Yahoo Tech would sometimes go weeks without running a single ad. Yahoo Food was twelfth in its market.

Katie Couric was unhappy. She had done several interviews with high-profile national figures, such as former secretary of defense Robert Gates. For some reason, Yahoo's users weren't gravitating toward the videos. Couric complained that Yahoo wasn't doing enough to feature her videos. She began planning to get back on TV somehow.

Yahoo's search market share continued to shrink. By the end of August 2014, it was hovering around 10 percent—half the 20 percent Mayer had once said would be easy to reach with some "simple and obvious improvements."

There was no revenue growth. Mayer's plan was to sell a new kind of advertising, in-stream ads in apps, and for her personally to build relationships with Yahoo's clients.

The problems were that the in-stream ad business was growing but still tiny, and Mayer was having a hard time building relationships.

It didn't help that Mayer had an awful year at Cannes Lions, the huge agency festival in June.

Mayer gave a keynote address to a roomful of ad buyers. Mayer hit them with a hard sell on Yahoo's advertising capabilities. She read a boring, corporate presentation from a teleprompter. It was entirely the wrong note for Cannes, where executives are supposed to tell stories and share their vision. The agency executives went to Twitter and complained while Mayer was still onstage.

Also during the trip, Mayer sat for an interview with Sir Martin Sorrell, the CEO of gigantic agency conglomerate WPP. It was an off-the-record interview. With no cameras around, Sorrell nuked Mayer. He asked her why she didn't respond to client emails. She said she responded to every one. Sorrell said that Mayer hadn't responded to his. He said Facebook's COO, Sheryl Sandberg, always responded and that he took Mayer's cold shoulder personally.

One of Mayer's last events at Cannes was a dinner with executives from ad agency IPG. It was scheduled for eight thirty—an inconvenient time for IPG CEO Michael Roth, but he shuffled his calendar so he could make it. Mayer didn't show until ten. Roth, furious, was leaving as she came in. She told him she had fallen asleep.

Throughout the summer, Mayer was in touch with executive recruiters, trying to find an ad sales leader who could replace De Castro. So far, the search was slow going. It was as though Mayer had gotten a reputation for being someone who was hard to work for.

In May, Apple gave Yahoo another design award—this time for Yahoo News Digest. That was nice, but then Apple dealt Yahoo a serious blow. It changed the default weather app that came with every iPhone from one featuring Yahoo's brand to one with branding by the Weather Channel. In a snap, Apple shrank Yahoo's reach on mobile by tens of millions of monthly visitors.

At an FYI in June, Adam Cahan said that when he heard the news, he "dug in with the team" responsible for Yahoo's relationship with Apple and found himself "honestly a little bit disappointed with Yahoo." It sounded like he was shirking responsibility—once again doing his best to look good for Mayer, even it meant throwing his team under the bus.

———

One thing Marissa Mayer had been able to do during her first two years at Yahoo was rebuild the company's relationship with Jack Ma, Joe Tsai, and Alibaba. The secret had been putting Jackie Reses on Alibaba's board as Yahoo's representative. Reses recognized the value of Alibaba to Yahoo and treated Ma and Tsai with deference.

Because of that, as the summer of 2014 ended and Alibaba's IPO loomed, Mayer faced a choice.

She could (a) go forward with the plan originally outlined in Tim Morse's deal and sell half Yahoo's remaining stake in Alibaba during the IPO. This would be a signal that Mayer thought Yahoo stock would grow faster if she took the $12 billion or so in proceeds and invested it in her plans for the Yahoo core.

Or, she could (b) sell less Alibaba stock during Alibaba's IPO. This would be a signal that Mayer believed Yahoo stock would grow faster if it were tied less to the strength of Yahoo's core and more to the growth of Alibaba. It would be a signal that she did not believe Yahoo was ready to come out from under the air cover provided to her by Alibaba during her first two years.

Mayer chose option B.

On July 15, Yahoo reported dismal second quarter earnings. Revenues were $1.04 billion. That was down 3 percent from the same quarter in 2013. Revenues had not been so small in almost ten years—not since September 2004, when Yahoo had yet to profit fully from Terry Semel's Project Godfather.

During a call to go over the earnings, Mayer announced that when Alibaba had its IPO in September, Yahoo would sell only 140 million shares, versus the 261.5 million shares stipulated in the original deal. She would use half the proceeds to buy back Yahoo shares.

Essentially, Mayer chose to punt—to buy herself more time.

She knew the fight to save Yahoo wasn't over yet.

How Do You Solve a Problem Like Marissa?

In late May 2014, Dan Loeb walked into the Westin Copley Place Hotel in Boston to attend the JP Morgan investor conference. In the hotel's cavernous America Ballroom, executives in suits sat at big round tables waiting for the show to start. At one of those tables, Loeb spotted someone he recognized.

It was Jerry Yang. Next to him sat Joe Tsai and Jack Ma.

Loeb hadn't talked to Yang since that one phone call back in the fall of 2011—the one where Roy Bostock hung up on him.

Never shy, Loeb walked over to Yang. They said hello and Loeb even sat down. So much time had passed that it wasn't uncomfortable.

Finally, Yang thanked Loeb for saving Yahoo—for making Marissa Mayer CEO.

Loeb took pride in the moment, just as he took pride when David Filo told him the same thing months before.

Loeb deserved the moment. If this story has a clear winner, it's him. Loeb earned his own investors $1 billion with his Yahoo trade. He left Yahoo better than he found it, if only because he removed Roy Bostock from the chairmanship.

But had Yahoo been saved?

By the time Alibaba held its IPO in mid-September 2014, the answer was still no.

Revenues were still not growing. They were shrinking. As a result, the market continued to value Yahoo's core business at less than zero dollars.

More than ever, the question was: Would Marissa Mayer be able to save Yahoo?

———

Maybe no person, no matter how talented, can save Yahoo.

If Marissa Mayer were to lose the fight to save Yahoo, she would not be the first extraordinary person to do so.

Jeff Mallett sold a company in his twenties. Then he took a popular website and turned it into an international, $128 billion company with billions of dollars in revenues and thousands of employees.

Terry Semel could have worked anywhere in Hollywood after he left Warner Bros. in July 1999. They put his handprints in the sidewalk in front of Mann's Chinese Theatre. He went to Yahoo and turned a $5 billion company into a $50 billion one.

Jerry Yang imagined Yahoo into existence. At a time when Yahoo had only $4 billion in cash, he bet $1 billion of it on an unheard-of Chinese startup called Alibaba.

Sue Decker was the top analyst in her industry and among the most trusted CFOs on Wall Street. Warren Buffett goes to her for advice.

Carol Bartz grew up on a farm in Wisconsin without a father or a mother. She ran a major sales organization in a chauvinistic, male-dominated world. Then she took over a flailing Autodesk, kicked out its beloved founder, and turned the place into a fast-growing machine.

All of them were heralded hires into Yahoo. All of them failed.

So might Mayer.

Ultimately, Yahoo suffers from the fact that the reason it ever succeeded in the first place was because it solved a global problem that lasted for only a moment. The early Internet was hard to use, and Yahoo made it easier. Yahoo was the Internet. Then the Internet was flooded with capital and infinite solutions for infinite problems, and the need for Yahoo faded. The company hasn't found its purpose since—the thing it can do that no one else can.

In 2012, Mayer tried to take Yahoo "back to the future" and recapture that original purpose. She believed the early mobile Internet was hard to use and that Yahoo could make it easier.

But Apple solved that problem with the iPhone, and Google solved it with Android. Just as Yahoo.com was a place users would go to learn about new products and services on the Internet in the late 1990s, smartphones and app stores were already the places mobile users went for solutions in 2012. That had been the case since 2008, if not before.

What's more, another reason the Yahoo of the 1990s was able to build so many web products that users wanted, and build them so much faster than its competition, was that Jeff Mallett figured out the trick of click-finding—following the path users took through Yahoo's directory. Yahoo no longer has that kind of huge advantage over its competition.

Yahoo also suffers from Marissa Mayer's inability to recruit talented executives. In fact, too often people get big jobs at Yahoo not because Mayer sought them out but because they sought out Mayer and sold themselves to her. Three of her most important hires—CFO Ken Goldman, COO Henrique De Castro, and CMO Kathy Savitt—came into Yahoo this way. Mayer didn't seek out Adam Cahan, either. Michael Wolf pushed him at her.

Because Mayer has a hard time hiring, she is working two jobs the Yahoo board expressly did not hire her to do. Brought on because Marc Andreessen told Michael Wolf that Yahoo needed a "products" CEO who could manufacture innovation, Mayer is now doing the work of a media executive—a job that would likely have been better done by Ross Levinsohn. Likewise, Mayer has been unable or unwilling to find a replacement for Henrique De Castro. After spending a decade all but ignoring the advertising business at Google, Yahoo's fate now depends on her understanding of the industry. Because she has to do both of those jobs, Mayer is unable to do what she does best: develop products.

Mayer's inability to recruit may have something to do with her difficulty connecting with peers. Worth $600 million and now one of the most famous business executives in the world, Mayer still remains painfully shy with all but a few trusted, junior confidants.

Even so, there is still hope for Marissa Mayer's Yahoo. Tumblr is growing. Though its user base is smaller than Facebook's or Twitter's, the users Tumblr has spend more time with the product.

Yahoo has more mobile users than before—430 million, as of the first quarter of 2014, up 30 percent from the year before. If advertisers adopted Yahoo's in-stream ads, it's possible that growth could outpace the rate at which Yahoo's desktop revenues are shrinking.

If Mayer can make it to the end of Yahoo's search deal with Microsoft, she will be able to sign a new one, with Google. That could add $1 billion in revenue almost immediately.

When Alibaba finally held its IPO on September 19, it sold $22 billion worth of stock in a single day. Almost $10 billion of that money went straight into Yahoo's bank account. Mayer pledged to give half the money to shareholders. Perhaps she will use the rest of the money to buy companies that could help Yahoo grow its revenues again.

Mayer's Yahoo might still launch a product as revolutionary as the iPod, which didn't come out until Steve Jobs's fifth year back at

Apple. She is still the CEO with a computer set up for coding. Her technical chops and supreme confidence allow her to make very fast decisions. If she can keep learning from her failures, Yahoo could iterate its way into some kind of megahit.

Perhaps when Filo and Yang thanked Loeb for saving Yahoo, they weren't thanking him for saving its financial prospects. Perhaps what they meant was that Mayer had brought a vitality to the place not seen in perhaps more than a decade—not since Jeff Mallett got off that plane in Zurich.

On August 1, 2014, Mayer announced that after two years of FYI meetings, URLs was finally going to be refurbished to host them every week. A new, permanent stage was coming. So was a giant screen. New TVs would be hung from the columns spaced throughout the cafeteria.

Then Mayer told a story.

This week, I've been doing town halls with a lot of the different groups and it's been fun, because a lot of the questions that people have been asking have brought up all kinds of memories.

For me, as you guys know, it's been about two years here at Yahoo, and one of the things that's come up in the past few weeks in these all-hands is: How do we feel about mobile; have we come far enough, et cetera?

It's been funny for me to think about.

I tell the story about when I first arrived at Yahoo. I was told that we had an award-winning mobile application that we should bet the entire company on, and it was called Yahoo Axis. In truth, it was a great and beautiful application.

But as I learned more about it, I found out it has twelve thousand downloads or thereabout. We had another beautiful application called TimeTraveler, which was really tremendous. It had seven hundred users.

Today we have nearly six hundred people in the company working on mobile. We have multiple applications that have millions of people who use them every day. We have a few applications that have tens of millions. We have three applications in Apple's top 100—Yahoo Mail, Yahoo, and Tumblr are all in the top 100. We used to have none.

But the real moral of the story is that one of the things I learned about Yahoo that I think is completely amazing is: When we put our mind to something, we can just unequivocally accomplish it.

We just decided to be good in mobile—to put enough people on it, hire the right people, build the right products. And we did it.

When we as a company put our mind to something, we do it and we do it really, really fast.

On July 22, 2014, Eric Jackson was in Sea Island, Georgia, on vacation with his family when he got an email from a major Yahoo shareholder.

The day before, Jackson had published a *Forbes* column arguing that Yahoo would be an attractive acquisition target for Apple, Facebook, Microsoft, or Google. Jackson's argument was once again based on a sum-of-the-parts valuation.

His point was: Even though Yahoo's market cap was now $33 billion—nearly double what it was when Marissa Mayer took over the company two years before—if you subtracted the value of Yahoo's Asian assets, the market was actually giving Yahoo a negative $4 billion valuation. Anyone who bought Yahoo now would essentially be getting the core business for free.

Over a series of emails back and forth, the Yahoo shareholder told Jackson he was on the right track, but that he should consider another, better outcome for Yahoo: an acquisition by Masayoshi Son's Softbank or Alibaba itself. Unlike any other acquirers, if either one of those companies bought Yahoo, they would be able to sell most of Yahoo's Asian assets without having to pay taxes—because they would just be reacquiring their own stock at a loss. The major shareholder suggested to Jackson that the tax savings would be somewhere around $18 billion.

Jackson saw the logic. But he wanted to know one thing. If Softbank or Alibaba bought Yahoo, it would probably mean the end of the Marissa Mayer era. At the very least, it would mean that Yahoo's current shareholders would not profit from any future growth her work brought about.

Jackson asked: Had the major shareholder lost so much faith in her after just two years?

The major shareholder said yes, he had.

The shareholder said that, according to his research, Mayer had lost all goodwill among advertisers, Yahoo employees, and Yahoo investors.

The major shareholder pointed to Yahoo's most recent quarterly results. After two years at Yahoo, Mayer reported on July 15 that Yahoo revenues shrank during the second quarter of 2014. She had wasted the two years of air cover that had been provided by Alibaba's massive growth and the subsequent inflation of Yahoo stock. She spent $1.3 billion acquiring thirty-six companies and none of them had gotten revenues growing again. She had failed to cut headcount. She spent $109 million on Henrique De Castro. She was trying to lead the sales force by herself now and was obviously failing.

The major shareholder seemed to want Jackson's help educating other Yahoo shareholders on the tax savings an Alibaba or Softbank acquisition would bring. He wanted Jackson to articulate that such a deal would be a far better bet than a wager on Mayer's ability to get Yahoo growing again.

Ultimately, the shareholder wanted Jackson's help getting Marissa Mayer fired—if that's what it took to get Yahoo to "unlock" the value of its Asian assets in a tax-efficient manner through a sale to Softbank or Alibaba.

Eric Jackson considered the shareholder's arguments.

Jackson had been an early, vocal supporter of Marissa Mayer. When Kara Swisher and another tech-industry commentator, Sarah Lacy, criticized Mayer's plans in September 2012, Jackson wrote a column for *Forbes* headlined, "Give 'Superman' a Chance at Yahoo."

But after two years of no revenue growth, Jackson had seen enough. He was particularly disturbed to hear that, after the Alibaba IPO in the early fall, Mayer planned to use only half of Yahoo's multibillion-dollar proceeds on shareholder buybacks. She intended to use the rest on Yahoo's core. Jackson didn't trust her with the money.

On July 23, Jackson published another *Forbes* column. In it, he outlined the Yahoo shareholder's argument: that Alibaba or Softbank should buy Yahoo and pass some portion of the roughly $18 billion in tax savings on to Yahoo shareholders.

The column tore through the investment community, and in the days following its publication Jackson fielded several calls from more Yahoo investors—including managers of large mutual funds and hedge funds.

Jackson realized the idea that Yahoo was better off selling to Alibaba or Softbank than it was continuing under the operation of Marissa Mayer was more than just fodder for blog posts. It was a perfect thesis for another activist investor campaign—just like the one he led years before to get Terry Semel fired, or the one Dan Loeb led in 2011 and 2012 to get Marissa Mayer hired.

Jackson considered how the very best activist campaigns he had studied over the years not only presented an alternative path that could create more value for shareholders but also made a clear case that the target company was being run by fools.

On July 29, Jackson wrote another column.

The headline: "How Do You Solve a Problem Like Marissa?"

In the story, Jackson blasted Mayer, criticizing her for bloating the company, hiring De Castro and wasting billions of dollars on acquisitions that weren't helping revenues grow. He argued that Yahoo's mobile user growth was nothing to brag about. "You would be hard-pressed to find a CEO who couldn't have taken Yahoo's top job in mid-2012 when they had 800 million monthly desktop users and not converted about half of them to mobile users two years later. This is the mobile world we now live in."

Once again, Jackson got loud and encouraging feedback from Wall Street.

He determined to make another activist campaign against Yahoo a reality.

His own fund didn't have the financial firepower to lead the charge. So he drew up a list of activist investors who might take up the mantle. Dan Loeb would have been perfect, but his agreement with Yahoo barred him from leading another campaign against the company until 2018. Jackson considered other big activists on Wall Street—names such as Ackman and Icahn. Near the top of his list was Jeffrey Smith from Starboard Value. Smith had led a successful activist campaign against AOL in 2011 and 2012, and Jackson figured Smith could quickly get up to speed on Yahoo's business since it was so smiliar to AOL's.

Still on his family vacation, Jackson used his Bloomberg

terminal account to find Smith's email address and reach out to him.

Within hours, Jackson was on the phone with Smith and a handful of associates from Starboard Value. Jackson made his case. He went over the tax efficiencies of a Yahoo sale to Alibaba or Softbank. He laid into Mayer. Smith didn't say much. His associates asked some basic questions.

During the next couple of days, the junior people from Starboard sent a few follow-up emails. They asked for Alibaba vice chairman Joe Tsai's email address. Jackson provided it.

In the following weeks, the line went cold. The deal seemed dead.

But then on September 19, 2014, Alibaba finally went public on the New York Stock Exchange. Its stock price spiked 38 percent— from $68 per share to a closing price of $93.80.

For two years, the hope among some Yahoo shareholders was that as Alibaba stock soared on its debut, so would Yahoo's. The theory was that Yahoo's core business had a certain value and that it was baked into its stock price. Therefore, went the theory, as Alibaba's price rose, so would Yahoo's.

That's not what happened. What happened was, as Alibaba's stock price rose, Yahoo's stock price remained steady. Then Yahoo's stock price began to sink, finishing the day down 5 percent. Essentially, the market value of Yahoo's core business was crashing.

Picture a pie chart of Yahoo's overall value. Throughout September 19, the pie itself did not grow in size. It actually shrank. Meanwhile, because Alibaba shares were going up in price, the wedge in the pie chart representing Yahoo's 401 million remaining Alibaba shares increased in size throughout the day. Since the overall pie wasn't growing, the rest of the slices got squeezed smaller— including the one representing Yahoo's core business.

The reality was this: Despite all the hope attending Marissa

Mayer's arrival at Yahoo and the progress she made fixing its culture, the market believed that the company was worth less than zero dollars.

A week later, on September 26, 2014, Jeff Smith made his move.

In an open letter to Marissa Mayer, Smith said she had failed to cut Yahoo's costs during her first two years and spent too much money on acquisitions that weren't adding to revenues. He said Yahoo's remaining stake in Alibaba was currently worth more than the entire enterprise value of Yahoo, and that the smartest thing the company could do was divest itself of those assets in a tax-efficient manner and return all the proceeds to shareholders. He said the best way for Yahoo to do that might be to sell to AOL, even if that meant the end of Yahoo as an independent company.

"We trust the Board and management will do the right thing for shareholders, even if this may mean accepting AOL as the surviving entity in a combination, should that be the best and most tax efficient structure."

Smith ended his letter: "We hope, and expect, that the management team and the Board will execute on the suggestions in this letter."

Behind those words was the same implicit threat behind all activist campaigns: Follow these instructions or we'll find someone else who will.

The fight was on.

The Long, Profitable
Death of Yahoo

The two questions people ask me most after reading this book are: "Do you like Marissa Mayer?" and "Do you think Marissa Mayer has been a good Yahoo CEO?"

The answer to the first question is that I admire Marissa Mayer quite a lot. Mayer was the CEO of a $40 billion public company before age forty. In terms of personal wealth, she's made at least $500 million. That's $300 million at Google and another $200 million or so at Yahoo.

Those finances are impressive, but Mayer's strengths go beyond her bank account.

I admire how when Mayer was finishing her graduate program at Stanford, she had a world of career options in front of her and she chose the option that was the scariest: working for a weirdly named startup no one had ever heard of, called Google.

I admire how at Google, Mayer was able to recognize her own weaknesses and build an incredible career there anyway. Mayer was hired by Google as a coder. Her first big project was to build Google's advertising system. It took her months and months to make any progress. Then Google went out and hired a star coder from DEC named Jeff Dean. Dean came into Google and in a matter of weeks built the system Mayer was trying to build. Mayer, who already decided she loved working at Google, realized she wasn't going to make her mark there as a coder. She would have to find other ways to be useful.

I admire how Mayer made herself useful by throwing herself at whatever problems Google needed to solve. She worked on marketing. She rigged servers. She helped PR. She ran Google CEO Larry Page's staff meetings. She turned that essentially administrative duty into serious influence over Page's and Google's agenda.

I admire how Mayer never seemed to worry too much about stepping on other people's toes. Throwing herself at all these problems, Mayer would sometimes throw herself at problems that other people were already trying to solve. Often, these people would get upset that Mayer was encroaching on their turf. Mayer didn't care. She ignored the haters.

I think young people, young women in particular, could learn a lot from these traits of Mayer. I sent the very last of my promotional hard copies of this book to the twelve-year-old daughter of a friend of mine. In my inscription, I told this young woman Mayer has provided her three lessons: (1) Choose the scariest option, (2) make yourself useful, and (3) ignore the haters.

So do I like Marissa Mayer?

You could say I'm dodging that question. And you would be right.

I am always tempted to answer the question by saying that I would never want to work for Mayer. I've heard too often that she's a micromanager and can, usually accidentally, be incredibly rude to people. But then I'm reminded of Henrique De Castro, the executive who made $109 million working for Mayer for just a year. I would take that.

The answer to the second question I always get—"Do you think Marissa Mayer has been a good Yahoo CEO?"—continues to get simpler every day.

It is, basically: not a very good one, no.

I finished writing the very first draft of this book in August 2014. The final draft was done in September. Then the first edition came out in January 2015.

On all of those dates, it almost seemed too soon to say whether Mayer was up to the task of saving Yahoo or not.

But then, suddenly, it was April 10, 2015, and Mayer had passed a significant milestone. After joining Yahoo in July 2012, she had been at the company for two years, nine months. She had been at the company longer than the delightful, infamous f-bomb dropping Carol Bartz. (The length of Mayer's tenure had long surpassed that of her immediate predecessor, Scott Thompson, who was flushed from the company thanks to his inaccurate biography.)

It was, of course, Eric Jackson who noticed Mayer had been around so long.

He wrote a *Forbes* column about it, comparing the tenures of Bartz and Mayer. He pointed out that Mayer, like Bartz, had so far been unable to grow Yahoo's revenues. Bartz, however, had grown Yahoo's profits—and Mayer had not. Mayer was able to grow Yahoo's stock price, but Jackson noted that this was due to its valuable stake in Alibaba.

Jackson concluded: "Mayer has gotten way too much of a pass from investors and the press because of the soaring value of Alibaba in the last 4 years. The core business has lost almost $8 billion in value and she should really start justifying how her turnaround plan is going to take hold. She has yet to get any tough questions from investors or the press and, as a result, hasn't answered them. Mayer of course does anything in her power to avoid tough questions."

Life at Yahoo has not gotten any less tumultuous since the conclusion of this book's story. In late 2014, Mayer began a reorganization of Yahoo's executive ranks. Adam Cahan, the shouter who ran mobile, lost a lot of power. Yahoo hired two new sales leaders. In early 2015, one of them quickly left.

In February, Yahoo and Mayer caved to activist investor Jeff Smith. She announced that the company would spin off its entire stake in Alibaba. This meant Yahoo's market cap would soon shrink from around $50 billion to something close to $5 billion.

It also meant Mayer would not get to spend any of the jackpot money Jerry Yang won for the company by placing a giant bet on a Chinese startup years before.

Worse yet for Mayer, even after winning this huge concession, Smith remained a Yahoo shareholder. He believed he could pressure Mayer into shrinking the company even further. He wanted Yahoo to spin off its stake in Yahoo Japan and return the proceeds to shareholders. He wanted Yahoo to sell its real estate. He wanted Mayer to fire thousands of people.

Soon, layoffs returned to Yahoo.

Revenue growth finally came in the second quarter of the year, but investors punished Yahoo's stock because of disappointing profits and a poor outlook for the rest of the year.

One reason Mayer has not done very well at Yahoo is that she has probably been asked to do the wrong job.

When Dan Loeb and Michael Wolf hired Mayer to save Yahoo, what they wanted her to do was to turn back the clock on the company. They wanted her to make Yahoo into a fast-growing Internet company with revenue growth that could compete with companies like Google, Facebook, and Uber.

Mayer's answer to this challenge was to turn Yahoo into an apps company. She put Adam Cahan in charge of hundreds of people and said to him: Go make the next great app. She went out and spent more than a billion dollars buying companies to staff the app-making team.

To Mayer credit, Yahoo produced several beautiful apps. Yahoo

Weather and Yahoo News Digest both won design awards from Apple. In the spring of 2015, Yahoo released yet another Flickr app. It was gorgeous and its functionality top-notch. In the summer of 2015, Yahoo released a video messaging app meant to rival Snapchat.

But despite their slick look and feel, none of these apps ever became very popular. By the summer of 2015, Yahoo had only one iPhone app in the top 50—Yahoo Mail, ranked fiftieth—and only two in the top 100. Tumblr, which Yahoo bought for $1 billion, was ranked in the eighties.

This failure rate may seem surprising considering Yahoo's resources. The problem is, even with those resources, Yahoo can make only a handful of apps per year. Meanwhile, it's competing against thousands of venture capitalists with billions of dollars to spend on thousands of new apps.

By 2014, 1.2 million apps had been created for the Apple app store. That same year, the venture capital industry raised $33 billion to invest in startups, according to Dow Jones.

This book concludes by wondering if anyone could have saved Yahoo. Perhaps that's not the right question.

If the definition of "saving" Yahoo means trying to restore its youth, the right question is: Should anyone try to "save" Yahoo?

It's possible that Yahoo's shareholders and employees would have been better off by now if, in 2012, Dan Loeb had taken a different direction. Perhaps instead of hiring Mayer to try and turn around Yahoo the way Steve Jobs once turned around Apple, Loeb should have pushed the company to quit investing in growth, lay off thousands of people, and return its massive, existing profits to shareholders.

Shareholders would have been able to take that money and, if they wanted to, give it to venture capitalists who are better at finding and placing small bets on app-making startups that are far more likely to be the next Yahoo than Yahoo itself is.

Meanwhile, many of those laid off Yahoo employees would be able to join some of those fast-growing, well-funded startups.

This was the tempting argument presented to me in December 2014 by Aswath Damodaran, a professor at NYU's Stern School of Business.

Damodaran has long argued about the danger of companies that try to return to the growth stage of their life cycle. These technology companies, he said, are run by people afflicted with something he calls the Steve Jobs syndrome.

"We have created an incentive structure where CEOs want to be stars," Damodaran explained. "To be a star, you've got to be the next Steve Jobs—somebody who has actually grown a company to be a massive, large-market cap company." But, he went on, "It's extremely dangerous at companies when you focus on the exception rather than the rule." He pointed out that "for every Apple, there are a hundred companies that tried to do what Apple did and fell flat on their faces."

In many ways, Yahoo's decline from a $128 billion company to one worth virtually nothing is entirely natural. Yahoo grew into a colossus by solving a problem that no longer exists. And while Yahoo's products have undeniably improved, and its culture has become more innovative, it's unlikely that Mayer can reverse an inevitability unless she creates the next iPod.

All breakthrough companies, after all, will eventually plateau and then decline. U.S. Steel was the first billion-dollar company in 1901, but it was worth about the same in 1991. Kodak, which once employed nearly eighty thousand people, now has a market value below $1 billion. Packard and Hudson ruled the roads for more than forty years before disappearing. These companies matured and receded over the course of generations, in some cases even a century. Yahoo went through the process in twenty years. In the technology industry, things move fast.

"Sometimes," Damodaran told me, "companies have to act their age." For Yahoo, embracing its maturity means settling for a business that earns close to $1 billion in profit every year. It has outlasted other formerly iconic Internet portals, from AltaVista to Excite, and even dwarfs more recent web sensations like MySpace and Ask.com. For a company that started out as Jerry and David's Guide to the World Wide Web, that's not a bad way to grow old.

A Note on Sources

This book is based primarily on firsthand reporting. That reporting included hundreds of interviews with more than a hundred sources with firsthand experience of the events described. I also obtained dozens of internal Yahoo documents.

I have covered Google, Yahoo, and Marissa Mayer as a beat reporter since 2006. I specifically began reporting on this story in October 2012. Since then, I visited California several times to meet with sources for this story. In April 2014, I spent two weeks living in Palo Alto, California, meeting with people who knew Marissa Mayer from their work and social lives.

This book is heavily reliant on anonymous sourcing. I would like to explain why.

When I first began working on this project, I reached out to Yahoo and Marissa Mayer, seeking their cooperation. Months and many emails later, I was told it would not be coming. It never did. I frequently attempted to change this through emails and phone calls throughout the process. The last time I heard from Yahoo public relations about the book was when I asked if Yahoo would like to help me fact check it. Yahoo PR told me: "We don't plan on participating in the book, including fact checking." Finally, when I completed my first draft, I offered to go over the facts reported in this book, if only as a courtesy. I never heard back.

Not only did Yahoo PR and Mayer not participate, each told

Yahoo employees, former Yahoo employees, personal friends, former colleagues, current colleagues, and admirers not to speak with me for the book.

The reason I used anonymous sourcing was that I needed those kinds of people to speak with me to get the unbiased (either way) truth about Yahoo and Marissa Mayer. Mayer is a very powerful person and Yahoo is a very powerful company in Silicon Valley. Many of my sources only agreed to speak with me on the condition that Mayer and Yahoo never find out they did. Many of the sources who provided me documents and agreed to be interviewed by me did so at the risk of their careers inside Yahoo, Google, and around the Internet industry.

And so, to protect those people, and to tell this story in a flowing, narrative fashion, I have not identified the sources of information for particular facts in this book, including thoughts and dialogue. I have not identified many on-the-record sources, because I did not want to allow the process of elimination to identify others.

I would caution readers against assuming that because I have reported a person's thoughts, that person is a direct source. A person will often share thoughts about pivotal moments in their lives with a large group of people—sometimes with other reporters, in front of large audiences or TV cameras.

The quoted dialogue in this book was carefully instructed from interviews, transcripts, and prior reports. Dialogue not in quotes should be considered a paraphrase of what was actually said.

This book would not have its level of detail without relying on years of work by other writers and reporters. I have outlined the reporting this book draws from, by chapter, in a bibliography. I am most especially in debt to the work of Karen Angel, Kara Swisher, Patricia Sellers, and Steven Levy.

Acknowledgments

I have so many people to thank for helping me write this book that I'm worried I will forget one or two.

I am so grateful to my parents for so many reasons. I will pick one for each. I am grateful to my dad, Mark Carlson, because he coached me in soccer for many years, and after every game we would sit in the car and talk about how it went. Win or lose, it was clear he loved and supported me. It made me feel secure in the world and free to take risks. Without that feeling, I'm not sure I would have ever tried writing a book, or writing at all.

When I was a kid, my mom, Dimity Carlson, would read stories to me and my brothers before school every day. I'd sit there enraptured by tales of kingdoms lost and won. I am grateful she shared her love of story with me.

I couldn't have written this book without support from the best employer anyone like me could ever dream of: *Business Insider. Business Insider* is run by two incredible people, Henry Blodget and Julie Hansen. For all the opportunities provided by them, I am also grateful.

I would not have written this book if an agent named Eric Nelson had not found me on Twitter and told me there might be widespread interest in this Marissa Mayer I had been writing about so much. Eric, a former editor, has been a huge help throughout the process.

I am grateful to Anne Giles for teaching me the five-paragraph essay, Cynthia Lewis for teaching me how to revise, and Douglas Glover for teaching me that a narrative structure is a physical thing.

Anna Carlson is my wife and my best friend. Every night for a year she listened to me say the same things over and over about this book. I would have gone crazy (crazier?) without her. I love you, Anna.

Lydia Dallet was my enthusiastic research assistant. I've never met a harder worker. I'm especially grateful for our early conversations about what pieces of my reporting she thought were most interesting and belonged in the book.

I got the opportunity to work with several editors at Hachette while writing this book. John Brodie brought me into the fold. Rick Wolff took over when John got a fancy new job. Sean Desmond of Twelve did all the really hard work, helping me finalize my outline, reading my copy, and getting me across the finish line. Thank you to them all. Thanks also to Libby Burton, a masterful wrangler.

Let's have a moment of silence for the hundreds of typos and awkward sentences that once lived in these pages—before copy editor Rick Ball wiped them out. Thank you, Rick.

This book got its start in a garage in Palo Alto. I am so grateful to my generous hosts Cece Long and Steve Long. I'm sorry I missed you two and everyone else in PML this year!

Kara Swisher is the best reporter in the technology industry, and no one has covered any company so well as she's covered Yahoo for the past decade plus. The reporting in this book would have been much weaker without her help.

Friends Zach Williams and David Crow read early drafts of this book and provided very useful feedback. Jay Yarow tried his best, but golf got in the way. He did write one really nice tweet about it. Dan Lewis gave me a few very encouraging words right when I needed it, twice.

Bibliography

Prologue

Eichenwald, Kurt. "Microsoft's Lost Decade." *Vanity Fair* (August 2012): http://www.vanityfair.com/business/2012/08/microsoft-lost-mojo-steve-ballmer.

Swisher, Kara. "'Because Marissa Said So'—Yahoos Bristle at Mayer's QPR Ranking System and 'Silent Layoffs.'" All Things Digital (November 8, 2013): http://allthingsd.com/20131108/because-marissa-said-so-yahoos-bristle-at-mayers-new-qpr-ranking-system-and-silent-layoffs/.

Chapter 1

Angel, Karen. *Inside Yahoo!: Reinvention and the Road Ahead.* New York: John Wiley & Sons, 2002.

Elgin, Ben. "Inside Yahoo!" *Bloomberg Businessweek* (May 20, 2001): http://www.businessweek.com/stories/2001-05-20/inside-yahoo.

———. "Yahoo!'s General Says 'Charge!'" *Bloomberg Businessweek* (February 18, 2001): http://www.businessweek.com/stories/2001-02-18/yahoo-s-general-says-charge.

Hardy, Quentin. "The Killer Ad Machine." *Forbes* (December 11, 2000): http://www.forbes.com/forbes/2000/1211/6615168a.html.

Levy, Steven. *In The Plex: How Google Thinks, Works, and Shapes Our Lives.* New York: Simon & Schuster, 2011.

Mangalindan, Mylene. "Yahoo! Is Pressed to Reveal More Numbers on Ad Revenue." *Wall Street Journal* (July 10, 2000): http://online.wsj.com/news/articles/SB963184612223420932.

Mangalindan, Mylene, and Suein L. Hwang. "Insular Culture Helped Yahoo! Grow, But Has Now Hurt It in the Long Run." *Wall Street Journal* (March 9, 2001): http://online.wsj.com/news/articles/SB984089525895733927.

Siklos, Richard. "When Terry Met Jerry, Yahoo!" *New York Times* (January 29, 2006): http://www.nytimes.com/2006/01/29/business/yourmoney/29yahoo.html?pagewanted=all&_r=0.

Vogelstein, Fred. "Bringing Up Yahoo." *Fortune* (April 5, 2004): http://archive.fortune.com/magazines/fortune/fortune_archive/2004/04/05/366371/index.htm.

Chapter 2

Angel. *Inside Yahoo!*

Arrington, Michael. "Yahoo's 'Project Fraternity' Docs Leaked." TechCrunch (December 12, 2006): http://techcrunch.com/2006/12/12/yahoos-project-fraternity-docs-leaked/.

Elgin. "Inside Yahoo!"

Hansell, Saul. "Yahoo's Growth Being Eroded by New Rivals." *New York Times* (October 11, 2006): http://www.nytimes.com/2006/10/11/technology/11yahoo.html?pagewanted=all&_r=0.

Hardy. "The Killer Ad Machine."

Levy. *In The Plex.*

Mills, Elinor. "Shareholders Blast CEO Semel for Yahoo Performance." CNET (June 12, 2007): http://news.cnet.com/Shareholders-blast-CEO-Semel-for-Yahoo-performance/2100-1030_3-6190546.html.

Siklos. "When Terry Met Jerry, Yahoo!"

Vogelstein. "Bringing Up Yahoo."

"Yahoo Memo: The 'Peanut Butter Manifesto.'" *Wall Street Journal* (November 18, 2006): http://online.wsj.com/news/articles/SB116379821933826657.

Chapter 3

Hansell, Saul. "AOL's Choice of Google Leaves Microsoft as the Outsider." *New York Times* (December 19, 2005): http://www.nytimes.com/2005/12/19/business/media/19aol.html.

Helft, Miguel. "After Deal Dies, Yahoo Weighs Its Next Move." *New York Times* (May 5, 2008): http://www.nytimes.com/2008/05/05/technology/05yahoo.html?pagewanted=all.

Levy. *In The Plex.*

Moore, Heidi. "Jerry Yang's Failure to Communicate." *Wall Street Journal* (May 6, 2008): http://blogs.wsj.com/deals/2008/05/06/jerry-yangs-failure-to-communicate/.

Chapter 4

"D7 Video: Yahoo CEO Carol Bartz and Kara Swisher." *Wall Street Journal* video, 9:33. May 27, 2009. http://live.wsj.com/video/d7-video-yahoo-ceo-carol-bartz-and-kara-swisher/EFFD4DE0-FC09-49C1-BFDB-816E9CA2D344.html.

Fussman, Cal. "Hi, I'm Carol Bartz...Are You an Asshole?" *Esquire* (May 3, 2010): http://www.esquire.com/women/women-issue/carol-bartz-bio-0510.

Lacy, Sarah. "Just Don't Call It Retirement." *Bloomberg Businessweek* (March 5, 2006): http://www.businessweek.com/stories/2006-03-05/just-dont-call-it-retirement.

Pepitone, Julianne. "Cranky Shareholders Blast Yahoo and Carol Bartz." CNNMoney (June 23, 2011): http://money.cnn.com/2011/06/23/technology/yahoo_shareholder/index.htm.

Sellers, Patricia. "Carol Bartz Exclusive: Yahoo 'F---ed Me Over.'" *Fortune.* (September 8, 2011): http://fortune.com/2011/09/08/carol-bartz-exclusive-yahoo-f-ed-me-over/.

Zachary, G. Pascal. "The Survivor." *Business 2.0.* (December 1, 2004): http://money.cnn.com/magazines/business2/business2_archive/2004/12/01/8192521/index.htm.

Chapter 5

Carlson, Nicholas. "The Truth About Marissa Mayer: An Unauthorized Biography." *Business Insider* (August 24, 2013): www.businessinsider.com/marissa-mayer-biography-2013-8?op=1.

"Marissa Mayer at Stanford University." YouTube video, 49:25. Posted by "Miraclemart," June 30, 2006. https://www.youtube.com/watch?v=soYKFWqVVzg.

Chapter 6

Edwards, Douglas. *I'm Feeling Lucky: The Confessions of Google Employee Number 59.* New York: Houghton Mifflin Harcourt, 2011. Kindle Edition.

Guthrie, Julian. "The Adventures of Marissa." *San Francisco* (February 8, 2008).

Guynn, Jessica. "How I Made It: Marissa Mayer, Google's Champion of Innovation and Design." *Los Angeles Times* (January 2, 2011): http://articles.latimes.com/2011/jan/02/business/la-fi-himi-mayer-20110102.

Holson, Laura M. "Putting a Bolder Face on Google." *New York Times* (February 28, 2009): http://www.nytimes.com/2009/03/01/business/01marissa.html?pagewanted=all.

"Introduction to Amit Singhal (at Google)." Vimeo video, 2:36. Posted by "Galactic Public Archives," January 3, 2014. http://vimeo.com/83265301.

"Keynote with Marissa Mayer, President and CEO, Yahoo!" YouTube video, 41:26. Posted by "Salesforce Video," November 20, 2013. https://www.youtube.com/watch?v=AdMW-2MVwks.

Levy. *In The Plex.*

"Marissa Mayer at Stanford University." YouTube video.

"Marissa Mayer's IIT Commencement Address." YouTube video, 16:53. Posted by "Google," May 16, 2009. https://www.youtube.com/watch?v=jaKoMCujc2k.

Sellers, Patricia. "Marissa Mayer: Ready to Rumble at Yahoo." *Fortune* (October 11, 2012): http://fortune.com/2012/10/11/marissa-mayer-ready-to-rumble-at-yahoo/.

Singer, Sally. "From the Archives: Google's Marissa Mayer in Vogue." *Vogue* (August 2009): http://www.vogue.com/873540/from-the-archives-marissa-mayer-machine-dreams/.

Warner, Fara. "How Google Searches Itself." *Fast Company* (June 30, 2002).

Chapter 7

Anderlini, Jamil. "Person of the Year: Jack Ma." *Financial Times* (December 12, 2013): http://www.ft.com/intl/cms/s/2/308e46a8-6189-11e3-916e-00144feabdc0.html.

Flannery, Russell. "Inside Alibaba: Vice Chairman Joe Tsai Opens Up About Working with Jack Ma and Jonathan Lu." *Forbes* (January 8, 2014): http://www.forbes.com/sites/russellflannery/2014/01/08/inside-alibaba-vice-chairman-joe-tsai-opens-up-about-working-with-jack-ma-and-jonathan-lu/.

Chapter 8

Cohan, William. "Little Big Man." *Vanity Fair* (December 2013): http://www.vanityfair.com/business/2013/12/dan-loeb-cuba-car-accident.

Gopinath, Deepak. "Hedge Fund Manager Daniel Loeb Skewers CEOs, Returns 28 Percent." Silicon Investor (August 18, 2005): http://www.siliconinvestor.com/readmsg.aspx?msgid=21622975.

Sellers. "Carol Bartz Exclusive."

Chapter 9

Swisher, Kara. "Dan Loeb Alleges 'Discrepancies' on Yahoo CEO Scott Thompson's Resume Related to Computer Science Degree." All Things Digital (May 3, 2012): http://allthingsd.com/20120503/dan-loeb-alleges-discrepancies-on-yahoo-ceo-scott-thompsons-resume-related-to-computer-science-degree/.

————. "In 2009 Interview, Yahoo CEO Does Not Deny He Has a CS Degree, and Calls Himself an 'Engineer' (Audio)." All Things Digital (May 3, 2012): http://allthingsd.com/20120503/in-2009-interview-yahoo-ceo-does-not-deny-he-has-a-cs-degree-and-calls-himself-an-engineer/.

Chapter 10

Carlson. "The Truth About Marissa Mayer."

Sellers, Patricia. "New Yahoo CEO Mayer Is Pregnant." *Fortune* (July 17, 2012): http://fortune.com/2012/07/17/new-yahoo-ceo-mayer-is-pregnant/.

Stone, Brad. "Can Marissa Mayer Save Yahoo?" *Bloomberg Businessweek* (August 1, 2013): http://www.businessweek.com/articles/2013-08-01/can-marissa-mayer-save-yahoo.

Swisher, Kara. "The King Is Dead, Long Live the…Whatever: Levinsohn's Management Moves at Yahoo (Internal Memo)." All Things Digital (May 17, 2012): http://allthingsd.com/20120517/levinsohns-management-musical-chairs-at-yahoo-internal-memo/.

————. "Ross Still Not the Boss (Yet): Yahoo CEO Selection Now Likely to Take Longer Than Many Expect." All Things Digital (July 12, 2012): http://allthingsd.com/20120712/ross-still-not-the-boss-yet-yahoo-ceo-selection-now-likely-to-take-longer-than-many-expect/.

Chapter 11

"Marissa Mayer: Distance from 'Feminism.'" Maker Studios video, 00:49. Posted by "MAKERS," 2012. http://www.makers.com/marissa-mayer/moments/distance-feminism.

McLean, Bethany. "Yahoo's Geek Goddess." *Vanity Fair* (January 2014): http://www.vanityfair.com/business/2014/01/marissa-mayer-yahoo-google.

Sellers. "Marissa Mayer."

Swisher, Kara. "'Physically Together': Here's the Internal Yahoo No-Work-From-Home Memo for Remote Workers and Maybe More." All Things Digital

(February 22, 2013): http://allthingsd.com/20130222/physically-together
-heres-the-internal-yahoo-no-work-from-home-memo-which-extends
-beyond-remote-workers/.

Weisberg, Jacob. "Yahoo's Marissa Mayer: Hail to the Chief." *Vogue* (September 2013).

Chapter 12

Cook, John. "What Happened to Lockerz? Heavily-Funded Startup Purchased by Chinese e-Commerce Company." GeekWire (January 14, 2014): http://www.geekwire.com/2014/happened-lockerz-assets-heavily-funded-startup-purchased-chinese-e-commerce-company/.

Goel, Vindu. "Yahoo Wants You to Linger (on the Ads, Too)." *New York Times* (June 21, 2014): http://www.nytimes.com/2014/06/22/technology/yahoo-wants-you-to-linger-on-the-ads-too.html.

Grigoriadis, Vanessa. "Welcome to the Dollhouse." *New York* (December 7, 1998): http://nymag.com/nymetro/news/media/features/2917/.

MacMillan, Douglas. "Marketing Chief Kathy Savitt's Star Rises at Yahoo." *Wall Street Journal* (February 25, 2014): http://online.wsj.com/news/articles/SB10001424052702304834704579405311104840146.

Shields, Mike. "Who Is Yahoo CMO Kathy Savitt? And Why Is She Running the Media Business?" *Adweek* (January 23, 2014): http://www.adweek.com/news/advertising-branding/who-yahoo-cmo-kathy-savitt-155131.

Swisher, Kara. "Kick the Can—Yahoo Mail Is a Consumer Disaster, but Company's Response Is Even Worse." All Things Digital (December 11, 2013): http://allthingsd.com/20131211/kick-the-can-yahoo-mail-is-a-consumer-disaster-but-companys-response-is-even-worse/.

"Yahoo CMO Kathy Savitt at Entrepreneurship Summit NYC 2013." Cornellcast video, 33:42. Posted by "Entrepreneurship@Cornell," December 11, 2013. http://www.cornell.edu/video/yahoo-cmo-kathy-savitt-at-entrepreneurship-summit-nyc-2013.

Chapter 13

Swisher, Kara. "He Was Fired: Here's Marissa Mayer's De Castro Buh-Bye Memo to Yahoo Staff." Re/code (January 15, 2014): http://recode.net/2014/01/15/he-was-fired-heres-marissa-mayers-de-castro-buh-bye-memo-to-staff/.

Yarow, Jay. "The Final Count Is In: Ex-Yahoo COO Henrique De Castro Gets a $58 Million Severance Package." *Business Insider* (April 17, 2014): http://www.businessinsider.com/yahoo-coo-henrique-de-castro-severance-pay-2014-4.

Epilogue

Atkinson, Claire. "Yahoo's Marissa Mayer Flops with Artsy Approach to Advertising." *New York Post* (June 17, 2014): http://pagesix.com/2014/06/17/yahoos-marissa-mayer-flops-with-artsy-approach-to-advertising/.

Goel. "Yahoo Wants You to Linger (on the Ads, Too)."

Hamburger, Ellis. "Tumblr Declares War on the Internet's Identity Crisis." *The Verge* (May 6, 2014): http://www.theverge.com/2014/5/6/5684212/tumblr-declares-war-on-the-internets-identity-crisis.

Jackson, Eric. "Marissa Mayer's Compensation and Stock-Selling Not Linked to Performance." *Forbes* (August 17, 2014): www.forbes.com/sites/ericjackson/2014/08/17/marissa-mayers-compensation-and-stock-selling-not-linked-to-performance.

Petrecca, Laura. "Yahoo CEO Takes Heat for Stilted Presentation in Cannes." *USA Today* (June 18, 2014): http://www.usatoday.com/story/money/business/2014/06/17/yahoo-ceo-marissa-mayer/10656221/.

Swisher, Kara. "As Weather Channel Blows Yahoo Off Apple's Upcoming iOS 8, App Storms Ahead for Mayer." Re/code (June 20, 2014): http://recode.net/2014/06/20/as-weather-channel-blows-yahoo-off-apples-upcoming-ios-8-app-storms-ahead-for-mayer/.

———. "Do Me a Solid? Alibaba Can Allow Yahoo to Keep Its Shares in the IPO (But It Probably Won't)." Re/code (May 6, 2014): http://recode.net/2014/

05/06/do-me-a-solid-alibaba-can-allow-yahoo-to-keep-its-shares-in-the-ipo
-but-it-probably-wont/.

Vranica, Suzanne. "How Marissa Mayer Fell Asleep and Kept Ad Executives Waiting for Hours." *Wall Street Journal* (June 23, 2014): http://blogs.wsj.com/
cmo/2014/06/23/how-marissa-mayer-fell-asleep-and-kept-ad-executives
-waiting-for-hours/.

Index

About the Author

Nicholas Carlson is *Business Insider*'s chief correspondent. His investigative reporting rewrote the histories of Facebook, Twitter, and Groupon. His coverage of Yahoo won Digiday's award for "Best Editorial Achievement" of the year. Carlson is a frequent guest on CNBC and contributes to the Bloomberg biography series *Game Changers*.